Arkady Vaksberg
Stalin Against the Jews

Arkady Vaksberg is a leading investigative journalist for
the weekly newspaper *Literaturnaya Gazeta*. Now fifty-
nine, he was trained as a lawyer (one year behind Mikhail
Gorbachev). He lives in Moscow and is a co-founder and
vice president of Russian PEN. Vaksberg's books *Stalin's
Prosecutor: The Life of Andrei Vyshinsky* and *The Soviet Mafia*
have been published in English, French, German, Swedish,
and Italian.

STALIN AGAINST THE JEWS

STALIN AGAINST THE JEWS

ARKADY VAKSBERG

Translated by
Antonina W. Bouis

VINTAGE BOOKS

A DIVISION OF RANDOM HOUSE, INC.

NEW YORK

First Vintage Books Edition, March 1995

Copyright © 1994 by Arkady Vaksberg

All rights reserved under International and Pan-American
Copyright Conventions. Published in the United States
by Vintage Books, a division of Random House, Inc., New York,
and simultaneously in Canada by Random House
of Canada Limited, Toronto. Originally published in hardcover
by Alfred A. Knopf, Inc., New York, in 1994.

The Library of Congress has cataloged the Knopf edition as follows:
Vaksberg, Arkadii.
Stalin against the Jews / Arkady Vaksberg:
translated by Antonina W. Bouis. — 1st American ed.
p. cm.
Includes index.
ISBN 0-679-42207-2
1. Antisemitism—Soviet Union—History.
2. Stalin, Joseph, 1879–1953—Views on Jews.
3. Jews—Soviet Union—History.
4. Soviet Union—Ethnic relations. I. Title.
DS146.S65V35 1994
305.892'4047—dc20   93-24120
CIP
Vintage ISBN: 0-679-75959-X

Manufactured in the United States of America
10 9 8 7 6 5 4 3 2 1

CONTENTS

STALIN AGAINST THE JEWS

I

NO SUCH NATION EXISTS

WE HAVE A MARVELOUS Georgian sitting and writing a big article for 'Enlightenment,' having gathered *all* [sic] the Austrian and other materials," wrote Lenin from Kraków to Maxim Gorky on Capri in February 1913. Both were living abroad—one in Italy, the other in Austria-Hungary—and, if not quite friends (Lenin had no friends), then close acquaintances with a rather active correspondence. The statement requires explanation. *Enlightenment* was the aboveground Marxist theoretical journal published in St. Petersburg. The article, then titled "The National Question and Social-Democracy," was later renamed "Marxism and the National Question"; and it would eventually enter, and for almost thirty years remain in, the circle of required reading and study for all Soviet citizens from cradle to grave. And the "marvelous Georgian" was naturally Stalin, so unknown in those days that Lenin did not bother mentioning his name, which would have meant nothing to Gorky. Contrary to his internationalist traditions, Lenin merely stressed the ethnic background of the "big article's" author.

It is more difficult to explain how that "marvelous Georgian," who found himself in Vienna and Kraków for a brief period (two months) between exiles, managed to gather "*all* the Austrian and other materials," that is, numerous theoretical works on the national question. Gather and read. And even discover stylistic errors in the translations. Stalin did not know any foreign languages and had no experience with theoretical articles. And the article was not being written for Soviet citizens who were required, even before reading it, to recognize each word of Stalin's as the highest wisdom, nor even for the condescending Bolshevik underground, but for a journal with a decent reputation, read by a wide and highly educated audience.

Those in the know were aware that the ideas of the fledgling theoretician had been instilled by Lenin, "all the materials" collected by Bukharin, and that the translations and other routine work on this article of such unmanageable length for him (40 typewritten pages) were assistance rendered the budding author by the Menshevik Alexander Troyanovsky (who did not become a Bolshevik until 1923). Despite his dangerous political past, Troyanovsky would be named Soviet ambassador to the United States in the thirties and would survive the Great Terror unscathed, and his son, Oleg, would also have a brilliant political career as a protégé of the Father of the Peoples. Apparently, Troyanovsky *père* did not threaten the vanity of the marvelous Georgian and managed to demonstrate his unwavering loyalty even then.

But back to the detective story–like plot of how a totally uneducated man entered the ranks of scholars and theoreticians, and of the influence that process had on the pathological vanity of the man. Decades later, Stalin would insist that he was the leading figure of all scholarship and science and declare himself the unquestioned authority on linguistics and political economy. But his first work—which in fact is not bad if it is seen as a polemic having no pretensions to infallibility—is interesting for another reason.

One of the main tenets of the work lies in the argument that "Jews do not form a single nation," that they constitute a "paper nation" with no basis in reality, one that in no way belongs among "the real, active, moving nations that demand attention." Jews are not a nation but "something mystical, intangible, and otherworldly," continues the author with ill-concealed delight, trying to impart his emotions, rather than his ideas, to the reader. How can they be a nation, he exclaims, if those "who consider themselves Jews live in different parts of the globe, never seeing one another, never acting jointly either in peacetime or in war?!" The question and exclamation point together speak for themselves, expressing the heat of the author's feelings.

Why was it so important for him to prove, and theoretically at that, that Jews were not a nation but an "assimilated group of persons" maintaining only "a certain communality of national character"? His line of "argumentation" includes the following conclusion: "Jews have no stable stratum connected to the soil that naturally unites a nation not only as its framework but as its 'national' market. Of the 5–6 million Russian Jews, only 3–4 percent are connected in one way or another with agriculture. . . . Jews service, primarily, 'other' nations . . . as industrialists and tradesmen, . . . naturally accommodating 'foreign' nations." Out of this Marxist and pseudo-Marxist theorizing, which at first seems to be only abstract mind play, suddenly flows an easily overlooked and yet obvious conclusion, clearly formulated by the author. "A nation has the right to determine its fate freely. It has the right to live as it wishes." But this inviolable right does not apply to Jews. After all, the author has just "proved" that neither within the framework of a single country (Russia) nor, especially, outside its framework ("different parts of the globe") does any such nation exist. And, therefore, nothing exists that has the right to determine its fate freely. That freedom, then, belongs to everyone except those the future great humanitarian calls "something mystical, intangible, and otherworldly."

There is much that is astonishing in this first and truly scandalous theoretical work by the young Russian-Georgian Marxist. The most amazing aspect is probably something that no one has ever paid attention to, at least in print. The laws, administrative orders, scholarship, and journalism of imperial Russia, as in almost every civilized country (then and now) related the concept of "Jew" only to religious adherence and not to blood. Jews who converted to Russian Orthodoxy were not discriminated against, and enjoyed the same rights as Russians. Even the ignorant, uneducated masses who were being pushed into pogroms against the Jews by obscurantists strictly upheld these rules. It was enough for a Jew to display an icon in his window or on his door to be left alone by the marauding crowd, with no further proof demanded. (We are not talking about individual acts by embittered drunkards.) Only Lenin's faithful student, who recognized no religions, even then perceived Jews solely in terms of their origins.

We will not be able to understand everything the author of this work did decades later when he was the absolute dictator of the Soviet empire if we do not return to the sources and follow the path of his thinking, disarmingly displayed on the pages of this screed entitled "Marxism and the National Question." These thoughts, whatever their utilitarian political meaning, are noteworthy primarily for the time of their birth. We must accept them in the context of the events happening in the author's homeland, the country where the article was printed, the events that preceded and accompanied its creation.

Just a year after the appearance of Stalin's masterpiece, in the pages of the legal press (the largest and most popular Russian newspaper, *Novoye Vremya*, or *New Times*), the chairman of the Council of Ministers—and idol of today's national patriots, the Pamyat Society, and their allies—Petr Stolypin, also denied Jews the right to consider themselves a nation. And he did it in a way that differs from Stalin's only in greater suppleness of expression, greater erudition, greater passion, and of course, greater directness without caution.

"It is important to understand," wrote the great Russian reformer, who would be mortally wounded by the young Social Revolutionary Bogrov, incensed by the monstrousness of his declaration, "that racial characteristics have so drastically set the Jewish people apart from the rest of humanity as to make them totally different creatures who cannot enter into our concept of human nature."

> *We can observe them the way we observe and study animals, we can feel disgust for them or hostility, the way we do for the hyena, the jackal, or the spider, but to speak of hatred for them would raise them to our level. The English have seen to it that there are no wolves in the British Isles, and no Englishman will ever speak of or even think about his hatred for that dangerous, vile beast. . . .*
>
> *Only by disseminating in the popular consciousness the concept that the creature of the Jewish race is not the same as other people but an imitation of a human with whom there can be no dealings, only that can gradually heal the national organism and weaken the Jewish nation so it will no longer be able to do harm or will completely die out. History knows of many extinct tribes. Science must put not the Jewish race but the character of Jewry into such conditions as will make it perish.*

This long but necessary quotation—if only for its color and passion—allows us to make an important comparison, one that I believe has never been made, of the positions expressed at the same time by two outstanding political figures, seemingly antipodes, of Russia. Of course, Stalin's work does not even hint at the zoological (literally and figuratively) chauvinism with which Stolypin is imbued. But both deny Jews the very modest honor of being considered a nation—one because Jews do not fit into *a priori*, narrow, "theoretical" schemes, the other because Jews do not belong to *Homo sapiens* at all. But for both writers, the Jewish people is not a subject that determines its own fate and has equal rights with all other peoples, but is instead an object to be manipulated by those in power in accordance with their political goals.

All these theoretical exercises belong to the period when Russian anti-Semitism was at its peak. In March 1911 in Kiev, a gang of thieves viciously murdered thirteen-year-old Andrei Yushchinsky, a close friend of the son of Vera Cheberyak, owner of a tavern. During a childish fight, Andrei cried out that he knew everything about the crimes committed by Vera and her friends, half of whom had just been arrested by the police, while the others wondered who had turned them in. This tragic coincidence sealed the fate of the miserable adolescent.

But in the overheated atmosphere of Russia of those years—after a series of bloody pogroms against Jews that occurred primarily in the Ukraine and Bessarabia, with the growing wave of anti-Semitism that was incited by the Union of the Russian People, the so-called "Black Hundreds"—a rather ordinary murder which would not have got beyond the police blotter in the local newspaper, unexpectedly took on a different aspect, captured the attention of the entire empire (and perhaps the entire world) for two years, and entered history. The boy was killed just before Passover and the corpse was found in a cave not far from the brick factory managed by the Jew Mendel Beilis. Now the task was to tie together these two unconnected facts. A peg was found: the bloodless body of Yushchinsky, with forty-seven stab wounds, was presented as evidence that this was no "ordinary" murder (why would a gang of able-bodied men need to make so many wounds to kill one child?) but a "ritual" murder. Rumors that Jewish monsters used the blood of a Christian child to prepare Passover matzos were prevalent throughout the Russian empire, even in print. There were dozens of court trials accusing the "nonexistent" nation of this bloody crime— even a brief retelling of all the cases would fill a volume.

But no trial of a "ritual" crime had the impact and resonance that accompanied the Beilis case. Two circumstances contributed to this.

This was the very height of the discussion about removing the humiliating limitations placed on Jews by Russian law (a ban on freedom of movement, their restriction to the so-called Pale of Settlement; a quota for entrance to mid-level and higher educational institutions; a limit on access to many professions; and so on). The reactionary forces had united in a search for new and "irrefutable" arguments to maintain these restrictions. The newspaper *Russkoe Znamya* wrote, "Let Russia beware of Jewish equality more than of fire, sword, and open warfare. . . . Our lickspittle liberals apparently do not understand what human breed [at least they say human—A.V.] they are dealing with in the Jews. . . . It is time for the Christian world to understand where its enemy is and against whom it must struggle, it is time to preach a new crusade against the Yids."

The need for a "scientific" basis for this crusade prompted the backstage organizers of this gigantic anti-Semitic campaign to look for an excuse to document officially a ritual killing, that is, one that took place as a matter of principle. This was the second circumstance that turned a purely criminal act into a political one. It required proof at any cost that Yushchinsky's death had happened after he lost blood, not before. Even though, strictly speaking, that fact does not confirm the ritual nature of the murder but speaks only to the means used to kill this particular victim, public opinion, deceived by propaganda as usual in Russia, would take this fact beyond pure accident and generalize from it. Celebrated and authoritative experts were found (are they not always?) who agreed to play their part—for a fee, of course. In the Beilis case, for instance, it was Professor Dmitri Kosorotov, one of Russia's greatest forensic scientists of the period. Decades later Stalin would successfully use the same method (expert confirmation of the procurator's version) as a "scientific" justification for falsified charges of terrorist acts against his "closest comrades-in-arms."

It was in this politically hysterical atmosphere that Stalin labored over his academic work on the national question. Living in the peaceful Austrian capital, the "marvelous Georgian" knew about the anti-Semitic bacchanalia raging in his homeland, but he did not devote a single line to this issue, which one would think had a direct connection to the national question. This amazing fact must not be attributed to the general Bolshevik position or to Lenin's direct influence. In fact, that comrade spoke about anti-Semitism in general and the Beilis case in particular, expounding the official position of the Bolshevik Party, not very often, but quite categorically, in those months and years. "The Beilis case," he wrote, "again and again turns the attention of the whole civilized world to Russia, exposing the shameful conditions that prevail in our country. There is not a trace of anything resembling legality in Russia. Everything is allowed to the administration and the police for unbridled and shameless persecution of Jews—everything is allowed, including cover-up of a crime."

The surge of anti-Semitism and its shameful culmination, the Beilis case, elicited protests throughout the country and the world. Everyone still then remembered the famous Dreyfus case, which had shaken not only France. Protesting that disgusting judicial sham, along with such Frenchmen as Anatole France, Marcel Proust, Victor Margerit, Marcel Prevaux, Claude Monet, André Gide, and Jules Renard, were many celebrated foreigners, including Anton Chekhov, Mark Twain, Maurice Maeterlinck, and Émile Verhaeren. Anatole France initiated a protest campaign over the Beilis case. Paul Langeran, Gerhardt Hauptmann, and other notables were not indifferent to the fate of an unknown Kiev Jew nor, more important, to the fate of calumnied Jewry in general. Major writers, scientists, and public figures sent a fiery appeal "To Russian society." Among the hundreds of Russian signatories were Maxim Gorky, Vladimir Korolenko, Alexander Blok, Leonid Andreyev, Alexei Tolstoy, Vladimir Nemirovich-Danchenko, and Academician Vladimir Vernadsky:

> *In the name of justice, in the name of reason and humanity, we raise our voice against the new surge of fanaticism and superstition of the unenlightened masses. . . . As usual, the very ones who oppress their own people instill religious enmity and ethnic hatred in them. Without re-*

specting the people's opinion or the people's rights, ready to punish them with the harshest measures, they incite national prejudices, increase superstitions, and stubbornly call for violence against compatriots of non-Russian origin.

In this lie is the same anger that once brought the ignorant pagan crowd out against the first followers of the Christian teaching. After that the base, criminal passions raged. Stupid anger tried to blind and dim the awareness of the crowd and to influence the course of justice. . . .

Fear those who sow lies. Do not believe the grim lie that has been covered with blood many times, killing some and damning others to eternal shame.

Maxim Gorky, who was very close to the Bolsheviks and to Lenin personally, considered it necessary to speak out separately on the Jewish question. "Naturally, I have not forgotten that people do a multitude of nasty things to each other, but I consider anti-Semitism to be the vilest of them all." And more: "Recalling the Jews, you feel shamed. Even though I personally, in my entire life, probably never did anything bad to the people of this amazingly enduring race, but still when you meet Jews you immediately begin to think about your tribal relatedness to the monstrous sect of anti-Semites and your responsibility for the idiocy of your fellow tribesmen." And more: "I find the Jewish people, so great in its suffering, very simpatico; I bow before the strength of its soul, exhausted by centuries of gross injustice, exhausted but boldly and hotly dreaming of freedom."

I have quoted a tiny part of the appeals and articles on the issue that concerned all of Russia then* and which underline the "theoretical" incongruity and inappropriateness at best of the position taken on this issue by the "marvelous Georgian," who became the Bolshevik Party's

---

* I will mention only the questionnaire prepared by popular Russian writers to be sent to the readers of *Otechestvo* (*Fatherland*) magazine. It was not sent out because the police raided the offices and confiscated all copies of the questionnaire. Here are the questions. (1) Do you think that anti-Semitism as a public phenomenon arose and developed widely in Russia under the influence of Western anti-Semitism? (2) What influence does the growth of anti-Semitism have on the cultural development of the Russian people and state? (3) What influence does the growth of anti-Semitism have on the economic development of Russia? (4) Do you feel that anti-Semitism is particularly dangerous because of the multi-ethnicity of Russia and its national prejudices? (5) What do you think is the role of Jews in history, science, and social and cultural life in Russia? (6) What do you consider possible measures for the active counteraction against the spread of anti-Semitism and racial and national prejudice in Russia?

best authority on the national question and as a result was made Commissar on National Issues in the first Soviet government after the October 1917 coup. It is only because the pseudo-scientific and politically colored opinions on every issue of the Bolsheviks and because the author's name, "K. Stalin," which hid the fugitive political exile Josif Dzhugashvili ("Koba"), meant nothing to anyone that this literary exercise, later to be declared a scholarly masterpiece, attracted no attention and was not properly appreciated. Years later, it was beyond criticism for the Soviet public, and the West was more interested in post-revolutionary practice than in pre-revolutionary attempts at scholarly essays.

The Beilis case is often (almost always) connected in people's minds and in literature with the Dreyfus case, but there is a substantial difference between them. The Dreyfus case was anti-Semitic in its very essence and in the reaction that it elicited, and inevitably elicited. But superficially, formally, there was nothing anti-Semitic about it. An officer of the general staff, Captain Alfred Dreyfus, was accused of state treason, of espionage for the Germans, not as a Jew but as a French citizen—it was the reactionary press and national patriotic circles that gave the case its Judeophobic coloration. Whereas Beilis was formally accused of murder as a Jew, the motive and method, according to the charges that were dictated by palace and government circles, were determined by the killer's nationality and by a ritual that allegedly existed among true Jewish believers.

It is also widely known that after a month's investigation Beilis was acquitted in the Kiev district court and that this acquittal was considered to represent the triumph of law and justice since the jury members did not succumb to threats or pressure and followed their consciences.

That is true, but not completely. Yes, Mendel Beilis was acquitted, but I repeat that the goal of those who created that elaborate sideshow was not to send that particular frail Jewish man, a pawn in a political game, to hard labor in Siberia. Their main aim was to affirm through the statements of the jury and the judge the ritual nature of the murder, the existence of a monstrous dogma belonging to that "nonexistent" nation. And that goal was achieved.

Here is how the first question put by the court to the jury was formulated. "Has it been proved that . . . thirteen-year-old Andrei Yushchinsky, mouth gagged, was dealt wounds with a sharp object to the parietal area, back of the head, and temples, damaging the brain artery, the arteries of the left temple and of the neck, which led to massive bleeding, and then, when Yushchinsky had bled five cups of blood, he was stabbed again in the torso, damaging the lungs, liver, right kidney, and heart, where the final blows were dealt, and that these wounds, totaling forty-seven in number, and causing terrible suffering, led to the almost total loss of blood and Yushchinsky's death?"

If the jury had been asked the only question that should have interested it—has it been proved that Yushchinsky's death was the result of multiple stab wounds?—and had answered affirmatively, that would have been no more than a statement of the indubitable fact that called for consequences determined by the law. But the persistent emphasis on the total blood loss before death as the killer's main goal, along with the terrible suffering of the victim, which were made to seem an obligatory attribute of the "bloody Jewish ritual," was not dictated by juridical considerations. And, strictly speaking, these medical details were not within the competence of the jury members (who were carefully selected—four peasants, two postal clerks, a railway ticket vendor, a wine warehouse watchman, a trolley conductor, a coachman, an assistant inspector, and a house owner; all members of the intelligentsia were challenged by the procurator) but of doctors. But in their desire to achieve their goal, the judges posed the main question in that formulation and received a unanimous yes. As they were leaving the courthouse, one of the jury members is said to have told a Moscow reporter, "The Jews do drink the blood of Christian infants, of course, but this Jew is not guilty." So the wretched Beilis was acquitted and thousands of strangers wept and embraced in the streets with joy. But this was a false victory, even though Beilis avoided possible future twists of fortune by immediately emigrating to America. In acquitting one man, the "twelve angry men" in fact confirmed a slander against an entire nation.

Even before this trial, Russia had lost almost a million and a half Jews who had moved to the United States to get away from the persecution of tsarist Black Hundreds, perhaps sensing what was to come from the "marvelous Georgian" a half century later. Of course, pathological anti-Semites did not consider this mass exodus a loss for their country, but thousands of immigrants and their descendants became the pride of America, enriching it instead of Russia with their achievements in science, technology, business, and culture. Beilis's acquittal did not decrease, in fact it increased, the desire of Jews to flee a country where the prime minister, before his assassination, dared publicly to call them hyenas and spiders. They were right to hurry. No sooner had the World War begun than Russian Jews were accused of sending gold to the Germans in airplanes, in coffins, under the wings of and inside geese, signaling the enemy, hiding small coins to undermine trust in Russian money, burning sown wheat. They were charged with being ready to overlook the interests of the country in which they lived for the interests of members of their race living on the territory of the enemy. This was the nation that Stalin considered nonexistent, the people whose members "never act jointly in peacetime or in war."

Perhaps there is no need to return to the battles that shook Russia eight decades ago.* But without that context it will be hard to understand what happened later, and what is happening today. Reading the major Bolshevik specialist on the national question, we will not find a single line on what was agitating the whole country in regard to the "national question." Stalin's discussion of the "nonexistent nation," which at that very moment was being mocked, humiliated, and persecuted as a nation that irritated chauvinists and was to be destroyed like the wolves of whose presence civilized Britain had freed itself—his discussion helps us understand what affected his feelings, how his views took shape, and how his future strategy for the final solution of the Jewish question evolved.

One of the major figures in this book, Ilya Ehrenburg, in Paris during those years, wrote to his anonymous French mistress:

* The echoes of those battles reverberate in the present. In late 1991 one of the bastions of contemporary anti-Semitism, the magazine *Molodaya Gvardia* (Young Guards), published a photograph of the corpse of Andrei Yushchinsky, calling readers' attention to the "mysterious order and distribution of the blood-letting stab wounds," which were supposed to form a "cabbalistic sign." The resurrection of this obscurantist billingsgate does not seem like historical curiosity to me.

Do not recall with a sweet smile
My country.
How I want you to forget
That I am a Jew.

But even then Stalin little resembled a delighted and naïve Parisian girl. He did not forget anything even then. And he remembered very well who was who.

2

THE "MARVELOUS GEORGIAN" IN HIS CIRCLE

THE FACT THAT STALIN was a convinced and even fanatical anti-Semite (as will be shown throughout this book) has only recently been discussed. The numerous books, articles, and booklets devoted to him in the twenties, thirties, and later speak of his most varied qualities, the many aspects of his personality that in no way can be considered virtues—his unbridled lust for power, his vengefulness, cruelty, treachery, rancor, hypocrisy, etc. But an equally powerful "antipathy" of his, which was a stimulus to a series of criminal actions, was never mentioned until quite recently. Even Trotsky in his classic two-volume study, *Stalin*, is completely silent on this important "detail" in his profound and subtle psychological portrait in the chapter entitled "Thermidor." He re-creates and analyzes, in a most thorough and systematic manner, the various motivations that moved Stalin in his struggle with his primary and "less primary" but still powerful and dangerous rivals. There is only one motivation that he does not discuss. Is it because he did not consider it significant? Did not take it into account? Or simply did not know it existed?

The passionate exposés written by the few men in Stalin's circle who found the strength and courage to throw weighty accusations in the face of the Great Leader—for instance, Martemian Rutin, author of the Rutin Platform; a candidate member of the Central Committee of the Communist Party; and one of the military leaders of the October coup, Ambassador Feodor Raskolnikov—accused Stalin of many grievous sins, but never hinted at his anti-Semitism, even though in those days that sin was considered a mortal one by the Bolsheviks.

Moreover, even Boris Bazhanov, Stalin's secretary who fled abroad in the late twenties and published articles denouncing him in France (and he better than anyone knew his boss's most private thoughts and feelings), touched on the Jewish theme only in passing, jokingly, which did not indicate that Stalin was guilty of the evil of ethnic intolerance. Only a half century later, in the early eighties, as he was preparing a newly revised edition of his book, *The Memoirs of Stalin's Former Secretary*, did he include vivid and convincing episodes which showed that Stalin's anti-Semitism did not first emerge in the late forties, as so many have believed.

The reason that "theme" rose to the surface and was so thoroughly developed only in the last part of Stalin's life will be discussed fully in later chapters. But why it was suppressed for so many years is one of the mysteries of the tragic history of twentieth-century Russia. In his post-humously published memoirs, *Through the Eyes of a Man of My Generation*, Konstantin Simonov, a popular writer in Russia during and after World War II, tries to explain that phenomenon in the following way. "For different reasons I encountered people of various generations who thought that Stalin did not like, or at least had little affection for, Jews. . . . I did not want to believe in his anti-Semitism. It did not correspond to my image of him, with everything that I read of his, and it somehow seemed incongruous, incompatible with the character of a man who was at the head of the world communist movement."

In these frank and astonishingly naïve reflections the popular Soviet writer was typical of his times. Chekhov had foreseen it with his immortal formula: "This cannot be, because it can never be." Stalin could be every kind of scoundrel, but he was a Bolshevik, and all Bolsheviks were internationalists, with their goal of world revolution and unity of proletarians of all countries, independent of race and nationality. This was the reasoning (for a long time) of many wise and observant people from the same Bolshevik milieu. And therefore while Stalin was accused of major crimes, the most nightmarish acts of evil, he was not charged with anti-Semitism until the mid-forties, when his anti-Semitism became overt.

Yet another circumstance psychologically kept people from suspect-ing Stalin of this "anti-Bolshevik" sin. Stalin was a Georgian, and anti-Semitism was always considered a Great Russian, Little Russian

(Ukrainian), Belorussian, and Polish phenomenon. Georgians themselves were considered an oppressed ethnic group (natsmenshinstvo, or national minority), and no one perceived them as antagonistic toward groups that were even more oppressed. Moreover (let us not forget), the "marvelous Georgian" was considered a specialist on the national question in the Bolshevik milieu and therefore, almost automatically, a specialist on national equality as well.

Anti-Semitism in Georgia toward Georgian and other local Jews was immeasurably weaker than anti-Semitism in Russia toward Russian Jews. But Stalin very quickly broke with his Georgian roots and moved into Russian revolutionary circles. And as Lenin justly noted in a different context, "Foreigners who become Russified always overdo it in terms of the real Russian mood." The future leader's vanity and ambition are well known, and therefore there is no need to prove the obvious. Let us keep these qualities in mind as we try to delve into the real world and the real milieu that formed Stalin's worldview and created the stereotypes that persisted in his mind for the rest of his life.

The people to whom he was closest during exile and at the top after the revolution, the ones on whom he depended as a figure in the Party milieu, were primarily Jewish. Later some would become his rivals in a power struggle, but even before that they became intellectual rivals, competing for a place in the underground Party hierarchy and for the respect of the rank-and-file members. The level of education (even if only self-education), erudition, and culture of his milieu was significantly different from that of the seminary dropout. Yakov Sverdlov, Lev Kamenev (Rozenfeld), and Filipp Goloshchekin* were better educated (especially Kamenev) and treated Stalin with a mixture of

---

* Filipp was the Party nickname of a prominent Bolshevik who was one of the main organizers of the murder of the tsar's family in 1918. The chief of the investigative commission in the case, General M. Diterikhs, calls him Isaac, the investigator N. Sokolov calls him Shai, and Richard Pipes, Isaiah. All the Jewish names come from the pre-revolutionary police file published by the historian Sergei Melgunov. The tsarist police don't seem to have known his real name either. The son of a small contractor, he became a Bolshevik in 1903, a member of the Petersburg Bolshevik Committee in 1905, and one of the seven members of the Central Committee (CC) and a member of the Russian Bureau of the CC with Sverdlov and Stalin in 1912. But Lenin did not like him. In 1917 Goloshchekin lost his place in the CC and returned only in 1924, after Lenin's death. He displayed boundless cruelty in the genocide of the Kazakhs when he became Party leader of Kazakhstan. He was executed without the ornamental formality of a trial in October 1941 on the personal orders of Beria and with the knowledge of Stalin.

superiority, condescension, and patronage. The "marvelous" but infinitely touchy Georgian never forgot these insults, even though the insulters probably never intended to humiliate their comrade.

Stalin's inferiority complex—intellectual, national, and physical (much has been written about his withered arm and his complexion that does not need repeating here)—influenced all his decisions and actions when he achieved unlimited power. The need to rid himself of his "Georgianness" and his accent, which gave him a special charm in the eyes of millions but was for him a great source of torment, must be seen in the general context of his ethnic complexes. When, much later, Alexei Diky, an actor at the Maly Theater who had been released from the camps on Stalin's personal orders, was given the role of Stalin in one of a series of toadying plays, he refused to do the Georgian accent—because he couldn't do "a good one." The chiefs of Soviet culture were terrified, anticipating Stalin's wrath. A few days after seeing the show, Stalin called the Commissar of Culture and asked him to convey his gratitude to Comrade Diky, for he alone had understood Comrade Stalin, who "was the true leader of the truly Russian people." The culture bosses pondered that "historical remark" for a long time (in particular, they did not know whether it was now politically correct to portray the great leader without any accent—in which case, did that mean they had to get rid of the Georgian actor Gelovani, Stalin's current favorite, who played him in all films with his own native Georgian accent?), but the reason for Stalin's "gratitude" was obvious.

But that came later. The roots of the tragedy that took place in the late forties and early fifties must be sought in the late teens and early twenties. While before the revolution it was emotional factors that pressed on Stalin and his burgeoning anti-Semitism, after the revolution more prosaic and concrete factors came into play. The vicious power struggle was organically colored in national hues. Every (not almost every, but literally every) one of Stalin's serious rivals in that struggle was Jewish.

THE QUESTION OF Lenin's will, or, put more precisely, of who would be the second person in the Party and the state, arose while Lenin was still alive, in reasonably good health, and full of leadership energy. "Legally"—before his early death—this second person was Yakov Sverdlov, but in fact the name that always came after Lenin's was that of Lev Trotsky, the founder of the Red Army. Lenin's closest allies were Grigori Zinoviev and Lev Kamenev. They, and they alone, formed the "leadership nucleus" and had every reason to expect to inherit the mantle of leadership from Lenin. The man closest to the "troika" (Trotsky-Zinoviev-Kamenev) after Sverdlov's death was Grigori Sokolnikov (Brilliant), a former advocate and perhaps the most outstanding Bolshevik leader after Trotsky, a member of the Central Committee, and at one time a candidate member of the Politburo. It was he who signed the infamous Brest-Litovsk Peace Treaty. He commanded armies and implemented monetary reform with equal panache. Stalin hated him passionately, and with cause. It was Sokolnikov who in 1926 would demand from the tribune of a Party congress Stalin's removal as General Secretary. All four men whom Stalin perceived as his rivals in the struggle for power were Jewish. This situation, of course, could have affected any non-Jewish Bolshevik leader, but Stalin was already even more susceptible than most to anti-Semitism.

But these four were not the only manifestation of the "Jewish presence" that Stalin found so undesirable in the Bolshevik leadership. Each of them, especially Trotsky, naturally had a large number of allies in the higher echelons of power who could influence the distribution of posts and positions and the political clout and popularity of the candidates. There was a certain ethnic "imbalance" here too. It was not obvious, nor would it be noted by anyone brought up in a different milieu, in a different country, with different traditions formed over the centuries, with prejudices, of course, but prejudices with a different historical basis.

In the cruel power struggle—which was presented as a battle between positions of principle, ideology, and tactical programs, but was in fact a clash of personalities, each fighting to scramble to the top of the heap over the bodies of their rivals—in these conditions in Russia with its many nationalities and ethnic problems, the obvious "alienness" allegedly uniting an entire bloc of candidates was a glaring circumstance. This dramatic plot was complicated further by the fact that the candidate on the other side of the struggle for the Russian "throne" was also an "alien." But at least he was Christian and could in terms of the old Russian mentality claim to be a manifestation of the Russian spirit. His rivals could not.

The writer Ivan Bunin, later a Nobel laureate, noted in his émigré memoirs Cursèd Days the "fierce anti-Semitism" that reigned wherever the Red Army passed. The army units had numerous Latvians, Poles, Ukrainians, Armenians, Georgians, and Tatars, yet no one recalls any fierce anti-Latvianism or anti-Armenianism or anti-Tatarism.

On the third anniversary of the October Revolution there was published a colorful album, which opened with a photomontage of a gallery of the founders of the revolution—Lenin surrounded by his closest comrades. To the right of Lenin is Zinoviev, to the left, Trotsky. There are sixty-one men in the photographs, but Stalin is not among them. We can imagine his frustration and anger. And of the pictured Bolsheviks, more than a third, twenty-two, are Jews. And the picture, moreover, does not include Kaganovich, Pyatnitsky, Goloshchekin, and many others who were part of the ruling circle, and whose presence on that album page would have raised the percentage of Jews even higher.

In doing this sort of mathematics, I place myself on the same path taken by contemporary fascist groups who seek out Jewish names among the Bolshevik leaders and find them even where they do not exist. And not only among the Bolsheviks. The fascists have reached the point where they claim that the outstanding Russian statesman of the late eighteenth century, Count Mikhail Loris-Melikov, an Armenian, was actually Leib Meerzon, and that the head of the Provisional Government, the Russian nobleman Alexander Kerensky, was Aaron Kuperstok. According to the latest theoretician of anti-Semitism, A. Romanenko of Leningrad, Kerensky's real name was Kirgus, and Bukharin was Pinkus, and Dzerzhinsky really Frumkin, and so on.

The goal of such speculations is obvious: to prove that the revolution of 1917 was the work of international Jewry. What is not clear is why, then, these exposers thirst for a return to the system imposed exclusively by the Jews on the vast expanses of the Russian Empire. The only way to argue with these obscurantists and Black Hundred fascists is with reason, objectivity, and reality.

Counting up these insulting percentages provides me with no pleasure. The very concept must seem strange to a person living in a different society. I remember a popular Soviet joke of the seventies. Leonid Brezhnev comes to America and President Nixon starts giving him a hard time about discrimination against Jews in the USSR. "Discrimination? In our country?" Brezhnev is indignant. He pulls out a piece of paper from his pocket. "Why, we have 2,143 Jews in the Academy of Sciences, 87 at Moscow University, and 35 in the Leningrad Symphony Orchestra. Well, how many Jews do you have in the New York Philharmonic?" "I don't know," replies Nixon. And that was the point of the joke.

But we Russians cannot manage without toting up figures, because it enables us to evade the issue. Of course, it is easy to refute the political basis of the blatant anti-Semitism of today's national patriotic groups—especially since it is not based on real figures and facts but on fabricated ones.

A very popular quotation today in Russia comes from a book by Henry Ford, the American industrialist and anti-Semite, called *International Jewry*. This quotation appears in one "patriotic" newspaper after another. "The Bolshevik government in the form it took in late summer 1920 was the complete triumph of the Jews. To show the distribution of power, here are some examples—in the Council of Commissars, 17 Jews out of 22 members (77%); in the Military Commissariat, 33 Jews out of 43 members (76%); in the Justice Commissariat, 20 Jews out of 21 (95%); and of the 41 leading journalists, 41 were Jews (100%)." Vyacheslav Molotov repeated similar nonsense, conversing in his dotage with his admiring confidant, the patriot poet Felix Chuev: "In the first government, the Jews had a majority in the Politburo." And certainly Molotov ought to know better.

But only the least educated, totally ignorant reader could accept these "facts" on faith. There was only one Jew in the Council of Commissars (the government) during the years of the Civil War—Trotsky. In the Revolutionary Military Council (which Ford calls the Military Commissariat), there were three (Trotsky, Sklyansky, Rozengolts, and for a very brief time, Drabkin). There wasn't a single Jew in the Justice Commissariat. And many of the "leading journalists" of that period were Russian Orthodox Christians, including Bukharin,

Osminsky, Pyatakov, Lunacharsky, and Skvortsov-Stepanov, so the hundred percent figure is simply false.

And the same picture holds for the Central Committee. The last Bolshevik congress in which Lenin participated took place in April 1922. The same four Jews (Trotsky, Zinoviev, Kamenev, and Sokolnikov) who had been members since the summer of 1917 were elevated to membership in the Central Committee in 1922. And the same four became part of the Politburo (thirteen members in all) elected right after Lenin's death. Three of them were relieved of their duties very quickly by Stalin, who then moved the fourth, Sokolnikov, into the background.

Be that as it may, the abundance of Jewish names in the higher and middle levels of power (in the Party and state apparat, in the military ministry, etc.) is indisputable, and it requires not so much analysis as evaluation. The greatest mistake is to look at this fact from today's point of view and to apply today's criteria. For anti-Semites now, this is an odious and outrageous fact; from the point of view of normal people not blinded by chauvinist hatred, it is meaningless. For people without prejudice, the question is what a statesman does, not the kind of blood in his veins.

But we will study this phenomenon from only one angle. We still try to look at it through Stalin's eyes at that time and to understand his feelings when he fought for power. The presence and influx of Jews to the ruling circles and their visible activism irritated and angered him. A late veteran of the Komsomol (Young Communist League) told me that Stalin had disliked the Komsomol from the start and was prejudiced against it—because it was founded by the "Jewish upstart" Lazar Shatskin.

STALIN MUST HAVE been vexed much more by other "upstarts" who had taken command positions in almost every front, army, division, and brigade created by Trotsky. There were only three "upstarts" (plus one for a few months) in the Higher Military Council, but there were dozens among the commanders, commissars, and members of the military councils of the fronts, armies, and smaller units. Some of them revealed brilliant military talents. They won victory after victory at the front, which created an opportunity for the Kremlin intriguers to fight among themselves. And when Stalin won the court intrigues and had himself declared a great strategist whose genius guaranteed the Bolshevik triumph in the Civil War, the fate of the true strategists was sealed. It would have been the same fate no matter what their ethnic background had been. But the ethnic element added a special color to the bloody drama.

In the 1930s, Stalin destroyed almost all the Jewish officers in the army. The few survivors had not seen combat but were commissars, fiery agitators, and propagandists. The most servile and insignificant survived—the illiterate academician, the country's chief atheist, Emelyan Yaroslavsky (Minei Gubelman); his brother, Moisey Gubelman; Lev Mekhlis, who would remain Stalin's right-hand man until the leader's death; Isaak Mintz, a close friend of Mekhlis who later became an academician and a specialist on Party history (he is ninety-six now and his vile character will be portrayed in the next-to-last chapter of this book); and finally, Rozalia Zemlyachka (Zalkind), a sadist and monster who would play a major role in the slaughter in the Crimea after the destruction of the last stronghold of the White Movement there. The rest died from the bullets of the Lubyanka executioners or in the GULAG.

None of them was part of Stalin's entourage, and they all knew the truth about the Civil War. Perhaps not the whole truth, but each knew his own small part. And there was no place for Stalin in that panorama. And they were all guilty in his eyes. What they had in common was their background, even though they themselves might not have given it a second thought. In those days the romantics believed that they were united only by the ideals of the revolution and the struggle for the happiness of the proletariat of the world. But Stalin had a different and more penetrating view of things.

Decades later, Molotov revealed (in conversation with Felix Chuev) Stalin's secret thoughts about that period. He said that Stalin, rather than allowing Kamenev to become head of government after Lenin's death, even though this seemed the most appropriate succession (Kamenev had taken Lenin's place as chairman of the Council of Commissars during the latter's final illness), preferred to give the position to Alexei Rykov, "so that the head of the government would be a

Russian. In those days Jews held many top spots, even though they formed a small percentage of the country's population. . . . Even though Kamenev did not even look Jewish. Only when you looked into his eyes . . ." (This statement, doubtless accurately recorded by his interlocutor, is a good clue to the way Molotov and Stalin thought.)

The point is not that among the organizers of the revolution and the first rulers of the new Russia there were "only Jews." That silly statement is easily refuted with facts and figures. And the point is not that after the success of the coup and after so-called peaceful construction began, they occupied even more leadership positions. That too can be refuted. But here is something that cannot be refuted and that gives us pause for thought. There was an astonishing number of Jews not in comparison with their colleagues and comrades-in-arms of other ethnic groups, but in comparison with the proportion of Jews in the political life of pre-revolutionary Russia, that is, just two or three years earlier. And that enormous and totally unexpected change was so striking, so eloquent, that it caused a distortion in the perception of the real role of Jews at the government helm—a distortion even among the un-prejudiced, and a need among the prejudiced to turn this new phe-nomenon in Russian history into something negative.

At the very top of the Kremlin, as we can now judge from memoirs, the Jewish theme was the focus of attention even then, although at the middle and lower echelons it was a taboo topic. The great interna-tionalists would not permit even discussions on national themes, con-sidering them counterrevolutionary, and so kept a monopoly on such discussions for themselves.

The Marxist historian Mikhail Pokrovsky, extremely popular in the twenties, noted that "Jews constitute from one-fourth to one-third of the organizing level of all revolutionary parties in Russia," that is, not only of the Bolsheviks, but of the Mensheviks (where their percentage was even higher), and the Socialist Revolutionaries. It would have been strange for everyone in that milieu to forget or even to pretend to forget who was what. The lawyer Moisey Uritsky, an exceptionally noble- and intelligent-looking man, was the scourge of Petrograd in 1918, terrorizing the citizenry as chairman of the local Cheka. He was killed by another Jew, Leonid Kanegisser, the talented poet and hope of young Russian literature. On the same day in Moscow, Lenin was wounded. Fani Kaplan was declared the attacker, and she was shot three days later without a trial, on Sverdlov's personal orders, inculcating her culpability in the minds of several generations. Today there is little doubt that Kaplan did not shoot Lenin at all, that he had not been "mortally wounded," and that there had been no poisoned bullets. The likely attackers, the laborer Novikov and the volunteer policeman Protopopov, were allowed to escape. It is thought that the real would-be assassins (although the "mortally wounded" Lenin was chairing a meeting of the Council of Commissars less than a week later) did not have the right profile because of their proletarian background, which violated the reigning class paradigm. But they may not have been suited ethnically either.

Russian history after October 25, 1917, is an endless chain of mysteries and dark spots, unexplained contradictions. The facts about Jewish participation in the fateful moments of that history are contradictory too, because the "ethnic presence" is seen on both sides of the visible and invisible barricade—with aims that are in direct contradiction to each other. But we are not studying the history of Russian anti-Semitism or the role of Jews in the revolution. In touching on these large and complex problems, we are following a single goal—to present Stalin in the historical context that fed and developed his anti-Semitic feelings, which certainly did not arise overnight but evolved inexorably over a long period.

Kremlin mores and work habits in the early post-revolutionary years exhibited a constant concern, expressed in a joking manner that usually hides heightened interest, with the Jewish question, which had to have had an effect on Stalin's sensitive mind. It is therefore interesting to see what detail his memory retained, if we are to judge from Molotov's reminiscences (it also reveals what Molotov retained). "Stalin told me," Molotov recalled when he was ninety years old, "that once when he was commissar on national problems he came to Lenin for approval of the makeup of some commission. He read off the names—so-and-so and so-and so . . . And Lenin said, 'What? Not a single little Jew? This commission won't accomplish a thing.' "

No matter how Stalin's attitude toward Molotov changed in the last months of his life (which will be discussed later), he had no one closer or more loyal to him than that "stone arse" (Lenin's description of Molotov). Molotov absorbed his manner of thinking, his attitude toward many facts and phenomena of the world around him, and particularly toward individuals. And so the opinions of the aged Molotov, who forgot no one and nothing, on certain political figures of the recent and distant past are of great interest, especially on those people who came to a tragic end, not without his direct participation.

After his immortal aphorism "Jews are the most oppositional nation," Molotov brings up Nikolai Krestinsky for no apparent reason. But there is in fact a good reason. Krestinsky, one of the most cultivated and educated men in the Bolshevik leadership, an economist and diplomat with entree into the Central Committee and the Politburo, was executed by Stalin in 1938. He was the only participant in all three major Moscow show trials who found the courage to deny publicly all the charges made against him. But he was broken the night of his trial through torture and blackmail. And so right after stating that "Jews are the most oppositional nation," Molotov went on to say, "Krestinsky, apparently, was a former Jew, a baptized one. That must be why he has such a strange name. [*Krest* is Russian for "cross" and *krestit* is "to christen."] . . . We didn't know what to do with him until we arrested him."

Of course, Stalin and Molotov found a place in a common grave for everyone whom they didn't know what to do with. But the distinctive element here is that Molotov was not thinking about Trotskyism, or terrorism, or opportunism when he brought up Krestinsky, but about his alleged (and hidden, which must have driven the great internationalists mad) affiliation with the "most oppositional nation," which determined his fate and which Molotov does not hide. And yet Nikolai Krestinsky, the son of modest Russian intellectuals, was neither a "former" nor a "real" Jew, and therefore suffered for no reason at all.

"Stalin was not an anti-Semite, as they sometimes try to depict him," Molotov maintained in the late 1970s. "He noted many qualities in the Jewish people—hard work, unity, political activism. Their activism is higher than average, that's for sure. . . . However, there were not too many of them in the tsarist prisons and in exile. But when we took power, many of them became Bolsheviks even though they had been Mensheviks before that."

Many people switched sides to the one in power then, and the switchers came from dozens of different ethnic groups that formed the huge empire. But that is not the point. As we will see, the qualities Stalin noted in the Jews can be interpreted in two ways. "Political activism," especially that which is "higher than average," was the very basis for accusing thousands and thousands of innocent people of terrorism, diversion, espionage, sabotage, and many other things that the feeble imagination of the "marvelous Georgian" and his henchmen at the Lubyanka could concoct. Attempting to remove the anti-Semite label from Stalin, Molotov merely added new arguments to support the case.

STALIN SPENT A LIFETIME justifying himself and portraying himself, without any apparent external stimulus for such declarations, as a determined foe of anti-Semitism. Psychology tells us why he kept returning to the question and proving what no one then disputed. And criminologists have long observed the maniacal need of a criminal to justify himself, even if he has not been accused of anything.

"I learned quite suddenly," recalled his former secretary, Boris Bazhanov, "that Stalin was an anti-Semite. . . . I learned it accidentally. I was standing and talking with Mekhlis. Stalin came out of his office and moved toward us. Mekhlis says, 'Here, Comrade Stalin, is a letter from Comrade Faivilovich [one of the secretaries of the Central Committee of the Komsomol; I have already mentioned Stalin's love for the Komsomol and its Jewish organizers]. Comrade Faivilovich is very unhappy with the behavior of the Central Committee.' Stalin exploded: 'Who does that lousy little Yid think he is!' Comrade Stalin sensed immediately that he had said too much, turned and went back to his office. . . .

"Why did Stalin, as an anti-Semite, have two Jewish secretaries—Lev Mekhlis and Grigori Kanner? I quickly learned that they were there for camouflage. During the Civil War Stalin had led a group of outlaws who hated Trotsky, his deputy Sklyansky, and their Jewish colleagues in the Military Commissariat, which led the Party bosses to suspect Stalin of anti-Semitism. When he moved to civilian work, Stalin took Kanner and Mekhlis as his closest associates to obviate those suspicions. . . . He never regretted that choice. Kanner and Mekhlis were always his loyal workers. However, he did have Kanner shot in 1937, just in case. Kanner had been involved intimately in too many shady affairs of Stalin's."

One such affair was the destruction of Efraim Sklyansky, Trotsky's deputy, and a leader of the Red Army during the Civil War and the first few years after the war. Sklyansky was drowned in a lake during a business trip to the United States along with the director of Amtorg (the Soviet-American trading corporation), Isaiah Khurgin, a good friend of Vladimir Mayakovsky. The murder of two Jews whom Stalin hated had been organized by two other Jews, Kanner and Yagoda. Let us add that Kanner's assistant, Bombin, and Mekhlis's assistants, Makhover and Yuzhak, were all Jewish. They all died, except for Mekhlis. Stalin held on to him as a shield to ward off all accusations of anti-Semitism. Although who could actually accuse him of anything?

More categorical and convincing evidence of Stalin's anti-Semitism comes from Nikita Khrushchev, who knew him well and for a long time. Khrushchev, however, thought that a "fit of anti-Semitism" happened "suddenly . . . after the war." But it wasn't a sudden fit at all, but instead a manifestation of what had been accumulating inside for many years, hidden by declarations of the unacceptability of anti-Semitism and condemnations of it—often harshly, in the strongest and most unambivalent terms. Konstantin Simonov in his memoirs also asserted that only "in his very last years did Stalin take a position on the Jewish question that was directly opposed to the one he stated publicly." But he expressed a negative attitude toward anti-Semitism at every stage of his life known to us. Why then was it only "in his very last years" that those same words suddenly began to be at odds with his private thoughts? Now we know with certainty that his words never coincided with his thoughts. And whenever the wave of anti-Semitism rose in him, the more persistently and energetically—psychologically understandable—he tried to prove, without any external stimulus, just the opposite in rather large gatherings of people, because he knew news of his words, especially on such a touchy subject, would quickly spread.

From that point of view the archives of a respected but almost forgotten musical figure are of great interest. The composer Dmitri Rogal-Levitsky has faded into obscurity even though he was the teacher of such important composers as Aram Khachaturyan and Rodion Shchedrin. His evidence is all the more interesting because he was Polish, an intellectual of the first water, a man with a flawless reputation and removed from all political passions. He spoke with Stalin on only one occasion, and quite by accident. In 1944 he was commissioned to orchestrate the new state anthem. After turning in the work, he was invited to a government banquet backstage at the Bolshoi Theater. That same night, with almost stenographic accuracy, he recorded the conversation. Only now, almost a half century later, has it become possible to gain access to his notebooks, which were carefully hidden by his family.

There is nothing seditious in his notes, by contemporary standards or even by the standards of those days. But the composer feared to his dying breath the prospect of their being made public, even though he knew their historical value. I will skip the fascinating details, the chitchat of Molotov, Beria, Malenkov, Voroshilov, the Kremlin leaders' thoughts on music, their jokes, or rather what they considered jokes. I quote only what has direct relevance for this book.

Stalin asked how many conductors there were at the Bolshoi Theater. They told him seven, of whom three were Jews, but Stalin did not ask because he wanted the answer, which he already knew.

"Do you have Golovanov* here?" Stalin asked slyly, smiling. {The slyness is understandable, for he knew the answer.—A.V.}

"We were planning to entrust two or three productions to him," began Tsazovsky {the chief conductor of the Bolshoi, a Jew, which, as we will see, is significant here.—A.V.}.

"And?" Stalin interrupted.

"He refused."

"Good thing!" Stalin said, striking a match. "I don't like him. . . . He's an anti-Semite. Yes, a real anti-Semite. A crude anti-Semite. He should not be allowed into the Bolshoi Theater. . . . It's like letting a goat into the cabbage patch," he said, and laughed.

---

* Nikolai Golovanov (1891–1953), opera and symphonic conductor, professor at the Moscow Conservatory, and husband of the great Russian singer Antonina Nezhdanova.

Then the conversation turned to a different topic, but awhile later, without any obvious connection, Stalin returned to the first theme.

> *"But that Golovanov is an anti-Semite," Stalin began insisting again.*
> *"I've not dealt with him in that sense."*
> *"Don't worry, you will, if you let him into the Bolshoi Theater. . . .*
> *Golovanov is a real anti-Semite, a dangerous, principled anti-Semite,"*
> *Stalin said angrily. "You cannot let Golovanov into the Bolshoi The-*
> *ater. That anti-Semite will turn everything upside down."*

The intention of Stalin's remarks is obvious, just as obvious as the fact that these remarks, spoken angrily in front of a handful of musicians, would immediately become the subject of discussion far beyond the musical and theatrical worlds of Moscow. His maniacal insistence on making his point is evidence of his desire to create the impression that he was a foe of anti-Semitism and that whatever might happen, he had nothing to do with it. If something were to happen, it would be done without him, and in fact done against his will.

In Chapter 7 we will learn what had dictated this unexpected explosion and unusual expression of Stalin's anger. A fine musician, Golovanov was in fact known widely as a person who, to put it mildly, did not like his colleagues of Jewish extraction. The Russian idiom "a goat in the cabbage patch" makes Stalin's point. If Golovanov were to have his way, he would "clean out" the Jews from the Bolshoi Theater, without any instructions from above.

Stalin's scenario was completed four years later. In 1948, Arii Pazovsky was removed as artistic director and chief conductor of the Bolshoi Theater and was replaced by Nikolai Golovanov. And the latter did behave like a goat in a cabbage patch, just as Stalin had predicted. For his behavior Stalin bestowed upon Golovanov the title of People's Artist of the USSR and three Stalin Prizes during the dictator's lifetime. This episode, more than any other, is a paradigm with farcical overtones of Stalin's treachery and hypocrisy on the "Jewish question."

LENIN HAD RUSSIAN, Kalmyk, German, Swedish, and Jewish blood. Of this wealth, contemporary Russian anti-Semites, with pathological pleasure, draw on only the Jewish blood for their exploitative conclusions. In former times, only the Russian blood was considered. Propaganda stressed the fact that Vladimir Ulyanov came from Russian nobility, and for the cause of the world proletariat's happiness he broke with his class, that there was no foreign admixture in his pure Russian blue blood.

Marietta Shaginyan, a Russian-Armenian writer working on a chronicle novel called *The Ulyanov Family*, managed in the late 1950s to get into top secret files kept in the Marx-Engel-Lenin-Stalin Institute, where she discovered a great secret. She established that Lenin's maternal grandfather was a baptized Jew whose name was Blank. This discovery created enormous trouble for the indefatigable writer (who joined the Communist Party fairly late in life, as a patriotic gesture during World War II). The book, which included the information from her sensational find, was removed from libraries and bookstores and destroyed. The archivists who were not vigilant and the censors who missed the book's sedition were harshly punished.

This episode seemed only a curiosity to me until I discovered a few fascinating documents in my mother's defense attorney files. During the years of the thaw under Khrushchev, she took innumerable cases for rehabilitation, that is, she tried to get legal rehabilitation—rarely for those still living, usually posthumously—for the victims of the Great Terror.

What I found were not documents but her handwritten copies, which she had made (I think illegally, since it was forbidden to do so) of fragments from sentences, pleas, and other materials to which a few advocates were given limited access. And I found the following extract in my mother's dossier on the case of one Zeilik Kamenitser, sentenced to ten years in the camps by a tribunal of the Moscow Military District in 1940:

> *Continuing his counterrevolutionary and hostile activity, Kamenitser spread slanderous thoughts at work and among his friends which calumnied the Soviet regime and the leaders of the Party and the Soviet state. . . . Witnesses Rodin, Lebedeva, and Golyshko stated that Kamenitser slanderously maintained that V. I. Lenin was part Jewish and that this fact is intentionally hidden in the biography of V. I. Lenin that is studied in middle and higher school and in the network of Party*

education. . . . The accused does not deny spreading these thoughts, but insists that he had no intention of performing counterrevolutionary acts. . . . Kamenitser has a higher education and therefore could not have been unaware of the counterrevolutionary character of his statements. Besides which, as witness Lebedeva testified, Kamenitser asked her "not to blab at every corner about what he had told her," which means he recognized the inappropriate and dangerous character of his slanderous words.

The dossier also has excerpts from a letter Kamenitser sent to Stalin from the camps. There is no date, but we can assume it was sent soon after his arrival in the camp. Kamenitser wrote:

Bolshevik's word of honor, dear leader and teacher, our own Josif Vissarionovich, that I do not understand what I did wrong, even if I were wrong and Vladimir Ilyich had no one in his ancestry but Russians. In telling a few of my friends there were representatives of the most varied nationalities populating our great Homeland in Vladimir Ilyich Lenin's genealogy, I wanted merely to stress his great internationalism, his belonging to many peoples of our land. Is there anything counterrevolutionary about this, or on the contrary, was I showing comrades who were not in the Party the great internationalism of our great Party?

From the questions of the chairman of the tribunal I realized that the "most slanderous" part of my statements was considered the part where I mention among Vladimir Ilyich's other ancestors, his Jewish ones. I tried in my answer to explain that even if I had been mistaken, this could not be considered counterrevolutionary slander because there is nothing criminal or flawed in having such relatives. . . . In our great country, where under the sun of the Stalin Constitution over one hundred nationalities live happily and in friendship, everyone can be proud of his ancestors and know that the rest are also proud of them. . . . I asked the chairman to explain to me what anti-Semitism was in that case, but he interrupted me harshly and said that the tribunal does not have to explain anything to anyone as it simply judged criminals. . . . What criminal am I, dear, beloved Josif Vissarionovich? Please explain that to me.

But the dear and beloved leader did not explain anything either. It is unlikely that he read Zeilik Kamenitser's naïve and touching (or was it wise and clever?) letter, but there was an answer. It came in the form of a new sentence. The camp court added another five years to his term in the GULAG because "while serving his time, he continued his hostile anti-Soviet propaganda among the inmates." The papers I found did not give the content of his propaganda.

Kamenitser died (or was killed) in the camps in 1946 and was posthumously rehabilitated in 1959. I doubt that he ever got an explanation of his guilt.

And really, what was it? Why did Stalin fear the spread of that innocent—for those days—information? Hating Lenin secretly (both for his testament and for his final letter in which Lenin said he was breaking off "all relations" with Stalin, as well as for many other reasons), Stalin canonized the founder, declaring him to be in fact the untouchable Communist saint. Nothing in Lenin's biography could contain anything that could contradict any twist in the Party line. That is why thousands of Lenin's documents have been hidden until quite recently (and most are still inaccessible today). That is why his partial Jewish ancestry was considered inappropriate, since the eagle eye of dearly beloved Josif Vissarionovich saw from far, far away the coming anti-Semitic windstorm, which he himself would organize. And in that storm the Jewish forebears of the canonized leader would be completely out of place.

Stalin's ability to see far, to understand, and to calculate was as highly developed as his cruelty and treachery.

3

JEWS AGAINST JEWS

STALIN'S ANTI-SEMITISM JUXTAPOSED to the unquestionable fact that a large part of his milieu—both professional and personal—was made up for almost a quarter century by Jews, may seem to pose an inexplicable contradiction. Yet this paradox is quite natural. In fact, the two phenomena are interdependent. The more people of "undesirable background" there were around him and part of his everyday life, the deeper and fiercer grew his truly biological hatred of them, gradually turning into a mania.

It is well known that people like Stalin do not feel gratitude for those who do them good, but on the contrary, feel hatred and a need to be rid of them. Their presence is a reminder of the good deed and so makes the beneficiary feel psychologically dependent. It is quite possible that some of them have no expectations of a favor in return, are not counting on special attentions, much less rewards; but they are doomed nevertheless, because it is impossible to change the mind of a maniac and fanatic. The episode involving Zinoviev is a good example. As many historians have noted, it was the unprincipled behavior of Kamenev and Zinoviev in their struggle for power with Trotsky that led them after Lenin's death to join forces with Stalin in a "triumvirate" and thereby stay on top for another two years, giving Stalin time to deal with his main rival, then with them, then with Bukharin and his associates, to become the sole and all-powerful dictator. A year and a half after their Pyrrhic victory, which would lead inexorably to their execution, Zinoviev asked Stalin at a meeting of the Presidium of the Central Committee: "Does Comrade Stalin know the meaning of ordinary gratitude?" Stalin replied, unperturbed, "I do, I know very well what it is, it's a dog's disease." He was not without wit.

As fate would have it, the people who surrounded Stalin and who had rendered him services in the twenties and thirties were mostly Jews. Among the first leaders of the repressive apparat created almost immediately after the revolution to terrorize the whole country, first in the form of the VChK, or Cheka (the All-Russian Extreme Commission), then turning into the GPU (the Main Political Directorate), the NKVD (People's Commissariat of Internal Affairs), and finally the KGB (Committee on State Security), the man who was closest to Stalin and worked totally on his behalf was Genrikh Yagoda. Two other leaders, both Poles—Felix Dzerzhinsky and Vyacheslav Menzhinsky—were more distant from Stalin and, paradoxically, from the institution they headed. While formally head of that typical Soviet police monster until his death, Dzerzhinsky focused most of his attention on agriculture, simultaneously as head of the Higher Council on Agriculture, and seemed to be more a member of the GPU than its director. His first deputy, Menzhinsky, was a sickly and totally indifferent man, a cynic and aesthete, who spent his time lying on a couch and reading books in the many languages he knew. That alone would keep him from learning (nor, probably, did he wish to learn) one more language, the most important for his career—that of direct contact with Stalin.

But Yagoda, another of Dzerzhinsky's deputies, knew that language—and no other. He was the real chief of the Lubyanka even when he was second deputy director.

Born in Nizhni Novgorod, Yagoda was trained as a pharmacist (which came in handy later when the NKVD under his direction began a secret laboratory for the preparation of poisons), but worked as an apprentice in the jewelry studio of Moisey Sverdlov, whose son Yakov (Yanekl) would be "president" of Soviet Russia for a brief time—November 1917 to March 1919—and whose granddaughter (Yakov's niece) Ida would marry Yagoda. These court marriages were much more popular among the Soviet elite than even among European royalty. Almost all of them married people of their own circle, and this tradition was continued with even greater intensity by their children and grandchildren. Yakov Sverdlov's nephew and Yagoda's brother-in-law was Leopold Averbakh, the chief supervisor of Party purity in Soviet literature. It was not easy for outsiders to break into the family network.

And Yagoda was the man Stalin trusted most within the repressive apparat without which no totalitarian regime can exist. The Soviet version of dictatorship and Stalin personally would not have survived without the "faithful watchdogs of the revolution" and their "punishing swords."

The Soviet political police had "aliens" in its makeup from the start, particularly Latvians, Poles, and Jews. It is important to note that "aliens" (including Armenians and Georgians) formed a very large percentage of all Soviet departments and ministries—for obvious reasons. Oppressed, or at least discriminated against, second- and even third-class citizens in the old Russia, they felt a new energy in the new regime and with fanatical dedication launched themselves on revolutionary careers. But their presence was most visible (again for obvious reasons) in the activities of the vicious Cheka-GPU, noticed by both the public at large and the leaders who paid attention to the national question. The very fact that the life and death of hundreds of thousands, of millions of people depended on these men caused them to be scrutinized closely. Certain characteristics were noted even by internationalists who were not in the least interested in ethnic background.

The revolution brought to the top not the intellectual Jews, who had suffered discrimination under the tsars and had had to struggle to get an education and a university degree, to be able to master a profession and practice it wherever they wanted. The majority of Jewish intellectuals emigrated or became "fellow travelers," the "specials," scornfully tolerated by the Soviet regime. And a huge number of them ended up in the GULAG, or exile, or mass graves. But the illiterate petty craftsmen, who had ambitious dreams of careers and power over their kind—power of any sort—rushed to the capitals, and because of their flawless social background they received Party posts. The rest depended on their zeal and capacity for intrigue to make connections and to advance themselves.

The percentage of Jews in key posts in the Lubyanka did not differ markedly from the percentage in other departments, but the other departments interested only the people dealing with them, while the

Lubyanka interested everyone. And therefore if someone named Rabinovich was in charge of a mass execution, he was perceived not simply as a Cheka boss but as a Jew, while if someone named Abramovich was in charge of a mass epidemic countermeasure, he was perceived not as a Jew but as a good doctor. This was natural and not surprising.

It was the same reasoning that led to portraying the vicious murder of the tsar's family in Ekaterinburg in 1918 as the work of Jews, even though the vast majority of the executioners were Russian. Inflamed anti-Semites proclaimed one of the main organizers—chairman of the executive committee of the Urals Soviet, twenty-seven-year-old Alexander Beloborodov—to be the Jew Weisbrot, even though Oleg Platonov, a leading contemporary exposer of "Jewish crimes," has been forced to admit that "research in archives does not support this version." In their desire to find Jewish roots for Beloborodov, some people gave his father's name as Grigori (which is common in Jewish families) when it was actually Georgy.

But there is no getting around the fact that the first violins in the orchestra of death of the tsar and his family were four Jews—Yanker Yurovsky, Shaia Goloshchekin, Lev Sosnovsky, and Pinkus Vainer (Pert Voikov). The concert master and conductor was Yakov Sverdlov. It is quite possible, taking into account the extreme character of this murder against the background of the others that had become mundane, Lenin consciously left the organization of this Bolshevik act to Jews, so as to channel the wrath of the Whites and the Russian diaspora against them and then be able to accuse the indignant Russians of being anti-Semitic.

Could Stalin, as a member of the Central Committee and part of the innermost circle of the Party elite, been unaware of all the undercurrents in this scheme? Apparently he did not play a direct part in the murder of the tsar's family, but he learned a good lesson from the method of organizing bloody intrigues and manipulating public opinion. It goes without saying that the organizers and participants in the murder of the tsar's family came to the same end. Sosnovsky was shot in 1937, Beloborodov in 1938, Goloshchekin in 1941. Yurovsky died of cancer on the eve of his arrest in 1938 (the warrant had been signed), and Voikov was assassinated by an émigré student in 1927 in

Warsaw, where he had been sent as ambassador, and became a Soviet martyr saint. His name (his Party pseudonym, that is) remains on a Moscow street and metro station, despite the trend of restoring old names to cities and streets.

Working side by side with Yagoda was another professional Chekist (a euphemism for professional executioner), Meer Trilisser. He joined the Party in 1901 (at the age of eighteen) and remained a little-known figure among Bolsheviks until he started working in the "organs" and came to Stalin's attention. With Stalin's intervention, this unknown Jew became a top-ranking Chekist by 1921, heading the foreign section of the Cheka (and later the GPU and OGPU—United Main Political Directorate). His work included keeping an eye on foreign Communists and reporting on their sympathies and antipathies and their contacts with various Bolshevik leaders. Stalin was impressed that Trilisser had an obviously negative attitude toward Zinoviev. Of course, Trilisser could tell which way the wind was blowing and whom his benefactor liked and did not like.

This successful Chekist quickly received a promotion to the same level as Yagoda—deputy chairman of OGPU—becoming the second Stalinist at the helm of Lubyanka. The many actions undertaken by Trilisser's agents included blowing up the cathedral in Sofia with the Bulgarian tsar and his government inside and a much, much more important action—an attempt in Paris on the life of Boris Bazhanov, Stalin's secretary who fled the country. The attempt was a failure, but even that did not cause Trilisser to lose Stalin's favor.

In 1927, on the tenth anniversary of "the revolution's punishing sword" (the traditional high-flown Bolshevik epithet for the Soviet secret police, which became part of the political jargon), Trilisser was given the Order of the Red Banner. The anniversary "luckily" coincided with the total defeat of Trotsky, as well as of Zinoviev and Kamenev, who three years earlier had joined in a conspiracy with Stalin against Trotsky. Now all three were expelled from the Party.

Stalin "gratefully" acknowledged Trilisser's role, his help in supplying the General Secretary with valuable secret information about his sworn "friends," and furnished a solemn motivation for bestowing the order on his informer that is meaningless to the uninitiated but

transparent to those who are familiar with the language of the apparat:
". . . for especially promoting the strengthening of the dictatorship of
the proletariat with his courage, loyalty to the revolution, and tireless
persecution of its enemies and for especially valuable achievements in
the struggle against counterrevolution, espionage, banditry, and other
organizations hostile to Soviet power." Along with Trilisser, and with
similar formulations, this glorious battle order was awarded to many
other famous Chekists who were part of Stalin's entourage and who
had already distinguished themselves with a talent for execution—
Yakov Agranov, Matvei Berman, Karl Pauker, and other representatives of the Jewish proletariat.

There is evidence that Trilisser used his close relations with Stalin
to dig up some "dark spots" in Yagoda's biography (hinting at former
ties with the tsar's secret police) and reported them directly to the
dictator in the hope of further improving his position. The fierce war
for the throne of the ailing Menzhinsky as chief of OGPU was being
waged behind closed doors, and all the deputies dreamed of replacing
him. Stalin did not act on the valuable information, but remembered
it. At that time Yagoda was, on Stalin's orders, preparing the murder
of Kirov, and his own hour had not come. But Trilisser was not fired
for his inappropriate initiative; rather, he was promoted.

Soon afterward Stalin made the professional punisher the chief figure
of the Comintern, the Communist International, as a member of its
executive committee, presidium, and political secretariat. He used the
banal pseudonym Moskvin. Amazingly, that name, demonstrating
with dreary literalness the bearer's loyalty to Moscow, was used by
several other Comintern members, including foreign Communists,
and I have no idea how they kept the "Moskvins" separated.

As secretary of the executive committee of the Comintern, Trilisser-
Moskvin was in charge of personnel, a key position. The job was
always held by someone from the organs, but in this case, it was of an
order higher, since Trilisser had direct access to Stalin and got his
orders from Stalin. On all personnel issues (which included leading
comrades of all the fraternal parties), his word was law. His word was
not only the word of the NKVD but also the word of Stalin. The
Comintern archives are filled with respectful letters from friends abroad

to Comrade Moskvin with requests to confirm someone, replace someone, appoint someone, report on someone. Remarkably, even in the
latest edition of the *Great Soviet Encyclopedic Dictionary* (1991)—not to
mention the earlier ones—there is no mention in Trilisser's biography
of the almost four years he spent as personnel head of the Comintern
at the peak of the nightmare, 1935–1938.

Meer Trilisser (Mikhail Moskvin) met the fate that was inevitable
for them all. His case was run by Jewish investigators, some of whom
he had hired and who later followed him into that cellar to be shot.
Trilisser was accused of "placing Trotskyites, spies and provocateurs in
the fraternal communist parties of Greece, Poland, England, Estonia,
France, Hungary, Latvia and other countries." Not a single Trotskyite, spy, or provocateur was named; nor was it necessary in those days.
His students and colleagues at his beloved Lubyanka also claimed that
he became a spy for Japan in 1920 and for England in 1925. They
could have added many other countries, but they were too lazy. Besides, Stalin did not like reading very long documents, and this transcript was sent to him.

Trilisser was executed on February 2, 1940, on the same day as the
great theater director Vsevolod Meyerhold; as Mikhail Koltsov (Fridland), a worker of the NKVD and the Comintern and the country's
premier journalist, close to Stalin, yet hated by him for his "pushi-
ness"; and as Stalin's comrade-in-arms Robert Eikhe, among many
others. They were very different men, but there was one factor that put
them all on the same level—a bullet from the same executioner and
burial in a mass grave.

EVEN CLOSER TO STALIN than Trilisser were two high-ranking
figures at Lubyanka—Yakov Agranov, Yagoda's first deputy, and Karl
Pauker, head of the operative department.

Pauker—one of the Hungarian Jews who took an active part in the
Russian revolution (another, Bela Kun, spread bloody terror in the
Crimea with Rozalia Zemlyachka-Zalkind and was executed by Stalin
in 1938; yet another, Matyas Rakoszy, became dictator after the Red
Army occupied Hungary)—pleased Stalin and became chief of his

bodyguards. An illiterate barber, he compensated for his pathological ignorance with pathological cruelty and unbounded toadying. Stalin's trust in Pauker was so great that he allowed him—and only him—to shave him with a dangerous razor.

This satrap participated in many operations personally developed and approved by Stalin, and showed especial zeal and readiness to serve. For instance, he was a member of the group who arrested Kamenev. But this was not his primary role for Stalin. The toady knew that Stalin adored Jewish anecdotes, and he was an incomparable storyteller, amusing his boss with an ever-new store of jokes.

Jewish jokes come in two models. The first is imbued with irrepressible Jewish humor, a mixture of sadness with a strictly measured dose of self-irony, always evidence of spiritual health and faith in the solidity of the national spirit.

Pauker was a masterful teller of such anecdotes, and he needed clever writers to keep his repertoire fully stocked. Pauker himself was incapable of creating anything. According to reliable though unchecked sources, his main creative partner was none other than Karl Radek, the notable Bolshevik columnist and political figure, whose real influence was much greater than his official posts would indicate. This very talented and absolutely unprincipled politician, of Jewish extraction, would have been happy to amuse Stalin himself with his anti-Semitic jokes, but he did not enjoy the leader's trust to that degree, and so had to settle for anonymous ghostwriting that improved Pauker's standing in the boss's eyes. Pauker had a wonderful way of rolling his R's, and did a small-town Jewish accent that made the usually affectless Stalin roar with laughter. He did not even get too upset if Pauker ran short of new material, but enjoyed hearing the old stories over again.

There is a fairly well substantiated story that Pauker was personally present at the execution of Zinoviev and Kamenev, and that he is the source of information about the final minutes of Lenin's closest comrades, who with him had formed the leading circle of the revolution. After a late party, Pauker did an imitation of Zinoviev being dragged away to his execution by two guards, and with a Jewish accent (which Zinoviev did not have), moaning as he grabbed hold of the guards' legs, "For God's sake, comrades, call Josif Vissarionovich. Josif Vissarionovich promised to save our lives!" Delighted, Stalin choked with laughter and demanded a reprise.

The defector Alexander Orlov (Lev Feldbin), who knew the backstage life of the Kremlin and Lubyanka well, recounts in his memoirs, *The Secret History of Stalin's Crimes*, that the performance did not end there. "Pauker," Orlov writes, "added a new element to his performance. Instead of falling on his knees now when he depicted Zinoviev, he straightened up, reached to the heavens, and shouted, 'Hear O Israel, the Lord is our God, the Lord is One!'* Stalin couldn't stand it and, laughing and sobbing, he waved at Pauker to stop the show."

Actually, the truth of this episode (I do not mean "Pauker-Stalin" but "Zinoviev-executioners") is seriously open to question. Zinoviev, as he (literally) licked the boots of his killers minutes before his death, certainly must have shouted out some words. But *those* words are least likely to have been the ones. Pauker, however, knew what would make his boss laugh. He knew his hobbyhorse. And he played on the string that would please.

Either his incredible stupidity or the blindness that afflicted almost everyone kept Pauker from seeing his inevitable end. The recipient of every possible medal and order, he was arrested on April 21, 1937, and shot less than four months later, on August 14. The comic element (if that word can be used at all in the context of the great tragedy) was that the Jewish Pauker was seriously accused of being a Gestapo agent.

A year later the same fate befell another Chekist who was even closer to Stalin than Pauker. Yakov Agranov, deputy chief of the OGPU and then Deputy Commissar of Internal Affairs, was no illiterate Pauker. Stalin probably did not consider the sensible and well-educated man a friend (he never had a friend in his entire life) but certainly a "close comrade." In any case, he moved him into the Kremlin and gave him a dacha next to his own in the village of Zubalovo near Moscow.

Agranov began his "Soviet work" in Lenin's apparat as secretary of the Small Council of Commissars, and then moved to the Lubyanka,

---

* This is the "Shema," a central affirmation of faith in Judaism; among Orthodox Jews, it is traditionally the final utterance of a person before death.—Trans.

where he remained until his dying hour. A list of the cases that Agranov was in charge of would be enough for the Russian reader to learn everything he needs to know about the man. The most controversial cases of "counterrevolutionary conspiracies" fabricated by the Bolsheviks in the early twenties were investigated by Agranov, and it is likely that he himself wrote the scenarios that he later produced. We can find his name in Solzhenitsyn's *Gulag Archipelago*, where one passage is particularly illuminating about him.

The case involved one of the first large-scale fabrications created by Iron Felix [Dzerzhinsky], the case of the Petrograd military organization—an invented anti-Bolshevik conspiracy (1921), headed allegedly by Professor Vladimir Tagantsev, of Petrograd University and the Mining Institute. Here is what Solzhenitsyn writes:

> *Professor Tagantsev kept heroically silent through forty-five days of investigation. But then Agranov persuaded him to sign an agreement with him:*
>
> *"I, Tagantsev, consciously begin giving evidence about our organization, hiding nothing. . . . I am doing all this to ease the lot of the defendants in our case.*
>
> *"I, Yakov Saulovich Agranov, with the aid of Citizen Tagantsev, undertake to end the investigation quickly and afterward turn the case over to an open trial. . . . I promise that none of the accused will be given the highest measure of punishment."*

"None of the accused"—Stalin similarly gave his personal word to Zinoviev and Kamenev that they would not be executed if they "honestly performed the will of the Party." They were executed, and all that was left of Comrade Stalin's word of honor was Pauker's drunken story that gave Stalin so much merriment.

And in the case of Tagantsev, sixty people (including fifteen women) were shot on the night of August 14, 1921. One of the people executed was the Russian poet, and Anna Akhmatova's first husband, Nikolai Gumilev. A man of immense talent and great personal courage, he had looked death in the eyes several times and met it with amazing and proud dignity. Six years before his execution, in one of his most famous poems, he foretold his death at the hands of an executioner.

Another of Yakov Agranov's achievements is the case of his colleague, a zealous Chekist and former left Social Revolutionary, Yakov Blumkin*—the killer of the German ambassador Count Meerbach. (He was forgiven for the murder—he was executed for his closeness to Trotsky, which was the case Agranov investigated.) Another case invented by the Lubyanka was that of the Labor Peasant Party, which never existed, and on whose account Professor Alexander Chayanov, a leading agrarian economist and writer (of socio-philosophical novels) was executed. But the most important case is that of the murder of Sergei Kirov, the Party boss of Leningrad and Stalin's great rival. Stalin took Agranov, along with the prosecutor Andrei Vyshinsky and the investigator Lev Sheinin (more of him later), with him in the government train that rushed to Leningrad upon news of the fatal shot. Therefore, Stalin knew whom to take and why.

Agranov justified the trust of his leader and teacher. He ran an investigation that removed any possible suspicions against Stalin. He beat the statements he needed for his boss out of the wounded Nikolayev and the other arrested suspects. And he became, in the course of just a few days, the head of the Leningrad NKVD, and soon after that, First Deputy to Commissar of Interior Affairs Yagoda. The show trial of Zinoviev and Kamenev in 1935, which ended with prison sentences for them for conspiracy and murder, had been prepared entirely by Agranov. He headed the investigation team and personally interrogated the former leaders of the revolution. And it was then, in addition to his high post, that Agranov received from his "close comrade" and mentor an apartment in the Kremlin (to always be nearby) and the dacha in Zubalovo, the village that Svetlana Allilueva describes with such nostalgic warmth in *Twenty Letters to a Friend*.

Agranov, one of Stalin's "main Jews,"† until recently was known in

---

* Let us note in passing that the Lubyanka used the stratagem most popular in the twenties and thirties against Blumkin, that is, one of their own agents. Genrikh Yagoda called in his associate Liza Gorskaya, "a pure Jewish maiden" in the form of a fiery revolutionary, and ordered her to make the passionate Jewish youth Yasha Blumkin fall in love with her. The seduction worked brilliantly. In performing her assignment, Liza kept Lubyanka apprised regularly. Feminine wiles are still an effective weapon of the Soviet (and Russian) secret service, but they were never as widely employed as in those years.

† A reference to the expression popular in tsarist Russia, "Every governor should have at least one smart Jew."

the Soviet Union only as a friend of the poet Vladimir Mayakovsky and his mistress Lili Brik (née Kagan), the sister of the French writer Elsa Triolet. Without divorcing her husband, the writer Osip Brik, she was considered (and according to the literature of recent years, is still considered) the wife simultaneously of several other men, including Mayakovsky and an outstanding Soviet military leader, Vitaly Primakov, who was executed with Marshal Tukhachevsky in 1937. Like Osip Brik, Lili collaborated with the NKVD, performing delicate assignments, not yet fully documented (but apparently on the friendly recommendation of Agranov), at home and abroad—in Latvia, Germany, France, and England. Lili Brik's "salon," which Anna Akhmatova described with undisguised scorn, gathered major literary and artistic figures of the period as well as major Chekists. These were not secret agents, but official staff personnel of the Lubyanka, who not only did not hide their work but were proud of it.

It is important to understand that in those years the attitude toward the OGPU-NKVD was not like that of any decent person today—if for no other reason than the fact that no matter how grievous the crimes of the Cheka in the twenties, this was still before the era of the Great Terror, and the country had not yet lived through the NKVD under Yezhov and Beria, had not yet been inundated by the blood of occupied Eastern Europe, had not yet started persecuting dissidents. There was still a revolutionary, romantic aura that permeated society, especially that milieu, and it particularly related to the activities of the "glorious Chekists." If a host introduced an acquaintance to a new guest as someone who worked for the OGPU, he could be sure that the guest would break into a polite smile and make a respectful bow.

I doubt that there was another poet (or novelist or playwright or artist) who was as surrounded by Chekists as Mayakovsky. And sadly, they were almost all Jewish. But not because it was a Jewish plot to harass a Russian poet, but because they were placed, according to Stalin's plan (more below), in every level of Lubyanka. The only other salon that could compete with Lili Brik's in terms of permeation by OGPU officials was that of the actress Zinaida Raikh, whose husband, the director Vsevolod Meyerhold, also a friend of Mayakovsky's, was surrounded by them. Of the twenty-seven people who signed the poet's obituary notice published in *Pravda*, in which they called him their "close friend" (eleven of them would soon be executed), at least three were generals in the Cheka—Yakov Agranov, lovingly called "Yanya" by the literary-theatrical world of Moscow, Moisey Gorb,* and Lev Elbert.† A fourth, Zakhar Volovich, could have signed (with as much right as the other three), but did not only because he was on "diplomatic" assignment in Paris under an assumed name.

Zakhar Ilyich Volovich was involved in many of the dirty crimes of the NKVD, crimes enveloped even today in deep secrecy. In 1928 he worked undercover as Vladimir Borisovich Yanovich, an attaché of the Soviet embassy in Paris. That is where he became close to Maya-kovsky. The true role of the "diplomat" was no secret in Paris. The French newspapers openly called him "chief of the Paris GPU." Volovich-Yanovich (aka Vilyansky) took part in the kidnapping and murder of the tsarist General Kutepov, who headed the Russian Mil-itary Union. This piece of banditry caused a lot of noise in its time. When he returned to Moscow, he became deputy to the chief of the Operative Section of the NKVD, Pauker. He personally participated in the arrest of Grigori Zinoviev. With Pauker, he guarded Stalin, not leaving him for a minute. On March 27, 1937, he was arrested and charged with planning a terrorist act against Stalin (why he didn't execute it, seeing him daily, was never explained) and with espionage on behalf of Nazi Germany. His chief, Karl Pauker, was also arrested on this latter charge. Both these Jewish "Nazi spies" were killed by the bullets of an unknown colleague on the same day, August 14, 1937.

If Mayakovsky had only known how high his friend Yanya, Yakov Agranov, would soar! Whose cases he would investigate! Life creates the most unbelievable scenarios. Agranov supervised the investigation of one of the de facto husbands of his close friend and associate Lili Brik. The husband was Vitaly Primakov, whom Agranov had met at Lili's salon many times. From his prison cell Primakov wrote the first

---

* Moisey (Mikhail) Savelyevich Gorb headed one of the special sections of the NKVD under Yagoda. He was arrested on April 19, 1937, and shot on August 21, 1937.
† Lev Gilyarovich Elbert (they called him "Snob" in the Mayakovsky-Brik circle) worked in the foreign section of the NKVD and specialized in foreign intelligence. He survived the terror and after the war recruited agents in the Soviet-occupied areas of Germany, where he died (officially) of a heart attack in 1946. In the late thirties he co-wrote with Osip Brik the screenplay for the documentary film *Vladimir Mayakovsky*.

deputy commissar (his acquaintance and his wife's friend), "Please interrogate me personally. . . . They are confusing me more and more, something I do not understand at all. I am completely innocent. I have heart spasms every day." Agranov heard his pleas and called the prisoner in, after which he "confessed" to everything. And at the so-called trial with other "confessed" defendants he was the chief exposer of himself and others. And got a bullet in the back of the head.

The fall of Stalin's man Genrikh Yagoda meant the fall of the leader's friend Agranov. Yagoda's arrest was preceded by a brief appointment as Commissar of Communications. And Stalin decided to follow the same approach, but in a farcical variation, with Agranov. Yagoda was arrested on March 27, 1937, and on June 1 his former first deputy was sent by the "marvelous Georgian" to Saratov as head of the local ministry of internal affairs and instructed to expose "the nests of German intelligence in the autonomous republic of the Volga Germans." Agranov was a smart man, but he did not understand the meaning of this "responsible assignment." Or did he just not want to believe it?

He took on his new job with such zeal that his provincial colleagues were stunned. In just a few days his unbridled imagination created dozens of "spying, conspiratorial, terrorist, and diversionary groups" on his new territory. People were arrested by the hundreds and thousands, the local prison could not hold them, and they all confessed, all of them.

There was a small hitch. Many of the people charged with creating "German nationalist, anti-Soviet organization" were Jewish—and the local Chekists, who knew their "clients" better, pointed this out to the new boss. Perhaps he had been thrown off by the similarity of German and Jewish names. But Agranov simply changed the organizations he had uncovered to "German-Jewish nationalist anti-Soviet" ones. The patent for this fantastic hybrid is his.

Agranov was trying to save his life—he had to show that in far-off Saratov he had discovered enemies living in Moscow. Among the German spies he found were Lenin's widow, Nadezhda Krupskaya, and Georgi Malenkov, just starting out on his Party and state career. Stalin hated Krupskaya, which Agranov knew, but he could not allow Agranov to take such liberties with an icon's widow, and he had plans for Malenkov to replace the government "enemies of the people" who had been destroyed. Agranov had overreached. Agonizing, he lost all his abilities as an experienced and clever intriguer. His crazy letter to Yezhov* (which was immediately forwarded to Stalin), with a proposal to arrest Krupskaya and Malenkov as "protectors of the counterrevolutionary, nationalist German-Jewish underground," speaks for itself.

By July 16, Agranov had been recalled to Moscow. He expected to be rewarded for his zeal. But Yezhov, who had orders from his leader, gave him a crude and ruthless chewing-out. The inexorable end was approaching. Other tenants had been moved into his Kremlin apartment. But Agranov had a spare flat in the grim ten-story building for the Cheka, at 9 Markhlevsky Street (that prisonlike edifice is still standing), where Yagoda had recently been arrested. And Agranov was taken there too. He knew perfectly well what awaited him. He did not resist. He signed without a murmur everything that his more fortunate colleagues (for the time being) had prepared. A year later, on August 1, 1938, an executioner's bullet ended his life. On August 26, his wife, Valentina Agranova, who had also been a friend of Mayakovsky, was shot. She was rehabilitated posthumously in 1957. Despite the efforts of their daughter (who in the fifties wrote to Voroshilov, Kaganovich, and other former colleagues of her father), Agranov was refused rehabilitation. He is still considered an agent of Germany and Poland, on whose orders he planned to kill Stalin (but for some reason did not, despite seeing him on a daily basis at work and socially, with their families). God is his judge and the judge of his judges.

THERE IS A WIDESPREAD belief that whenever Jews find a niche, they start protecting one another and helping other Jews get on board too. Soviet reality, created by the genius of Stalin, refutes this point of view. A much more general and obvious rule was mutual destruction, and the desire not to be suspected of protectionism and

---

* Nikolai Yezhov (1895–1940), People's Commissar of Internal Affairs of the USSR after Yagoda. The Yezhovshchina, the nightmarish peak of the Great Terror (1936–1938), is named for him.

nepotism prompted many well-situated Jews, especially those in positions of power, to bend over backward to show their "objectivity" and unlimited loyalty to the Party and its beloved leader. This was supposed to confirm in a monstrously deformed way Lenin's concept of solidarity based on class rather than nationality and Stalin's idea that there was no Jewish nation.

But that nation existed for the author of the idea that the nation did not exist. In examining the factors that shaped Stalin's anti-Semitism, which grew fiercer with every year, we cannot limit ourselves to the political sphere and the power struggle. A great influence on Stalin was his personal entourage and the daily life of the Kremlin—especially in the twenties, when the Party leaders saw one another socially, including families, with the spontaneity of the recent pre-revolutionary past and of the Civil War, before the socializing became formalized into a Party ritual.

There were not that many Jewish leaders, but there was a plethora of Jewish wives. Their presence created an atmosphere in the Kremlin that would go unnoticed only by a normal person without prejudices. But the Kremlin's chief specialist on ethnic issues was by no means a normal person.

The wives of Zinoviev (Zlata Lilina) and Kamenev (Olga Bronstein, Trotsky's sister) were not only their husbands' helpmeets but political activists in their own right. Lilina held important posts in the Party and Soviet apparat (she was fortunate to have died a natural death in 1929), and Kameneva was in charge of culture (she was shot in September 1941 in a forest near Orel). Some authors use the fact that the leaders of the "right opposition" (the last opposition to Stalin in the late twenties) were almost all "pure-blooded" Russians to show that Stalin was not anti-Semitic in his struggle with his political foes. Konstantin Simonov stressed, "At the head of the right opposition, with which Stalin . . . dealt ruthlessly, were people with Russian names and Russian background, as if they had been specially selected."

But both Bukharin and Rykov, leaders of the right, who lived in the Kremlin, were close neighbors of Stalin, and shared the family table with him, were married to Jewish women. Nina Rykova (Marshak) was active in Party and administrative work in various districts of

Moscow and was in leading elective Party organs (she died in the GULAG). Bukharin's second wife (although they never made the marriage legal, which was not an issue in those days) at the period of his greatest closeness to Stalin, who called him "Bukharchik," was Esther Gurevich, Party member and famous economist. Soon after, he married the young and lovely Anna Larina (Lurie), who was the daughter of Mikhail Lurie, a prominent Bolshevik and friend of Lenin, economist, member of the parliament of the Union and of Russia, and a writer under the pen name Yu. Larin. This marriage elicited envy and jealousy in Stalin and left a deep wound in the rancorous leader.

Sergei Kirov, "beloved friend and brother" of the great leader, was also married to a Jew. Of Stalin's closet entourage, Molotov, Voroshilov, and Andreyev all married Jewish women. There was nothing remarkable about this. Jewish girls from poor families (primarily the families of village craftsmen) joined the revolution in great numbers and gave it their passion and fire. And it was among them that the future leaders found their love. Voroshilov, for instance, married Ekaterina Gorbman in 1907 or 1908. Molotov found his love, Perl Karpovskaya, in 1921 in Moscow, where the twenty-four-year-old Communist had come for a conference from the Ukrainian city of Zaporozhie. She would later take the name Polina Zhemchuzhina and become famous in the Party and the country.

But surely it was no accident that these two comrades-in-arms, Molotov and Voroshilov, who passed unharmed through the maws of the Great Terror and escaped its revival in the late forties and early fifties, were suspected by Stalin toward the end of his life when he was completely paranoid. In Voroshilov, Stalin saw a British spy and in Molotov, an American one. It would be a grave mistake to consider these family particulars as being incidental or insignificant and unworthy of historical analysis. By virtue of circumstance, every detail of Kremlin life, the life of that building which was basically a communal flat, willy-nilly became a factor in politics. For a man of a different mentality, a different upbringing, roots, and character—in other words, a man from the intelligentsia influenced by culture—the ethnic background of his colleagues' wives would not have mattered. But Stalin was made of other stuff; and as the years passed, the constant presence of the wives became harder and harder to deal with for Georgian leader of the Russian people.

Let us also add the wife of a man extremely close to him for almost two decades, his personal secretary and a Lubyanka general, Alexander Poskrebyshev. Bronislava Solomonovna Poskrebysheva was the sister of the wife of Lev Sedov, Trotsky's son. That alone doomed her. Poskrebyshev dared to defend his wife, but Stalin's sole response was: "We will find you another wife." And one evening, when Poskrebyshev came home, he found a woman selected by Stalin going about the housework. I need not say that she was not an "alien." But still, in 1952, when the fear of a Zionist conspiracy drove Stalin to his final madness, he not only planned the liquidation of Molotov and Voroshilov (the only two survivors out of the entire ruling elite) but also fired Poskrebyshev, the most loyal of the loyal. His logic (if it could be called that) is clear. If not for the grace of God, all three would have followed the millions of other victims, many of whom had died thanks to them.

THE FIGURE OF Lazar Kaganovich stands out, and deserves separate discussion. The last of Stalin's entourage, Kaganovich, who died recently at age ninety-eight, spent almost three decades as the leader's favorite and closest comrade. For some time (in the first half of the thirties) he was the second most important man in the country. Many letters from the provinces on current questions of party or economic life were addressed to "Comrades J. V. Stalin and L. M. Kaganovich." It was he who was designated by Stalin to announce to the Politburo that Stalin's wife, Nadezhda Allilueva, had shot herself. Until then, Stalin had told his party comrades that Nadezhda had "died suddenly."

When Stalin took a vacation, Kaganovich, as acting General Secretary, replaced him. He chaired the meetings of the secretariat of the Central Committee and the Politburo. It was probably that exceptional position that gave him the "moral" right to be rude to Krupskaya, which Stalin liked (and which Kaganovich knew he liked). In particular, in 1930 Kaganovich announced at a regional Party conference in Moscow, "Krupskaya shouldn't think that just because she was Lenin's wife that she has a monopoly on Leninism." Not many people would have dared to say something like that publicly, even in 1930.

A cobbler by profession, from a poor Jewish family, uneducated, writing with an enormous number of grammatical and spelling mistakes, Lazar Kaganovich was brought into the Bolshevik underground before the revolution by his older brother, Mikhail, but he did not earn any fame in the Party. In July 1936 an unnamed versifier sent "A Message from the Belorussian People to Comrade Stalin," which said, "Kaganovich's word resounded, He grew our Party in Gomel." But in fact no one heard Kaganovich's word and no one had any idea that he was "growing the Party," if only in Gomel. In the thousands of letters, notes, notations, and resolutions by Lenin, lovingly preserved in the Party archives, innumerable names appear, most of which are forgotten even by specialists in Party history and require footnoting, but Kaganovich's name does not show up even once.

But Stalin, with his unerring nose, found Kaganovich in the mass of middle-level Party apparatchiks and elevated him as soon as he himself became General Secretary of the Party (1922), bringing him into his innermost entourage. Just two years later, on Stalin's direct "recommendation," the previously unknown Kaganovich became secretary of the Central Committee, and a short while later a member of the Politburo.

This dizzying career, created by Stalin himself, might seem to disprove the idea of Stalin's anti-Semitism. But in fact, no matter how paradoxical it may seem, it confirms it. First of all, with the very large number of Jewish Party apparatchiks and officials at all levels, the question of ethnic background was not an issue in the twenties—and personal loyalty was much more important for Stalin than data in a curriculum vitae. Kaganovich suited him because he had never been part of Lenin's group (even at a great remove), or of a leading nucleus, had no ties to the old cadres who were fighting for the inheritance of their respected founder, and owed his job solely to Stalin. Secondly, the presence of at least one Jew in the leading elite (Trotsky, Kamenev, and Zinoviev were gone by then) automatically obviated any possible accusations of discrimination. In those days a hint of even hidden anti-Semitism was a grievous sin that in some cases meant expulsion from the Party. Stalin, almost to the very end, maintained his image as a militant internationalist.

When in the late twenties Kaganovich was sent by Stalin "to bring order" to Ukraine, he showed his boundless energy and organizational abilities through merciless beatings of the cadres on any demagogic excuse. Two other Ukrainian leaders—Grigory Petrovsky and Vlas Chubar—came to Stalin to beg him to recall Kaganovich from Ukraine before he beat up all the most talented workers. Defending his man, Stalin accused them of anti-Semitism. That was a favorite tactic of his, allowing him to kill several birds at once. He not only rejected accusations against Kaganovich, who was merely doing what Stalin told him to do, but he made it impossible to accuse Comrade Stalin of a sin unbefitting a Communist. Of course, Stalin did recall Kaganovich from Ukraine a year later and made him secretary of the Central Committee again, which brought them even closer because of the zeal with which Kaganovich did Stalin's bidding (the zeal that so upset Petrovsky and Chubar). Eventually Chubar was shot, Petrovsky was removed from all his posts and left to anticipate arrest, Petrovsky's son was arrested and executed, while Kaganovich remained on the Party Olympus as the only Jewish representative, demonstrating the absence of state anti-Semitism in the most international and most democratic country in the world.

Kaganovich actively participated in the forced collectivization of agriculture, in the cruel campaign against Cossacks in the Northern Caucasus (that is, in the deportation and killing of Cossacks only because they or their fathers had belonged to the Don Cossack Army in tsarist times). He ruthlessly purged the transport sector and for a time was the Commissar of Transportation. The list of his villainous deeds is enormous.

Kaganovich's virtuoso hypocrisy is demonstrated in a little-known statement by the former secretary of the Central Committee of the Komsomol, Alexander Milchakov, who survived the GULAG. He was arrested on December 21, 1938, with the sanction of Kaganovich, Beria, and Vyshinsky. Kaganovich's official sanction was needed because at the moment of his arrest, Milchakov was the head of the main directorate of the gold industry (Glavzoloto), which was under Kaganovich, who was secretary of the Central Committee. "Relishing his power over people," wrote Milchakov after his rehabilitation, "Kaganovich ruthlessly and criminally played with the fate of people and their families, turning over thousands of innocent people to be destroyed by Yezhov and Beria." That "unprincipled two-faced intriguer," as Milchakov characterized him, was personally involved in the killing of all the first secretaries and lesser secretaries of the Komsomol Central Committee in its history—Oskar Ryvkin, Lazar Shtiskin, Efim Tseitlin, and many others. He derived special pleasure from turning over Jews, knowing that this would make Stalin happy and would prove his high Party principles. Need it be said that thousands of innocent Russian victims were on this man's conscience, as were thousands of others from every ethnic group inhabiting the Soviet Union.

Among his victims, and this is significant, was the entire management of the Transportation Commissariat (at a time when Kaganovich was solemnly declared the Chief Honorary Railroad Worker of the land). I recently received a letter from Professor Naum Fufryansky, son of Alexander Fufryansky, head of the Omsk Railroad, shot in 1937. The professor made a study of Kaganovich's role in the destruction of his own apparat. He determined that every file of those victims holds either Kaganovich's direct suggestion for his arrest, or his sanction for arrest, or a letter from the prisoner begging for help. The letters went unanswered. Every one of his deputies, every department chief (and even those who had held the posts before them), every chief of the railroads of the Soviet Union and their deputies turned out to be "spies," "saboteurs," "terrorists," and "wreckers." The mind boggles trying to understand how this army of spies and terrorists could have been headed by the immaculately honest and pure Commissar Kaganovich, Stalin's favorite.

Even more vividly, Kaganovich's slavish devotion to Stalin and his animal fear for himself were manifest in his attitude toward his own family. His older brother, Mikhail, was also a leading comrade. He was a member of the Central Committee, a deputy of the Supreme Soviet of the USSR, Commissar of Defense and Aviation Industry. In early 1941 he was unexpectedly subjected to harsh criticism at the Eighteenth Party Conference, and then Stalin created a commission to check on his work, headed by Anastas Mikoyan. Lazar Kaganovich not only did not speak up for his brother, he publicly announced that the affair did not concern him, since "it is within the competence of the investigative organs." Mikhail knew his brother well, and knew what this distancing boded. When he arrived at Mikoyan's office, he asked for the toilet and there shot himself in the temple. No word of this event traveled beyond the Kremlin walls. A rumor was started that Mikhail, working at a lower but still responsible administrative position, had developed ties with the Gestapo and was being considered by Hitler for premier of the puppet government of conquered Russia.

The first half of this Lubyanka-created story was believed even by Roy Medvedev, who maintained in his articles and interviews that Mikhail Kaganovich committed suicide after the war. In fact, it had happened in the spring of 1941, and with his silence Lazar Kaganovich supported and spread the slander against his brother.

His two other brothers were unharmed. One, Yuli, was also a Party official, first secretary of the Gorky Committee and then a member of the collegium of the Ministry of Foreign Trade. He finished his career as trade representative in Mongolia, and died in the early fifties after a lengthy illness. Had he lived longer, he might have been among the victims of genocide. But instead he was living proof, like his brother Lazar (in a more modest way), of the absence of anti-Semitism under the sun of the Stalin constitution.

If not in content, then in the manner in which he expressed his loyalty, there was no equal to Kaganovich. It was his idea to rename Moscow "Stalin." The leader rejected the notion; his modesty was well known. And yet, the overheated passion that he tirelessly demonstrated apparently did not evoke a reciprocal response from Stalin. The leader kept Kaganovich at a distance. In 1932 he shamelessly proposed himself to Stalin for the post of chairman of the OGPU. The result is easy to imagine. He would not have been worse than Yagoda or Yezhov, but certainly no better. Stalin, however, wanted to be fully in charge of that principal lever of power. Yagoda, and Yezhov after him, executed his every whim without a word. Kaganovich in that post would have followed orders certainly, but he would have brought so much personal initiative to the job (as he had to every other) that he might have become uncontrollable. Kaganovich did not move to the Lubyanka, but his concurrences, often filled with unprintable words and expressions, ornament dozens of lists of people to be executed. Of course, so do the concurrences of Molotov and Voroshilov. Kaganovich did not distinguish himself from his comrades in this respect.

At the same time Kaganovich figured in the secret transcripts of the Lubyanka in two ways. Iosif Pyatnitsky (Tarshis), a leader of the Comintern, was charged, among many other things, with "developing a plan to prepare a terrorist act against Comrade Lazar Moiseyevich Kaganovich and trying to implement that plan." Analogous charges, just as abstract, were made against some of the defendants of the second Moscow show trial (the Pyatakov-Radek case). Stalin himself decided who would be an intended victim of these trumped-up terrorist acts and who would not. He approved Kaganovich but crossed Molotov off the list, which horrified the "stone arse." If Stalin decided that no one had tried to kill Molotov, that could mean he was being moved from the ranks of faithful comrades-in-arms to the other side: the renegades. And that could mean a role as victim not of counter-revolutionary terror but of revolutionary terror. But nothing came to pass.

These were events of 1937. In 1938 Kaganovich's name began to appear on the pages of Lubyanka transcripts in another context. Two particularly fierce executioners (both illiterate Ukrainians—one from a small Jewish village, the other from Melitopol, which had a large Jewish population), Boris Rodos and Lev Shvartsman, tried to force several prisoners to state that they had conspired with the "foreign spy and Zionist agent" Lazar Kaganovich. This was what Rodos wanted Vasili Chimburov, secretary of the Uzbek Party Central Committee, to confess. Chimburov was supposed to name Politburo member Andrei Andreyev, whose wife was Jewish, as another "spy and Zionist agent."

Even the highest-ranking Lubyanka investigators would never dare to mention Politburo members, "the great Stalin's closest comrades-in-arms" as the newspapers called them daily, without direct orders from above. And their bosses would have had to be ordered to do it by someone even higher, or heads would roll. After Stalin's death, when Rodos, Shvartsman, and others of their colleagues (alas, not many) were charged with crimes, Rodos gave evidence that it was Lavrenti Beria who ordered him in 1938 to "beat people to confess to espionage and Zionist ties with Kaganovich." It is clear that on Stalin's orders this material was being collected just in case, to be taken out of a safe when needed and shown to Kaganovich whenever he would go from being a member of the Politburo to being one of the Lubyanka's many clients.

Kaganovich probably did not know about this, but he must have had his suspicions, for he was well informed about the goings-on in the NKVD. The switch from one condition to another, diametrically opposed state had happened before his very eyes to many of the faithful, including Politburo members (Psotyshev, Chubar, Rudzutak). Why not him?

This made him toady even more, flatter even more sweetly, and put up with Stalin's crudity, perceiving it almost as a reward. Pietro Nenni, according to Khrushchev, once told Ilya Ehrenburg, "One day Stalin came up to Kaganovich and said, 'Want a punch in the face?' He covered his face with a newspaper and said, 'Don't hit me. I'm a member of the Politburo.' Stalin thought about it and changed his mind. He didn't hit him. He just laughed." That was their typical humor.

Another example of Stalin's "jokes" with Kaganovich came from a later period. According to Jean Cathala, then French press attaché in Moscow, at a farewell banquet in the Kremlin on December 9, 1944, for Charles de Gaulle, Stalin raised an unexpected toast to Kaganovich. This was the toast: "Let us drink to Kaganovich, a brave man who knows that if the trains do not run on time, I will have him shot." Everyone laughed merrily, especially Kaganovich.

However, Stalin did not listen to or tell anti-Semitic jokes in front of Kaganovich, or raise any such topics with him. There is only one known case before the war when Stalin forced Kaganovich to feel like a Jew. He alone of all the Politburo members was not invited to the reception on August 23 for their dear guest, Nazi Minister of Foreign Affairs Ribbentrop.* And from that moment until the beginning of

---

* Not long before his death, Lazar Kaganovich tried to make the tyrant seem more than he was in his conversation with Chuev. He told him that during that "historic" reception Molotov was the toastmaster, who gave Stalin the floor. Josif Vissarionovich allegedly offered a toast "to our Commissar of Transportation, Lazar Kaganovich," and Ribbentrop was forced to lean across the table, clink glasses with a hated Jew, and drink to his health. Perhaps it is merely that in his nineties, Kaganovich was confused. But the confusion has a definite tendentiousness to it and is symptomatic of his other statements.

the war with Germany, Kaganovich's name stopped appearing with the same frequency in the newspapers.

He responded to this anti-Semitic gesture in the Stalinist spirit. Kaganovich once had a fit because the translator who was doing the voiceover for an Italian movie he was screening at his dacha had a Jewish accent. At least his sensitive ear, because he had come from a small Jewish town, caught the accent. And the translator lost a prestigious job. Gradually and ubiquitously the tradition was entrenched. A Jewish boss, worried about being thought nationalistic, would not allow any Jews to work for him. Jews were helped by Russians, not by other Jews.

Kaganovich took everything that Stalin dished out. And he remained faithful to the end, even after he had learned many things about Stalin and the way Stalin had treated him. "Kaganovich even today is such a proponent of Stalin," Molotov confided to Felix Chuev in 1976, "that you can't say anything bad about Stalin in front of him. He was the two-hundred-percent Stalinist among us. He thought that I didn't praise Stalin enough." And Kaganovich, as he approached his hundredth birthday, told Chuev, "Stalin's greatness is that he understood historical necessity. The will of the Party and the will of the people were manifested in him." In other words, he could not speak in anything but the old Soviet propaganda clichés. He never learned.

For almost thirty years Lazar Kaganovich was the only Jew in the higher Party Areopagus, as the representative of all the besmirched and persecuted, refuting the "bourgeois slanders." Molotov was right when he told Chuev, "The Jews do not like Kaganovich. They would have liked a more intelligent man in the Politburo."

Correct. A more intelligent (even better, an intelligent) and decent man instead of a sadist, ignoramus, and lackey. There were people like that among the Bolsheviks, certainly people who were much more decent and of a higher cultural level. Grigori Sokolnikov (Brilliant) had been friends with Boris Pasternak since high school, and his circle included the composer Dmitri Shostakovich and the writers Isaac Babel and Boris Pilnyak. What people of culture could have been friends with Kaganovich? Sokolnikov was killed by a criminal planted in his prison cell; Kaganovich stayed with Stalin to the end and broke all records for long life among the Kremlin fanatics and killers.

4

THE HOUR
OF RUSSIAN JEWRY

AT THE VERY END OF 1930, the Jewish Telegraph Agency of the United States asked Stalin to explain the official attitude of the Soviet regime toward anti-Semitism. The answer was not long in coming. On January 12, 1931, Stalin replied categorically and un-equivocally: "Anti-Semitism is dangerous for the workers as a false path that takes them from the correct road and leads into the jungle. Therefore Communists . . . must be implacable and sworn enemies of anti-Semitism. Anti-Semitism as an extreme form of racial chauvinism is the most dangerous vestige of cannibalism. . . . Active anti-Semites are punished with death by the laws of the USSR."

Actually, if one were to stretch the point, some Soviet laws in force then could be interpreted as being against anti-Semitism, and some of them did call for the death penalty. So if Stalin had sud-denly been asked to clarify his declaration and produce the actual laws, it would not have been very difficult for him to do so. But Stalin was clearly exaggerating. There had never been trials for anti-Semitism ending in a death sentence. I have a dossier on one case tried by a famous defense counsel of the late twenties, Ilya Bauder. I was his assistant for the last eighteen months of his life. A Russian laborer, the young husband of a lawyer of Jewish origin, constantly insulted her national dignity, publicly mocked and humiliated her, and in the heat of an argument poked her eye out with a finger. He was tried—and found guilty—of doing bodily harm, but neither in the charges nor in the sentence was there a word about another crime, no less grievous (and if Stalin's answer to the Jewish Telegraph Agency is to be believed, even more heinous)—active anti-Semitism.

And yet we would not be mistaken in calling the period of the twenties and the first half of the thirties one of state protection for Russian Jewry. In that period many Jews moved up into leadership posts in all spheres of Party, Komsomol, state, union, economic, and cultural life. This phenomenon is easily explained. A *priori* (and not without foundation) considered victims of discrimination under the tsars, Jews were assumed to be faithful allies of Soviet power and therefore to be trusted in promoting policy. Their ethnic background was a guarantee of loyalty and heightened activism in strengthening the position of the new regime in all its command structures. Ilya Bauder told me, recalling the twenties, "It was prestigious being Jewish then." The words that were so true of that brief period sound almost unbelievable today.

We remember that in Stalin's pre-revolutionary conception the absence of a territory compactly settled by Jews, and, more important, their lack of permanent ties with the land (in other words, the absence of a social stratum like the peasantry) deprived them of the right to be considered a nation. But Stalin and those who were at the helm of power with him (he was not the sole ruler yet) did not settle for a simple statement of that far from uncontroversial fact—on the contrary, they tried to improve the situation and give Russian Jews the chance to be reborn as a nation.

In 1924 two organizations were formed—KOMZET (the Committee on Land for Working Jews) and OZET (Society for Land for Working Jews). The Crimea was the place selected for settling Jews, who had mostly come from the towns and villages of the Ukraine and Belorussia (the former Pale of Settlement). The creation of a national hearth in Palestine then seemed in the distant future, and so foreign charitable organizations and business sponsors ardently supported the Crimean variant and sent the bulk of their material aid to the Crimea—tractors and other agricultural equipment and pedigree cattle. The aid reached the first settlers who had gathered in the Crimean steppes (not the seaside, which was inhabited by Tatars) for national rebirth.

The chairman of the Central Executive Committee (TsIK), Mikhail Kalinin, the erstwhile President of the Soviet Union, who followed

Yakov Sverdlov in that post, came to the 1926 Congress of OZET and appealed to them to cultivate the Crimean land: "The Jewish people are faced with a major task—the preservation of their nationality [an enormous step forward compared to Stalin's concept: not to be reborn, but to be preserved.—A.V.], but a significant part of the Jewish population has to be turned into a compact population, measuring at least in the hundreds of thousands. Only under these conditions can the Jewish masses have hope for the future of their nationality."

Here it is important to note not the dilettantish and politically expedient discussion of the conditions for preserving a nationality (a literary and scientific error), but the strategic course of the Party, so astonishing to anyone who knows what happened later. The massive concentration of the Jewish population on a single territory—what later was feared most by Stalin and his heirs—was then considered of major state importance. Logically, such a concentration, if the Kalinin (Stalin) line were to be realized, would inevitably have led to the creation of an autonomous or Union Jewish republic within the USSR. This official, state, and Party strategic plan must be borne in mind when we see into what it was transformed and to what it led.

A Jewish mass—mostly poor—poured into the Crimea. There weren't a hundred thousand, but tens of thousands of settlers filled the almost unpeopled Crimean steppes. The so-called Jewish land cooperatives, which later became collective farms, lived and flourished. The country followed their achievements. At least the newspapers covered them extensively and propagandized their successes. The leaders of the farms, the tractor drivers, and the agronomists were turned into heroes of labor by the enterprising press. Jewish names, so unusual at first, became commonplace in the lists of record-breaking grain harvesters and cattle breeders.

Those years could justifiably be called the years of the flowering of Jewish culture in the USSR— primarily in literature and theater. That huge, complex, and very convoluted theme calls for special examination beyond the scope of this book. Here it is important to stress the political aspect of that brilliant fireworks display which ended so tragically. Yiddish literature developed at an incredible pace, with thousands of readers in the original and hundreds of thousands in translation into Russian, Ukrainian, and other languages of the USSR. But, even more important, there were many talented people who could create a literature in that language. The demand created the supply, and the system of state stimulation accelerated the process of forming a large contingent of Jewish writers who were concentrated primarily in Moscow, Kiev, Odessa, and Minsk. Their names became familiar even to people who had not read their works, thanks to the publicity campaign mounted by the press. Jewish writers formed groups that eventually were transformed into the Jewish sections of the Writers' Union of the USSR when that organization was founded. Jewish publishing houses sprang up, printing literary journals and magazines in Yiddish and then the newspaper *Der Emes.*

But it was the Jewish theater that garnered the most fame, thanks to its talented directors, actors, artists, and composers, who enthusiastically undertook the creation of a Jewish *Soviet* theater (I stress the word "Soviet" intentionally). The Moscow Jewish Studio Theater, Habima, which based its work on biblical epics and ancient religious themes—that is, returning to the deep roots of Jewish history—did not suit the Communist Kremlin. It was soon accused of Zionism, nationalistic isolationism, and mysticism. Habima was forced to emigrate (which was not too difficult then), and after traveling all over Europe and America, it found a home in Israel. But a Jewish theater where "the voice of the Revolution resounded powerfully" (I quote a reviewer) and whose founders (I quote him again) were "internationalists by conviction, who believed in the free and happy brotherhood of workers of all races and tribes and that they would definitely reign over the ruins of the former prison of peoples"—that theater had the sympathy of the Soviet regime, first under Lenin and then under Stalin.

That theater was born in Petrograd and later moved to Moscow. Originally called the State Jewish Chamber Theater and later simply the State Jewish Theater (GOSET), it played a prominent role in the cultural life of Moscow and the country. After its founder and head, Granovsky-Azarkh, a student of the great German director Max Reinhardt, emigrated, he was replaced by the actor Solomon Vovsi, who had taken the stage name Mikhoels back in 1919. The theater's success and enormous prestige were due in great measure to the artists who played a pivotal role in its productions—Marc Chagall, Natan Altman, Isaak Rabinovich, Robert Falk, David Sterenberg, and Alexander Tyshler. The music, equally important, was the work of the composers Alexander Kreim and Lev Pulver. The theater attracted the most promising talents of Soviet Jewish literature—Aron Kushnirov, Iekhezkil Dobrushin, Naum Oislender, Peretz Markish, Isaak Nusinov, David Bergelson, and Samuil Galkin, all of whom wrote in Yiddish. And Mikhoels also surrounded himself with a group of gifted Jewish actors, the brightest being Veniamin Zuskin.

The government gave the Jewish theater a first-class building in the middle of Moscow and large state subsidies for its work, and its creative figures received generous titles and medals, which guaranteed them privileges and material comforts within the Soviet system. The press, and not only the professional press, raved about the productions of this theater and the books of Jewish writers. There were Jewish theaters and studios outside Moscow too, and some of them (for instance, the theater in Kiev) enjoyed both success with audiences and, much more important, state support.

Jewish themes were widely represented in the burgeoning Soviet film industry. In 1925 there appeared a film that set the public tone with its title alone. It was called *Jewish Happiness* and was based on the stories of Sholem Aleichem, the classic of Yiddish literature. Involved in the production were Mikhoels and Isaac Babel, who wrote on Jewish themes in Russian, presenting in another language the intonation and melodiousness of Jewish speech, the psychology, mind-set, and palette of emotions of the Jews of Odessa—and, of course, not only of Odessa.

In this same period there was also an influx into Russian culture—literature, theater, and film in particular—of people of Jewish descent who had little to do with Jewish culture per se. Many of them were an organic part of the "gold reserves" of Soviet culture (I stress Soviet) and enjoyed the great and unconditional support of the authorities. A short list would include the film directors Sergei Eisenstein, Grigori Kozintsev, Leonid Trauberg, Dziga Vertov (Kaufman), Fridrikh Ermler, Abram Room, Iosif Kheifits, Grigori Roshal, Alexander Zarkhi, Yuli Raizman, and Mark Donskoi; and the writers Vassily Semenovich (Iosif Solomonovich) Grossman, Eduard Bagritsky (Dzubin), Ilya Selvinsky, Mikhail Svetlov, Ilya Ilf (Fainzilberg), Lev Kassil, Vladimir Lidin

(Gomberg), Semyon Kirsanov, Samuil Marshak, Vera Inber, Iosif Utkin, Agnia Barto, and Mikhail Golodny. They were studied in schools
and written about constantly in the newspapers. These were the ones
who were pampered and officially recognized, and therefore this list
does not include the disgraced Osip Mandelstam, who was persecuted
for reasons other than his origins. But Boris Pasternak could be added
to the list. Even though he was a baptized Christian, he was always
considered Jewish, because for the Kremlin and the Lubyanka it was not
religion but blood that determined Jewishness. Pasternak was subjected
to harsh criticism, but the accusations of extreme individualism, apo-
litical attitude, separation from the people, etc., were never anti-
Semitic in character. He received a definite, though not publicized,
degree of protection from Stalin—and probably not only because he
translated Georgian poets, both classic and contemporary.

The writers and directors listed above, and many others, were showered with orders and medals, were published, praised, and never distinguished from people with Russian roots. When Stalin needed a
two-part film series on Lenin (*Lenin in October* and *Lenin in 1918*) that
would assert the decisive and leading role played not by Lenin but by
Stalin in the revolution, the leader chose two Jews to execute his
plan—screenwriter Alexei Kapler and director Mikhail Romm.

THE IDEA OF A territory of their own for Jews was like a splinter
in Stalin's brain. The Crimea was no longer a simple administrative
unit, but an autonomous republic because it was the original homeland of the Crimean Tatars who inhabited it. The hypothetical division of the Crimea into Tatar (the seacoast) and Jewish (the steppes)
entities could lead to an ethnic conflict and did not suit Stalin's plans
at all. He needed a Jewish "territory," not for the sake of the people
he loved so much but because he could then collect them all in one
place, and enjoy the "moral right" to clean out the cities and regions
that in his opinion were too densely populated with Jews. He camouflaged this reason with others.

The necessity of giving "working Jews the chance to create their
own state" allegedly could be realized only in the reaches of the Far
East, in the desert foothills of the Maly Khingan Mountains, along the

banks of the Amur River. Jews had never lived there. This idea would have to be called utopian. Stalin's attitude toward it was serious, but not for utopian reasons. He was thinking ahead fifteen or eighteen years, when the existence of a national area for Soviet Jews would make his dream of a huge ghetto legal, justified, and realizable. Let us not forget that the first half of the thirties was marked by an almost hysterical apotheosis of "revolutionary romanticism"—its second stage, after the Civil War, and its theme, according to the propaganda, was creation, rather than destruction. An important component of this romantic surge, masterminded in the Kremlin, was the cultivation and mastery of the Soviet Far East. Thousands of sincere young volunteers went off to build, for instance, the city of Komsomolsk, near the future Jewish Autonomous State. They were told that the greatest danger to the Soviet Union was from Japan and that the unpopulated expanses of the Far East would make it easier for the samurai to penetrate Soviet territory. A popular song went, "On the high banks of the Amur, the homeland's guards stand watch."

The Jewish settlers were expected to play the homeland's guards. Or perhaps not even to play, but actually to be, for then Stalin knew that the creators of the new Jewish state he was herding there, to the joy of snakes and mosquitoes, were no traitors, no Zionists, no hidden enemies, but loyal inhabitants of the socialist paradise, and that on the border with puppet Manchuria, Japanese territory, the Jewish settlers could be a good buffer.

The several thousand families that made the journey in the early thirties did not change the demographics of any region, including the one on "the high banks of the Amur." Even given the low density of population overall in the Far Eastern territories, they formed a tiny percentage. But Soviet propaganda exaggerated the "enormous economic and cultural transformations" that allegedly began in the territories where Jews settled. Stalin did not go as far as creating a Jewish Autonomous Republic. Whatever the decorative and propaganda role of the Stalin republics, they nevertheless had the external attributes of statehood—Supreme Soviets, governments, and a constitution, seal, and flag. But Stalin did not stint on a Potemkin village of a cultural renaissance for the area. The scribblers who wrote in Yiddish were declared writers, accepted in the Writers' Union, and published. The newspaper *Der Stern* was printed, even though much of its run was immediately thrown away into containers for recycling. A new Jewish theater was opened and named for Lazar Kaganovich.

But this autonomous region left its biggest mark in film. The history of the Jewish settlers, created for its political effect, provided the foundation for a movie that lives in the memory of several generations of Soviet viewers and which influenced them in a way not intended by the Leader. This was *The Seekers of Happiness*, starring Veniamin Zuskin. The mother was played by the Russian actress Maria Blumental-Tamarina, who embodied that touching and charming role as well as any Jewish actress could have. The plot was based on a desirable but totally unrealistic notion: A large group of Jews comes from America, passionately dreaming of working the Soviet land, not just anywhere, but in their new homeland, Birobidzhan, the Jewish Autonomous Region created by Stalin. The hero, Pinya (played by Zuskin), hopes to find in Birobidzhan the happiness he naturally lacked in damned capitalist America. He wants to prospect for gold and become the equal of Rothschild himself—Rothschild being the pejorative symbol in Russia of the rich Jew.

But instead of being an exposé, the film turned out to be touching and heartfelt. That was due not only to the brilliant acting but to the music of the most popular Soviet composer of the thirties, Isaak Dunaevsky. The songs from the film score, like Dunaevsky's other songs about the happy life under the great Stalin, were sung everywhere. In the 1930s the country lived from one song to the next. Most of them came from the movies, then were produced as records and played on the radio and in concerts, at youth dances, at industrial and Party meetings, in the home. They were the work of composers whose pictures were in all the newspapers and whose names were known by every schoolboy—Dunaevsky, the brothers Dmitri and Daniil Pokrass, Matvei Blanter (author of the legendary song "Katyusha"), Sigizmund Kats, Viktor Bely, and Yuli Khait. They were later joined by Yan Frenkel, Mark Frandkin, Arkadi Ostrovsky, and Oskar Feltsman. Only a small part of the enormous wealth of Soviet songs of that period was written by the Russian composers Vasili Solovyov-Sedoi, Nikita Bogoslovsky, and Boris Mokrousov.

It is obvious that this was not only permitted but encouraged by Stalin. His plans for the destruction of his ideological foes and potential rivals and the gathering storm of the Great Terror had to be muffled by the drumbeat of the wildly happy denizens of Stalin's paradise. Everything that promoted this happiness was hailed and supported. There were not many who saw an attack directed at Jews in the mass repressions that had just begun. And it was not directed solely at them. The Stalinist machine of destruction fell on everyone— Russians, Jews, Ukrainians, and Belorussians. If there seems to be an incommensurate number of Jewish names in the lists of victims, it is only because in the twenties they held positions in every sphere of political and social life, in all structures, and when the time for payment came, they paid with their lives not for being Jewish but for holding those posts. But the Jews whose music played in the background, drowning out the noise of this action, were considered allies—whether they wanted to be allies or not, and only for as long as they were deemed useful.

Besides which, no matter that most people saw only an ideological basis for the persecution of former leaders of the Party and the state, Stalin, like every criminal, worried that his secret thoughts were obvious to everyone. There is a Russian saying, "A thief's hat burns on his head," meaning a criminal's guilt feelings make him feel conspicuous. Stalin knew that in his growing sadism there was an ethnic element, especially in the first and second Moscow show trials. That is why he kept stressing his alleged pro-Jewish feelings throughout the first half of the thirties, to a much greater degree than was necessary to confirm his proletarian internationalism.

An episode that took place on January 11, 1935, serves as a vivid illustration. It was the fifteenth anniversary of Soviet film, celebrated at the Bolshoi Theater. Less than six weeks earlier, the provocateur's shot that killed Kirov in Leningrad had laid the groundwork for the Great Terror. With lightning speed, the killer Nikolayev and those falsely accused of conspiring with him were executed, mass arrests and deportations of "suspicious elements" began, and Zinoviev and Kamenev were under arrest waiting for the start of a falsified and closed trial that would end with a prison sentence. It would be followed by a new, public trial and a death sentence. All of Stalin's thoughts were concentrated on the fact that his hour was near, the hour of triumph and revenge over the hated and now humiliated and defeated Zinoviev and Kamenev.

At that moment the film industry was celebrating its birthday, and Stalin attended the subdued celebration. Nothing revealed the fierce storm inside him. He was imperturbable and calm, amiable and cheerful—as usual. There was no master of ceremonies because no one needed an introduction. The standing-room crowd knew everything about each of the performers. And two men came out quickly onto the stage, both of medium height and incredibly funny to look at, one in front, the other behind him. The audience applauded, instantly recognizing the actors Solomon Mikhoels and Veniamin Zuskin. They quickly walked around the stage, stopped at the footlights, and stared out into the audience as if they simply could not understand what was going on. They exclaimed in unison, "Oh!" And went around the stage again. They reached the footlights once more, and this time they did not express surprise but total disbelief. They seemed to be saying, "What are you doing here, dear people?" The audience was roaring with laughter. The man in the state box, also of medium height and with a mustache, was having a very good time.

The short mime scene was over, and Mikhoels and Zuskin went offstage and then returned to take a bow. The man with the mustache, still laughing and applauding, stood up and hailed the artists with small, steady claps. The theater was in confusion. That audience (any audience in those days) could not remain sitting while the leader stood and applauded. But they were accustomed to giving standing ovations only to their leader, not to their colleagues. Mikhoels and Zuskin saved the day. They walked toward the state box and applauded Stalin wildly. The whole audience got to its feet, and the Bolshoi thundered with ovations. Now they were addressed to the man with the mustache. But it was still his initiative—he had stood to express his delight over two brilliant Jewish actors. It was a memorable episode. Which was the point. It was January 1935. The first of the stars of that evening had thirteen years (and two days) to live. The second had seventeen and a half years.

It is unlikely that anyone besides Stalin perceived this spontaneous delight (yes, it probably was spontaneous rather than planned) as a political act with a definite goal and subtle calculation. Stalin was thrilled by the actors' art, and it didn't matter whether they were Jews—except to him. He knew why he played out that masterful little scene.

At that time, truly talented young musicians were achieving incredible popularity, fanned by the press, for winning prestigious international competitions in Warsaw, Vienna, and Brussels. Their popularity, their great fame, were deserved, but were not commensurate with the place classical music held in the cultural needs of the mass audience. The triumphs of young Soviet artists in the international arena were part of the propaganda program to deflect attention from Soviet reality. The enthusiastic shouts for the graceful successes of Soviet polar explorers, pilots, athletes, border patrols, and musicians were designed to drown out the sounds of executioners' bullets and the groans of innumerable victims. But the sweet phrases addressed to the musicians who were supposed to conquer the world with their mastery held a special meaning.

With very few exceptions, they were Jewish. It was then that the firmament was filled with the heretofore unknown names of David Oistrakh, Emil Gilels, Yakov Flier, Yakov Zak, Elizabeta Gilels, Roza Tamarkina, Boris Goldshtein, Arnold Kaplan, Mikhail Fikhtengolts, and Tatyana Goldfarb. The newspapers carried babbling reviews and photographs. Stalin gave them medals and showered them with money. The whole country called the fourteen-year-old violinist Wunderkind Boris Goldstein by his family pet name, a typically Jewish one, Busya. Stalin received him in the Kremlin and wished success and happiness to "the marvelous Soviet Pioneer Busya, of whom the whole country is proud." He "materialized" his wish— Stalin gave Busya from Odessa a three-room apartment in Moscow along with three thousand rubles—a gigantic sum in those days.

When Henri Barbusse decided to write a biographical apologia for Stalin (or, to put it more bluntly, a sycophantic biography), a special team was created by the Central Committee to prepare material for him. The episode of little Busya being petted by Stalin and receiving his generous gifts was put into the pile marked "Facts for Mandatory Inclusion." This puff piece was intended not only for Western simpletons but for the domestic market as well. Barbusse's book became required reading in schools, universities, and political education clubs. And so these marvelous musicians who had every right to take the signs of public acclaim and state recognition as their due probably had no idea that they were expected to play a political role as well.

Probably no more so than the outstanding chess player Mikhail Botvinnik, champion of the USSR and soon to be world champion. He too had become an object of Stalin's heightened attention and concern. The medal-winning chess player's name was always in the papers and on the radio. This helped to create the image of Stalin as friend of all the peoples, who supported the worthy no matter their race or religion, and helped them achieve their full potential and be rewarded for their labors. No one in his right mind could possibly have regarded Stalin as anti-Semitic. His hidden thoughts were truly hidden. The time for them to surface had not yet come.

THIS ANTI-ANTI-SEMITISM that Stalin imposed not only on the masses but on what were called the "competent organs" (i.e., the secret police) produced concrete and eloquent results. Even in the twenties, when the times were more suited to such charges, there were not as many political trials for anti-Semitism as there were in the thirties. Anti-Semitic behaviors—real or alleged, in this case it did not matter—were perceived as counterrevolutionary acts covered by the political article of the Criminal Code: Article 58, which struck fear and horror into the whole country. Interestingly, most of these trials were held in strict secrecy, behind closed doors, and most frequently were in absentia by the infamous special sessions (the NKVD troikas). They were, therefore, not intended to have public resonance. That means that the center and the local outposts regarded the struggle with anti-Semitism as a real assignment from the Party, the state, and beloved Comrade Stalin, and not just window dressing.

The papers of the lawyer Ilya Bauder contain a few pages showing that in 1936 he was approached by the wife of one Petr Prokopyevich Golubnichy from Kharkov to represent him. Bauder could not have accepted, if only because the case had gone to a special session, which did not permit defense attorneys to be present. Indirect evidence of the charges against him is the record of speeches at a Party meeting (apparently someone had risked taking notes and passing them on to the wife), in which the arrested Golubnichy is branded "a vicious anti-Semite, attacking the Leninist-Stalinist friendship among peoples." A clumsy phrase attributed to the regional Party instructor reads, "Slanderously spreading rumors of some Jewish establishment in the leadership, he sings the songs set by the German fascists."

Archival discoveries of the last few years have revealed the secrets of some of the literary trials of that period (which were also secret, of course), where accusations of anti-Semitism were the connecting thread and the dominant tone. Highly instructive is the case of the ten-man "anti-Soviet group of Siberian writers." Among them were at least three poets of quality—Pavel Vasilyev, Sergei Markov, and Leonid Martynov, who lived to write several books. In 1958 Martynov would join in the attacks on Boris Pasternak on the occasion of his Nobel Prize.

The charges against this group of writers stated that they "set as one of their goals widespread anti-Soviet agitation, . . . anti-Soviet education of young people and strata of society hostile to Soviet power, . . . with fascism as their ultimate political goal. . . . As their main support in realizing these goals, the group chose anti-Semitism as a means for working in an anti-Soviet, counterrevolutionary spirit with the backward strata."

The confessions forced out of the defendants bear evidence of the same goals as the investigation (which was supervised personally by Genrikh Yagoda). Pavel Vasilyev's statement includes the following: "Once or twice Anov [one of the group of ten] tried to figure out how many Moscow poets were of Jewish descent. 'Pasha,' he would say, 'What's Utkin? A Jew. Bezymensky?* A Jew. Altauzen's† a Jew. Krisanov, Selvinsky, Bagritsky, Inber. . . . And they call that the great Russian literature? Tolstoy and Dostoevsky are turning over in

---

* Alexander Bezymensky (1898–1973), one of the "Komsomol poets," author of a widely popular Komsomol anthem of the twenties, "We are the young guards of workers and peasants."

† Jack (Yakov) Altauzen (1907–1942), poet popular in the twenties and thirties. Died in the war.

their graves. You guys just don't know how to work. You should learn from the Jews. One Utkin gets to the top and he pulls five Altauzenovs with him. You just don't have the imagination.' "

Leonid Martynov, Sergei Markov, and Nikolai Anov survived the GULAG and exile, but Pavel Vasilyev was executed at the age of twenty-seven. He was not forgiven his anti-Stalin poem, shocking in its hatred ("O Muse! sing today of Dzhugashvili, the son of a bitch, who combines the stubbornness of an ass with the slyness of a fox. He made thousands upon thousands of nooses, and got to power through violence. What have you done, where are you, tell me, ridiculous seminarian!"), or his promise to "shove a laurel wreath up the dictator's ass," or his openly anti-Semitic verse proclamations, which the prosecutor characterized as "vicious anti-Soviet, counterrevolutionary attacks." Here is one of his typical verse miniatures, its vileness apparent, as is the desire of the Lubyanka to portray this chauvinist hatred as a blow against Stalin and his international policy.

> A Greenland whale, king of the seas,
> Once swallowed a lousy Yid.
> It raced back and forth.
> On the third day the sovereign got sick,
> It couldn't digest the Yid.
> And so, Russia—the comparison will scare you—
> You too will die of indigestion like the whale.

Vasilyev took Stalin's anti-anti-Semitism at face value and hated Stalin because he loved the Jews. But he at least was punished for real anti-Semitism and not on trumped-up charges of anti-Semitism. His friend the Leningrad poet Boris Kornilov unfairly bore this suspicion because of his closeness to several of the Group of Ten, Vasilyev in particular. Even the fact that his second wife was Tsipa Bornstein, whom he married when she was sixteen, did not save the poet from these charges, which in those days were very serious in various cities and regions of the country.* In the twenties, people had been similarly imprisoned, but the sentence was often reduced or commuted because

---

* Boris Kornilov was executed. His small poetic legacy, showing undeniable talent, includes the song "The morning greeted us with coolness," with music by Dmitri Shostakovich, which still lives sixty years later.

they were considered to be under the influence of prejudices left over from tsarist times.

ALL THE TRIALS I have mentioned, like so many others, took place behind closed doors, and that means they could have no propaganda effect. Stalin needed that effect, and a case turned up that could accomplish his goal. It can be said with certainty that if it had not existed, Stalin's henchmen would have invented it. But it came to them, and at the most appropriate moment.

In January 1935 on Wrangel Island, above the Polar Circle, in the eastern part of the Arctic, a mutilated body was found. It was that of Dr. Nikolai Vulfson, a member of the polar station. His wife, Gita Feldman, also a physician, suspected that his death was not an accident (falling from the dogsled on his way to visit a patient in a blizzard, smashing his face on the ice, and freezing to death) but murder, organized by the chief of the station, Semenchuk, with whom Vulfson and Feldman had been feuding. Gita Feldman wrote to Moscow, to the procurator general of the USSR, Andrei Vyshinsky. It took a long time—there was no communication for weeks at a time with the mainland—but when the investigators arrived, they got action. Vyshinsky, who knew his leader's moods and desires, started the case immediately, entrusting it to his closest associate, investigator of special cases Lev Sheinin, who understood his laconic chief's orders.

There was no investigation and Sheinin had no intention of investigating. There was neither time, nor energy, nor technical capability, nor, most important, desire or necessity. An investigation assumed a trip to the scene of the crime, a forensic examination of the corpse, questioning of witnesses and information from them about facts, and not personal suspicions and suppositions. None of these conditions was fulfilled. Sheinin simply sat in his Moscow office and clipped newspaper articles quoting incensed letters demanding swift punishment for the killers. The letters were elicited by articles on the arrest of "criminals who perpetrated a vicious murder on Wrangel Island." The accused were Konstantin Semenchuk, chief of the station, and a local man, Stepan Startsev, a kayur (dogsled driver), who allegedly carried out Semenchuk's orders. They were declared the killers, by name, before any trial; the article also stated that they would be tried very soon. And this article provoked an avalanche of outraged letters and telegrams. When the case was reexamined in 1988, the file revealed nothing but newspaper clippings.

The very fact that the victim was a doctor with a Jewish name and the "killers" people with non-Jewish names gave the case a distinctly ethnic coloration. But Stalin needed more than hints, more than reading between the lines, more than guessing and speculation that might be too difficult for the simple Soviet man-in-the-street. He wanted clarity. He wanted everyone to understand that a crime committed for anti-Semitic reasons was being punished severely and that he would spare no one who attacked the great friendship among the Soviet peoples. And so the motive of the crime (or, rather, one of the main motives) was not hidden, pushed into the background, or referred to euphemistically, as it might have been at another time in Russian history. This time it was proclaimed and used. I do not discount the possibility that Semenchuk and others at the polar station were anti-Semitic, but in this instance that prejudice was being exploited for other reasons.

Why did Stalin need this case? The trial took place in late May 1936. The preparations were in full swing for a more important trial, the first Moscow show trial. In August, just three months away, sitting on the defendant's bench would be Grigori Zinoviev and Lev Kamenev, and the third, invisible, defendant would be Lev Trotsky, who was in exile. It is quite likely that no one would see any anti-Semitism in this trial, just as Trotsky did not in the many wrathful pamphlets he wrote. But Stalin knew his own secret thoughts and was afraid that others would learn them.

The trial of Semenchuk and Startsev lasted seven days, and took place at the Hall of Columns at the House of Unions. Vyshinsky, the USSR's chief procurator, came to try the defendants. There was nothing distinctive in legal terms about this run-of-the-mill murder case. Every year murders occur for many kinds of reasons. In all his years as procurator—in the twenties and thirties—Vyshinsky had never prosecuted a murder case. But this one was heard by the Supreme Court of the RSFSR, one of the constituent republics of the Soviet Union.

Established practice called for the republic's procurator, not the procurator of the USSR, to present the state's case.

This was a brilliant move. The exotic villainy of the crime allegedly committed at the edge of the earth under cover of the polar night was bound to attract attention. It heightened the mystery of the crime. Vyshinsky's presence and his passionate opening statement gave the case a scope that it would have been unlikely to achieve with a different prosecutor.

And there was yet another significant detail. The defendants denied their guilt. No one forced them to confess, even though the specialists from the NKVD and the procurator's office could easily have done so. The defense—two excellent lawyers, Nikolai Kommodov and Sergei Kaznacheyev—did not accept the charges and argued with determination and vigor. There was nothing at all about this case that smelled of a rehearsed show trial. This alone suggests persuasively that the organizers did not care about the trial per se or its results. The mere fact that the defendants were charged served to demonstrate the state's position on anti-Semitism—and that was the trial's main goal, which it achieved through intense publicity, without particular interest in the course of the arguments or even in the outcome, which was predetermined.

The mouthpiece of the "concept" of the state's case (in effect, Stalin's voice) was Vyshinsky. Some passages from his summation show his intention to turn the case of Semenchuk and Startsev into a Beilis case in reverse. In the Beilis case, it was important to prove the ritual character of the murder, which made the trial anti-Jewish, while here they had to prove at any cost the anti-Semitism of Semenchuk and his friend, the biologist Vakulenko, another defendant who mysteriously did away with himself. Thus this case was pro-Jewish.

"All of Semenchuk's activity," exclaimed Vyshinsky, "was directed at undermining the authority of the Soviet regime, filling people's hearts with a feeling of hurt and deep, undeserved insults, creating a blow against the basic principles of nationality policy, against the Leninist-Stalinist nationality policy in general. Semenchuk acted crudely and criminally, violating all the principles of Leninist-Stalinist nationality policy, permitting himself monstrous perversions of the instructions of our party and the leader of the peoples of the Union of the SSR, Comrade Stalin. . . . Semenchuk dared not only to ignore but to directly violate the marvelous instructions of our leader and teacher on the inviolable friendship of the peoples of our country."

Even more revealing of the undercurrents of this trial were the words Vyshinsky used to sing an anthem to the dead Vulfson and to his wife. "The only person," Vyshinsky intoned, more accustomed to slandering than to praising, "who represented a light of morality in the grim, black background of the polar night, who raised a voice of protest, who began the struggle and brought it to an end at the cost of his own life, was Dr. Nikolai Lvovich Vulfson and his faithful and supportive companion, Gita Borisovna Feldman. If not for them, perhaps we would not have been able to lance this shameful anti-Semitic boil so quickly. . . . The memory of Dr. Vulfson will live in the heart of every honest citizen of our Soviet land. . . . Our awe and gratitude go to Dr. Feldman, whom Semenchuk and Vakulenko planned to kill after murdering her husband, discussing the best way 'to get rid of that Yid woman,' still mocking their victim Vulfson, calling him a 'filthy Yid.' . . . Vakulenko said that, and Semenchuk supported him because he hewed to the same line himself."

In my archives is a letter from Mikhail Goloshchekin, a paramedic in Leningrad, who met with Gita Feldman in the fifties, when she worked at the Botkin Hospital in Moscow. Even though Vyshinsky had not stinted in his flattering words about that "fragile but heroic woman," she had only unflattering things to say about him. When he received her before and then after the trial, he was crude and insulting. The fate of a real person, like the fate of the humiliated and injured people whom the prosecutor was so passionately protecting, interested him not in the least. His only goal was to execute his leader's secret order, to create an image for himself as an incorruptible guardian of legality on the eve of the first of the three show trials, the "trials of the century," and for the leader, the image of a great fighter for the friendship of the peoples and an implacable foe of anti-Semitism. Vyshinsky's demand that Startsev and Semenchuk be shot was satisfied. However, for that to happen, Semenchuk and Startsev's alleged crimes had to be requalified under a different article of the Criminal Code. They were no longer anti-Semitic acts or even murder, but "banditry," which was from a juridical point of view clearly absurd.

Three months later, when the curtain rose to reveal yesterday's tribunes and leaders of the revolution now turned into "fascist spies," no one could suspect the "marvelous Georgian" vacationing in Sochi of attacking his Jewish rivals or settling personal accounts or being subject to the very prejudices against which he fought so fiercely. He needed this moral alibi particularly because, of the sixteen defendants, eleven were Jewish. But there is no mention of their origins in the case. Moreover, all but one are given their Party pseudonyms, and there was no question of adding their Jewish names in parentheses, a practice that would become quite popular some twelve or fifteen years later. So, for instance, Kamenev was tried and executed as Kamenev and not as Rozenfeld, even though that was his legal name. The only exception was made for Kruglyansky, a Comintern worker, because the name he was going by, Fritz David, was one of his espionage cover names, and he could not be tried under it.

And the man who sat at the prosecution desk had just earned respect and popularity as an erudite and incisive protector of the law, the very embodiment of truth and justice. The organizer of this trial did not need a mechanical functionary in that role, he needed a clever, passionate, and popular man. And in Vyshinsky he got him.

MANY FOREIGN POLITICAL figures, writers, and journalists visited Moscow in the 1930s. Probably all of them would have been happy (or at any rate, very interested) to meet briefly with Stalin, and quite a few would have written a book about it. But Stalin was very choosy about his interlocutors, requiring maximum effect from each meeting. And it was no accident that on the eve of the second show trial (the Pyatakov-Radek case) he picked Lion Feuchtwanger—not only because he had a full dossier of reports on the writer's readiness to support Stalin on the grounds that Stalin would fight against Hitler, not only because this émigré writer was very popular in the USSR and had a good name abroad, but also because Stalin felt it exceptionally important to have among his agents and propagandizers a European writer who did not belong to any party, who was independent, and who was Jewish. His name alone would remove all suspicions of anti-Semitism from Stalin. Stalin kept imagining skeptics everywhere who suspected him of a secret sin.

Stalin even managed to persuade Feuchtwanger that Karl Radek (Sobelson), who was well known in Germany and who in a few days would be appearing as a defendant in the October Hall of the House of Unions, was a close friend of Stalin's, who grieved over his betrayal and wanted to help, but couldn't. And then, in fact, Stalin did help. Of the four main defendants (Pyatakov, Radek, Sokolnikov, and Serebryakov), two were Jewish, and Stalin spared their lives. Pyatakov and Serebryakov were executed, Radek and Sokolnikov lived on, only to be killed two and half years later in their prison cells. (But that was done secretly.) Many researchers tried to figure out the basis of Stalin's decision. Various hypotheses were proposed, and none can be discounted out of hand, because each has some truth to it. Probably there was no one single reason.

But one was most important, and as far as I know, no one else has considered it. The same reason that would be the cause for the execution of tens of thousands of people just a few years later was the cause of the temporary salvation of Radek and Sokolnikov. After the exposure of the "main Jew," Trotsky, and the start of the hunt for him, after the execution of Zinoviev and Kamenev, despite Stalin's promise (news of which spread quickly in the upper echelons of the Bolsheviks), Stalin could not destroy the last two Jews who stood at the very top (Radek held no high post officially, but was close to Stalin). This would give rise to unwanted suspicions. So Stalin let them live.

Yet if he had in fact turned over Radek and Sokolnikov to the Lubyanka executioners right then, the world would not have seen any intentional "nationalist" element in it. Stalin's pathological wariness, which would soon turn to paranoia, prompted him to see things that were not there. He listened to his suspicions, and won again.

Lion Feuchtwanger, charmed by Stalin, wrote, "In general I consider the behavior toward the Soviet Union of many Western intellectuals to be short-sighted and unworthy.

"They do not see the historical achievements of the Soviet Union, they do not want to understand that you cannot make history in white gloves. . . .

"Stalin is sincere when he says his unfinished goal is the realization of socialist democracy."

Stalin had to act hypocritically for many years in order to mislead Feuchtwanger and other Western intellectuals. One of the buttons Stalin pushed was the Jewish issue, of great concern to the West. Thanks to this, the hour of triumph for Russian Jewry—its hope for real equality in the Soviet Union—lasted almost a decade. And perhaps a bit more.

5

The Attack Begins

It would be pointless to seek out the exact day when the era of ostentatious protection of the Jewish nationality and Jewish culture ended and was replaced by its opposite. The time had not yet come when Stalin could push a button, invisible to the rest of the world, and one policy would instantly be replaced by its opposite. Not much later, this situation would indeed arise, and we can determine almost to the day when the command to commence a campaign of state anti-Semitism was given, if not in so many words, certainly in a way that was clear to everyone. But in the later thirties, when such a campaign was in the works and had even yielded its first results, it was not yet a frontal attack. One era was smoothly passing into another, and the outlines of both remained friable and amorphous.

The Israeli researcher Ludmila Dymerskaya was perhaps the first to notice that back in January–February of 1936, under the guise of a discussion on drafts for new schoolbooks on Russian history, *Pravda* unexpectedly published a series of articles praising the Russian people in a spirit that was from a Marxist internationalist standpoint quite unusual. The unexpectedness lay not in the fact that Karl Radek was the executor of Stalin's new plan but that the object of his wrathful philippic was Nikolai Bukharin. A real surprise was Radek's ascribing to Bukharin the well-known definition by Lenin (and surely Radek and Stalin knew him as the author of the definition) of the Russian people as a "nation of Oblomovs."* Lenin used the terms "Oblomov" and "Oblomovism" frequently as symbols. For instance, in a speech on March 22, 1922, he announced, "There was this type in Russian life, Oblomov. He was not only a landowner, but also a peasant, and not a peasant, but also an intellectual, and not an intellectual, but a worker and a communist." In other words, all the people.

In an unsigned editorial, Stalin juxtaposed his own concept of the Russians to Lenin's (attributing it to Bukharin): "A nation that gave the world such geniuses as Lomonosov, Lobachevsky, Popov, Pushkin, Chernyshevsky, and Mendeleyev, such giants of humanity as Lenin and Stalin, a nation that prepared and realized the October Socialist Revolution under the leadership of the Bolshevik Party—only a man who does not realize what he is saying could call this nation a 'nation of Oblomovs.' " The direct goal of such bathos was to attack Bukharin, and the oblique intention (though one obvious to a great number of contemporaries) was to wound Lenin. But beyond that, almost in passing, as something that went without saying, it turned the "marvelous Georgian" into a giant of humanity, a gift to the world from the Russian people.

There was also a third aim, one that was for the most part deeply hidden. It becomes more evident in subsequent articles in *Pravda*, which push the idea of "the great Russian people, who have stood at the head of the historic process," "shown the proletariat and workers of capitalist countries the path to freedom"; of "the great Russian people, the first among equals"; and the idea that "the lot of the Russian workers is the honor of helping the workers of other nationalities to become truly free members of the socialist community of peoples and thereby to earn their greatest love."

Just how great that love was we can see today, when the reflexive

---

* Oblomov is the eponymous hero of a novel by the classic Russian writer Ivan Goncharov (1812–1891). The author imbued his hero with indolence, lack of initiative, and contemplativeness and juxtaposed him to the other main protagonist, the German colonist Stoltz, a man of energy, drive, and persistence. The term "Oblomovism" became a mainstay of literature, sociology, and philosophy to define the Russian national character. In the film version of the novel (1980), Nikita Mikhalkov tried to rethink the canonical interpretation of Oblomov and Stoltz, presenting the former as a spiritual, naïve, trusting, and ennobled person and the latter as a soulless pragmatist, a cold-hearted businessman with no human feelings.

hatred of everything Russian has reached astronomical proportions in the republics of the former Communist empire. But in the late thirties the persistent emphasis of the true Russian origins of the revolution had a narrower and specific significance. Stalin decided to destroy the "myth" of the decisive role of the Jews in the planning, organization, and realization of the revolution, and along with the unnamed but assumed Trotsky, Zinoviev, and Kamenev, Stalin is burying Marx as well, whose role in the creation of the theoretical underpinnings for the revolution is not mentioned at all. Gradually the first two names of the traditional quartet "Marx-Engels-Lenin-Stalin" fell away, the better to turn the diminished duo into Stalin's triumphant solo.

The entire campaign, with its short-term and long-term goals, cannot be regarded as an open call for the establishment of state anti-Semitism. These were just distant rolls of thunder warning of a storm to come. Only a very sensitive ear and eye could have seen the global, catastrophic consequences at that early stage. Perhaps Stalin himself did not intend a campaign of that scope, if only because Berlin was not yet defeated and in ruins, and psychologically he did not then perceive himself to be the ruler of the world, allowed to toss away any ideology and do whatever he felt like.

But Jews were swiftly disappearing from political life. As suggested, they usually vanished not as Jews but as people who held a certain post, and there were many Jews in many posts. But for whatever reason they moved from their desks to execution pits and concentration camps, and other people took their places. And the vast majority of the replacements were young people from Russian villages, without a revolutionary past or any preparation and experience—theoretical or professional. They learned their professions "on the job" and were totally indebted to Stalin, and him alone, for their promotions. Even a microscope would not reveal a trace of a "Jewish presence" in this new wave. There were a few individuals—"remnants of former glory" who survived the terror and who were allowed by Stalin to finish out their lives in unimportant positions, their very existence proving "Stalin's friendship of the peoples" (like Zemlyachka, Mekhlis, Yaroslavsky, and of course, Kaganovich). But these were the remains of the old cadres. New people were not allowed into the severely delimited and closed circle.

And another note: the process of pushing Jews out of political life was gradual. The Central Committee (members and candidate members) elected at the Eighteenth Party Congress had at least 25 Jews out of 139 members. Amazingly, among the 139 members and candidate members elected at the Seventeenth Party Congress, there were also 25 Jews. Only 6 carried over from the old Central Committee, and the other 19 Jews were from the nomenklatura, but from the economic and military sectors, not the Party. Decorum was maintained, and we cannot speak of a wide-ranging anti-Semitic campaign or a powerful attack. By early 1939, when the Eighteenth Party Congress took place, Stalin was merely preparing the artillery.

But three or four months later, the attack had begun. The signal was the sudden—and incredibly crude—removal of the Commissar of Foreign Affairs, Maxim Litvinov, on May 3, 1939. And that same night, the building of the Commissariat (now Ministry) of Foreign Affairs, situated across the street from the NKVD, was surrounded by Beria's troops. This event was more than a change in foreign policy, it was an action directed personally against Litvinov, who had miraculously survived the Great Terror.

Discussing it almost a half century later with Felix Chuev, Molotov admitted, "In 1939, when Litvinov was fired and I took his place, Stalin told me, 'Get the Jews out of the commissariat.' Thank God that he said that! You see, the Jews were the absolute majority in the management and among the ambassadors. That is not right, of course. Latvians and Jews. . . . And each one had a long tail dragging behind him. [Molotov repeats that phrase in his conversations with Chuev many times—in various years and in various contexts. Apparently, the idea of the mythical tail gave him no peace.] And they looked down on me when I came there, they mocked the measures I began instituting."

By arrangement with Beria, that is, on Stalin's instructions, the major diplomats either were moved directly into Lubyanka cells or had faked compromising materials gathered against them. As early as May 10 Beria arrested one of Litvinov's closest colleagues, the chief of the foreign ministry's press division, Yevgeny Gnedin (Gelfand), son of the notorious Parvus.* In the first round of interrogation (May 15–16), after terrible torture, Gnedin signed what was wanted, that he was part of a "counterrevolutionary, terrorist, espionage group in the system of the People's Commissariat of Foreign Affairs," and that the group was headed by Maxim Litvinov (Vallakh).

The assignment Stalin gave Molotov (and therefore Beria also) went according to a plan. This is supported by the names of those who were arrested and against whom dossiers were being made. After Stalin's death, Senior Ministry of State Security (MGB) Investigator Voronovich, who had tortured Gnedin and was later arrested for his methods, testified (September 20–21, 1954) that Beria and his deputy, Bogdan Kobulov, personally beat Gnedin in a commissariat office for forty-five minutes, demanding that he sign a statement about "an espionage-terrorist organization that was headed by Litvinov and whose members were Soviet ambassadors and management figures in the Commissariat of Foreign Affairs"—all Jewish.

The archival materials that I obtained despite the desperate resistance of Lubyanka's guardians give convincing evidence that a large trial of diplomats was being prepared and that it would have been the first undisguised anti-Semitic trial. With only one exception (Alexandra Kollontai, ambassador to Sweden and before that to Mexico and Norway), all the defendants and their untried cohorts in the "espionage group" (who were already executed for individual sins) were Jewish—Ivan Maisky (Israel Lyakhovetsky), ambassador to London; Boris Shtein, former ambassador to Finland and Italy; Yakov Suritz, ambassador to France (and before that to Germany); Konstantin

---

* Parvus was the Party pseudonym of the German Social Democrat Alexander Gelfand (1869–1924), who was also a member of the Russian social-democratic party of Mensheviks. His Menshevism did not keep Lenin from doing dark and rather dirty deals with him. There is a large amount of literature on the subject, but their relationship is not fully clear to this day. Parvus helped organize the passage of Lenin and other émigré Bolsheviks from Switzerland to Russia through warring Germany (March 1917) in a sealed railroad car and was the main intermediary in delivering German money to Russian Bolsheviks for their subversive activity, money that was meant to bring about (and did) the total collapse of Russia, which was fighting Germany in the war. The newspapers naturally uncovered this unparalleled political affair. Lenin protested energetically, using the strongest and most vulgar words, but the more he lambasted the "vile inventions of the bourgeois press," the clearer it became that he was the one doing the inventing. Parvus's name was compromised and he spent the last years of his life in total obscurity, far from the political scene.

Yurenev (Krotovsky), former ambassador to Japan, Italy, Austria, and other countries; Marsel Rozenberg, ambassador to Spain; Lev Khinchuk, former ambassador to Germany and trade representative in England; and many other ambassadors (Yakov Davtyan, Leonid Stark, et al.). The envoys were to be joined by officials from the foreign ministry, including Mikhail Koltsov (Fridland) and Vera Inber (Trotsky's niece). A leading role in this spy play was going to the ambassador to the United States, Konstantin Omansky. And the scenario was being brought to life by the investigative team of Israel Pinzur. Following Stalin's favorite model, Jews were destroying Jews.

The name of Israel Lvovich Pinzur, captain of state security (the equivalent of a colonel), comes up in many falsified political cases. At one time he headed the investigation division of the Moscow Directorate of State Security, and then was promoted to assistant chief of investigation of the Chief Directorate of State Security of the NKVD USSR. On April 27, 1940, he received a medal for valor. Judging by the dates, it was for his successful work on the diplomats' case. Pinzur had plenty of valor, but it wasn't very highly valued by then. In 1936–1938, similar exploits had merited more distinguished decorations as well as monetary awards.

The "ambassadors' trial" was not intended to be part of the Great Terror show trials, even though it would generate an enormous amount of publicity because of the defendants' profession. It had more far-reaching goals. A cardinal shift in national policy was planned to end with Stalin being proclaimed the great son of the Russian people and its leader. But Stalin's plan for this trial underwent constant modification as the international situation changed. The Molotov-Ribbentrop Pact of August 23, 1939 (and before that the complex negotiations with the British and the French and the obvious approach of war), inevitably had an influence on the fate of the intended victims from the diplomatic sphere. They played too great a role in the country's foreign policy. The situation kept changing, and so the final decision kept being postponed. That is why Gnedin was held in prison for over two years without a sentence. If it had been a question of him alone, isolated from the rest, the NKVD would have summarily decided his fate. The usual time between arrest and execution was three or four months, more rarely five or six. But Gnedin's case was dragged out. There were no instructions on canceling the trial, yet without Gnedin it could not proceed (at least, as the scenario was written). It became clear only after Hitler's aggression on June 22, 1941, that there would be no diplomats' trial. After prosecutors hastily threw together a one-page "summary of charges," Gnedin was tried individually, and on July 9, 1941 (July 5–12, 1941, saw an enormous number of people sentenced who had not been tried earlier for one reason or another) he received a "humane sentence"—a mere ten years in the camps. He would be brought back from the Karaganda steppes and rehabilitated on August 13, 1955.

The diplomats' trial had been intended to set in motion a general plan of action, and when the trial collapsed, implementation of that plan was, fortunately, postponed. Rozenberg, Khinchuk, Stark, Yurenev, Davtyan, and others were executed as individuals, while some escaped completely. Maisky was arrested much later and on different charges. Neither Shtein nor Suritz was touched—they were merely "transferred to other work." Vera Inber would actually receive the Stalin Prize seven years later. Konstantin Omansky—yet another "leader of an espionage group," who had begun his career as an OGPU informer about foreign (and domestic) Communists in the Comintern—survived unscathed. His death in an airplane crash, en route from Washington to Costa Rica, where he had been appointed ambassador, terminated his climb up the professional ladder. We can only guess what would have happened to him in 1949–1952, when Stalin's anti-Semitic campaign was unleashed.

As for Litvinov, the case that was begun against him secretly in May 1939 was closed just as secretly in October. Stalin decided to limit himself to stripping him of his commissar's portfolio. It may have been Stalin's friendship with Nazi Germany that saved Litvinov, paradoxical as that may sound: Destroying the diplomat whom Hitler hated so openly would have been too demonstrative a step. It would never be too late to accomplish, if circumstances called for it. Litvinov was removed from the Central Committee, that is, from all power. A bloodbath was planned. Molotov told Felix Chuev about it with amazing candor. "Such a bastard," he said. "He deserved the highest measure of punishment. . . . He was a real bastard. Litvinov was spared only accidentally."

The American journalist Maurice Hindus expressed his opinion about the Molotov-Litvinov relationship in his book *Crisis in the Kremlin* (New York, 1954).

It is well-known in Moscow that Molotov always detested Litvinov, but not, as has been often alleged in Moscow's foreign colony, because Litvinov was a Jew. In his personal life, at least in the prewar years, Molotov never manifested racial bias. His wife is Jewish, and her brother once told me that despite Molotov's atheism, he was always respectful of his mother-in-law's observance of Orthodox Jewish dietary laws. Molotov's detestation for Litvinov was of a purely personal nature. No Muscovite I have ever known, whether friend of Molotov or of Litvinov, has ever taken exception to this view.

A humorless man, Molotov chafed under Litvinov's blunt and often scorching wit, which Stalin, by contrast, always enjoyed in the days when he trusted Litvinov more than anyone else as the executor of the Kremlin's foreign policy. A Russian of Russians and fiercely fanatical, Molotov was as resentful of Litvinov's fluency in French, German, and English as he was distrustful of Litvinov's easy manner with foreigners. Never having lived abroad, Molotov always suspected that there was something impure and sinful in Litvinov's broad-mindedness and in his appreciation of Western civilization. Had Molotov possessed the power, he would have dismissed Litvinov from the office of Foreign Commissar long before May 3, 1939, when he himself ascended to that office.

This detailed and insightful analysis of the characters of two opposites and their relationship could be considered flawless if not for one circumstance. The removal of Litvinov and his replacement by Molotov were not the result of their relationship, and not even of foreign policy considerations. Molotov may not have had anti-Semitic feelings about Litvinov, but Stalin did. And Litvinov's downfall was part of a global anti-Jewish action in which it did not matter in the least how fluently Litvinov spoke in how many foreign languages. He was "guilty" not of what he was accused of but of his origins.

At the Eighth Extraordinary Congress of Soviets (November 1936), the "great bastard" Litvinov, calling the Soviet Union an impregnable fortress, went on to say, "This confidence continues to grow with the knowledge that the fortress is led by and its keys are in the hands of

a commandant like our glorious and great leader, Comrade Stalin."
The commandant, no fool, knew the value of that declaration of love,
but he spared the speaker, knowing that he could still come in handy.

Litvinov's replacement by Molotov naturally caused astonishment
throughout the world, especially in Germany, but the real reason for
these events was not suspected, as we can see from documents now
available. On May 4, 1939, Germany's Chargé d'Affaires Tippelskirch
cabled Berlin from Moscow:

> The unexpected change has elicited great wonder here, since Litvinov was
> in the center of negotiations with the British delegation, and at the May
> Day parade he had appeared on the tribune next to Stalin,* and there
> was no recent evidence of the instability of his position. There are no
> commentaries in the Soviet press. The Commissariat of Foreign Affairs is
> not giving any explanations to the representatives of the press.
>
> Since Litvinov had received the British ambassador as recently as May
> 2, and yesterday his name was listed in the press as one of the honored
> guests at the parade, his removal seems to be the result of an unexpected
> decision by Stalin. . . . Molotov (not a Jew) is considered "the closest
> friend and comrade-in-arms" of Stalin. His appointment undoubtedly
> guarantees that foreign policy will be conducted in strict conformity with
> Stalin's ideas.

It could have been conducted in conformity with those ideas by
Litvinov as well. Naturally, Tippelskirch did not suspect that the
NKVD had started a case against Litvinov as a spy for Germany (yes,
Germany), for no matter how strongly the chargé d'affaires held Nazi
ideas, they did not deprive him of reason or of the ability to think
logically. In fact, it would have made much more sense in fabricating
a case to have Jewish Litvinov and Jewish Surits spying for a regime
that was closer to them—for instance, Litvinov for the Americans and
Surits for the French. But Stalin thought it much more effective to
accuse two or three famous Jews, and with them all of Soviet Jewry,
of selling out to the Nazi regime. After all, he had already turned
Trotsky into a Gestapo agent.

---

* This is not quite true. Litvinov was not on the reviewing stand on Lenin's Mausoleum but
on the tribune for honored guests. It would be more correct to say that he was not next to
Stalin but was not far from him.

. . .

IN THE MEANTIME, the Jewish theme took its place in the transcripts of the other arrests that probably would have been tied in with the diplomats' trial when it took place. Mikhail Koltsov, the country's leading journalist (editor-in-chief of the magazines *Ogonyok, Krokodil,* and *Za rubezhom,* member of the editorial board of *Pravda,* deputy of the Supreme Soviet of the RSFSR, and corresponding member of the Academy of Sciences of the USSR), was openly accused of having ties with a "Zionist nest in the Foreign Office," directly with Gnedin, Girshfeld, Surits, and Omansky. Through his friend André Malraux, then a young man in love with Soviet Russia, Koltsov allegedly had "access to corresponding circles in Europe and the USA." In this context "corresponding circles" means "Zionist circles." Malraux's part in this is totally inexplicable, but his name figures in various Lubyanka cases fabricated against cultural figures of that period. And Koltsov allegedly had access to "corresponding circles" inside the Commissariat of Foreign Affairs through his good friend Matvei Berman, chief of the GULAG and later Deputy Commissar of Foreign Affairs.

This motif is heard even more in the case of the writer Isaac Babel, who was also arrested in May 1939. He was accused of Trotskyism and terrorism, the usual charges. But he was alleged to be working with a "band of conspirators" that included Ilya Ehrenburg, Boris Pasternak, Sergei Eisenstein, Solomon Mikhoels, Leonid Utesov (founder of the first Soviet jazz orchestra), and other cultural luminaries of a certain ethnic origin (along with representatives of other national groups as well—Stalin never forgot to dilute a strong ethnic brew to avoid suspicions of anti-Semitism).

Beria's scenario writers also tried to get Babel involved in the military case. Babel had been in the Civil War, where he had met many of the men who became the top brass in the Soviet armed forces. Some were sworn enemies, others close friends. His main adversary was Semyon Budenny, later an illiterate marshal, who was angered by Babel's world-famous cycle of short stories *Red Army,* in which Budenny's glorious cavalry was not depicted in the romantic light of official propaganda. The publication of those stories prompted a wrathful reply from Budenny, who accused the writer in print of "distorting the image" of the First Cavalry, which had fought under Budenny's command. One colorful detail is telling: In his *Pravda* article, Budenny accused Babel of "acting from the image of a crazy Jew."

The polemic might have had no further ramifications if Maxim Gorky had not entered the fray. The acknowledged Soviet classic mortally insulted the vainglorious "red commander." Budenny, Gorky said, was judging Babel's book from the level of a horse rather than from the level of art.

While Budenny was an enemy, other comrades from the Civil War became Babel's good friends. Commander Iona Yakir (shot in the Tukhachevsky case), chief of the Kiev Military Region, and division commanders Dmitri Shmidt (David Aronovich Gutman)* and Yakov Okhotnikov were the three closest. Budenny hated them because they were rivals and opposites. Compared to him, these military leaders were practically models of intellect and culture, and they were in the orbit of many famous writers, directors, and actors. Besides envy of talent and intellect, hostility to their position, and consciousness of his own inferiority, Budenny's seething enmity toward his "colleagues" was fed by yet another powerful feeling—all three were Jewish.

But until Stalin intervened in Babel's fate, until the opportunity arrived to involve his name in a general conspiracy, there was the hope of keeping him out of trouble. And that came, of all places, from Yezhov himself. Babel had known Yezhov's wife, Yevgenia Solomonovna, for a long time. (Yes, the horrible executioner of the Lubyanka shared the Kremlin predilection for Jewish wives.) Babel remembered Yevgenia Khayutina (later Gladun, by her first husband),† ten years his junior, as a little girl frolicking on the Black Sea beach back in Odessa. They kept in touch, and became closer friends, when she took over as editor of *USSR Under Construction* and started looking for work from celebrated writers for the magazine. Despite his great fame, Babel did not appear in print too often after the scandal

---

* Dmitri Shmidt's biographical details are evident in the image of red commissar Boris Erlikh, the hero of Babel's unfinished novella, *The Jewess*.

† Alexei Gladun, a diplomat, was shot for being a Trotskyite and spy. His wife had become close to Yezhov before the end of their marriage, and he knew the bloodthirsty dwarf well. The materials in his case file attest that Gladun had used his wife to recruit Yezhov into an "anti-Soviet organization."

over *Red Army*. The commissions from his friend from Odessa were just what he needed, especially since what she wanted coincided with his own plans for a "collective farm novel."

Ilya Ehrenburg's memoirs describe Babel frequenting the Yezhov house even after the husband became the feared Commissar of Internal Affairs. He went there knowing he was taking a risk. An invisible force pulled him into the mysterious lair—there were not many people of his circle who had such easy entree into theirs. As a family friend, perhaps Babel was contemplating a future novel that would use his first-hand observations.

He knew both sides of the family. At the Yezhov house on Kiselny Alley, the highest-ranking NKVD officials met with Babel and other writers. Though Yezhov (with the involvement of his wife) saved him when he had the power to do so, Babel would have to share the commissar's fate when Yezhov's luck turned. The sentence read, "Organizationally tied in anti-Soviet activity with Gladun-Khayutina, the wife of enemy of the people Yezhov, Babel was lured by her into anti-Soviet conspiratorial terrorist activity, sharing the goals and aims of that anti-Soviet organization, including terrorist acts . . . against the leaders of the All-Union Communist Party (Bolshevik) and the Soviet government."

On October 29, 1938, six weeks before Yezhov lost his post as Commissar of Internal Affairs to his deputy Beria, a brigade of Kremlin doctors visited his wife and demanded that she be hospitalized immediately. All evidence indicates that the "patient" did not call them in. Their "diagnosis of the main illness" confirms it (therefore there were also "not main" symptoms, we must assume): "asthenia-depressive state (cyclothymia?)."* But probably the most amazing part is that the patient, who was apparently in urgent need of hospitalization, was taken not to a hospital but to a government sanatorium in the country, where she was attended round-the-clock not by psychiatrists, but by the country's leading physicians (Professor Dmitri Rossiisky, Professor Vladimir Vinogradov, et al.), who treated Stalin and his immediate circle. More important, they had just falsified the medical ev-

---

* Cyclothymia is a light form of manic-depressive psychosis. Note the question mark used by the diagnosticians.

idence for the Bukharin-Rykov trial and always signed whatever certificates were required without a murmur.

From the sanatorium Yevgenia Yezhova (Gladun-Khayutina) sent her husband a strange note (which would be used as evidence in the case against Yezhov): "Nikolai! I beg you . . . persistently check my entire life, all of me . . . I cannot accept the thought that I am suspected of double-dealing, of crimes I never committed." Of course, one could see evidence of persecution mania, a symptom of schizophrenia, in that letter. But there are no signs of madness in the note. It is the cry of a woman desperately fighting for her life and knowing full well what awaits her. And why did she need to write to her omnipotent and loving husband—who could stand in the way of his visiting her? And who could give her anything in her hospital bed as she was treated by the country's best physicians?

On November 21 (just two weeks before Yezhov was fired), Yevgenia Yezhova died at the age of thirty-four. The death certificate was signed by Vinogradov, Rossiisky, Professor Spasokukotsky, and Professor Busalov, chief of the Kremlin hospital and sanatorium department—a full deck of celebrities who "scientifically" confirmed the passing of members of the Politburo and of Stalin's favorite commissars. "Cause of death: luminal poisoning." In other words, suicide.

Less than a half year later, the dead Yezhova will be accused of espionage for British intelligence and of belonging to a conspiracy (with Isaac Babel) against the Soviet leadership, and her husband will be accused of killing her by sending her a horse's dose of sleeping medication, because she knew too much about him. But what could she have known? That Yezhov passionately enjoyed sex with men, as much as he did with women? But everyone in the Kremlin knew that. What else? That he was covered in the blood of innocent victims? Who didn't know that? Besides, Yezhov was not accused of his real crimes. And Yevgenia could not have known that Yezhov was a foreign spy because he wasn't one.

Then who killed the woman who suddenly decided to take on the dangerous Lubyanka Olympus, and why? There is no doubt that Yezhov was at the center of that bloody operation—perhaps the last in a long line of murders he organized (because by early October, even though he was still formally Commissar of Internal Affairs, he was no longer working), but could he have risked using the trusted medical luminaries to kill his wife? The signature of the Father of the Peoples is recognizable here. He liked arresting the wives of his loyal comrades-in-arms (or rather, his loyal lackeys) and watching them display even greater docility. Let us recall Molotov (there will be more in a later chapter), Kalinin, and Poskrebyshev. He dealt with Yezhov with even greater virtuosity, keeping his position among the Soviet leaders in mind. He gave Yezhov orders to kill his wife and then—with every justification—accused him of murder. Brilliant dramaturgy, borrowed from the history of ancient Rome in its decline and the medieval Inquisition.

As fate would have it, Babel first was saved from death thanks to Yevgenia Yezhova and then died thanks to her. He was at her funeral and wept bitterly without hiding his tears. Was he mourning only the death of a friend? Or was he also contemplating his own imminent demise, which, as one of the wisest men of his era, he could not have doubted?

The poet Semyon Lipkin recounts in his memoirs how he heard Babel say to the poet Eduard Bagritsky in the early thirties, "I've learned to watch calmly as people are executed." To this Vassily Grossman* responded: "How sorry I am for Babel, sorry not only because he died too young, that he was killed, but because he—such a smart, talented and high-spirited man—could say those words of madness. What had happened to his soul? Why did he spend New Year's Eve with the Yezhov family? . . . Why were such extraordinary people—he, Mayakovsky, Bagritsky—so drawn to the GPU? What was it—the attraction of power?? And why did Babel hang out with shady characters?"

Attempting to answer these puzzling questions would lead us off on a tangent. The attraction felt by some major talents for the grim Lubyanka lair—a seduction that cost some their lives and others "merely" moral degradation—is a topic deserving of separate consideration. For Babel, it was a tragedy on more than just a personal level. It gave

---

* Vassily Semyonovich (Iosif Solomonovich) Grossman (1905–1964), author of the banned and confiscated novels *Life and Fate* and *Forever Flowing*, which were published posthumously. He was harshly criticized for such works as the novel *In the Righteous Cause* and the play *If the Pythagoreans Are to Be Believed.*

the Kremlin's Playwright an opportunity to create a plot that threatened to throw a multitude of outstanding people into the execution pits, tying them together with a chain that existed only in the author's feverish brain. It was an alarm bell warning of the coming—or at least possible—Holocaust. When one juxtaposes the data in the still strictly classified archives, the cases, the formulas of the investigation documents, the dates, the names of the Lubyanka bone-breakers who obtained "confessions" from their victims, one can see the clear contours of a case, enormous in scope and consequences, that would be a single case even if it were broken up into several cases. They all had a common goal. There was one plot element that would have tied together all the military leaders, NKVD officials, diplomats, writers, directors, and actors—their tendentiously homogeneous origins would have been evident to all, even if the Party propagandists did not emphasize them.

There is evidence of this plot being constructed then in other cases, and that is no accident, but Stalin followed all of them closely and they were all directly supervised by Beria. There is convincing, reliable evidence that Stalin had personally read, pencil in hand, the cases against Koltsov and Babel. The phrase that investigators attributed to Babel tells us much about their plans. He is alleged to have said, "I, Babel, was the leader of the counterrevolutionary organization in literature; in film it was Sergei Eisenstein, and in theater it was Mikhoels." All Jewish names. Ten years later Mikhoels will figure in the Lubyanka transcripts not only in theater, but as leader of a gigantic Zionist conspiracy. The name of another conspirator "exposed" by Babel will also surface then, that of Professor Leonid Tumerman, whose arrest was postponed because Stalin's plans changed temporarily. There is no doubt about the direct connection between the events of the very end of the thirties and those of the late forties.

From the beginning, Beria and his team designated Ilya Ehrenburg as chief of this band of spies, killers, and hirelings of international capitalism. His name figures in every list in the files of arrested writers and actors and in many of the files of diplomats. Here is what the investigators forced Babel to say about Ehrenburg: "Naturally, when Ehrenburg found a fellow thinker in me, he readily entered into anti-Soviet conversations, in which we determined our common views and came to the conclusion of the need for an organization [this was the Lubyanka's main task, to show that there was an organization] united in the struggle against the present regime." In this organization invented by the Lubyanka we will find the poets Mikhail Svetlov and Mikhail Golodny (Epshtein), to whom we will return in Chapter 9.

Stalin must have come across Ehrenburg the "spy and Zionist agent" every time he read the files of Babel, Koltsov, and the others. But he did not ask Beria, "Why is such a spy and agent walking around freely, what is your ministry thinking?" And he decided the fate of Ehrenburg and many others who were considered spies—Pasternak and Eisenstein, Utesov and Svetlov, Suritsa, Maysky, and Shtein. Why? Ehrenburg, who was acutely aware of the sword dangling over his head* but was unlikely to have an idea of the charges already made against him, responds briefly in his memoirs, "I don't know." In the fifties he was attacked mercilessly with this question ("Why were you saved?")—I heard him at an evening dedicated to him at the Polytechnical Institute and at an evening for the public to meet the actors and friends of the Sovremennik Theater. He could say nothing but "I don't know." And who did? Who does? Was there a clear and obvious logic (albeit criminal) in any of Stalin's decisions?

There was some sort of logic, probably. The swiftly changing international situation—primarily the alliance with Hitler—had to bring corrections to the scenario Stalin had originally developed. It was not even that the diplomats with international importance could still be useful (in that sense Ehrenburg with his excellent foreign connections and refined pen could be considered a diplomat too). It was more that the world perceived Nazism first and foremost in relation to the Jewish question. To embark on an anti-Jewish action at the moment of uniting with Nazi Germany and carving up the map of Europe would have meant demonstrating solidarity with Hitler's ideology as well. It was too early to do that.

---

* For instance, he could not have disregarded this: N. Matsuyev's bibliographical work on Russian literature was published at the very beginning of 1940. Volume 1933–1938 does not mention Ilya Ehrenburg at all, despite the fact that about ten of his books were published in those years. Matsuyev, of course, included them in his reference work, but they were removed by the censor, Glavlit (the book was passed in 1939), which got lists of banned names from the Lubyanka with lightning speed.

Stalin never clung fanatically to his own schemes. He was quick to respond to shifts in the situation and changed his plans without the slightest concern of how it might appear to others. The strategy never altered, but the tactics were adjusted to new circumstances. And that is what happened this time.

THERE WAS YET another circumstance, not visible to an observer, that could have influenced Stalin's decisions, especially in this area.

The siege of Trotsky continued, and many millions of dollars were expended on his liquidation. Nothing compared with the successful completion of this operation for Stalin. Trotsky's political discredita-tion could have no additional effect. Stalin had done everything pos-sible in that regard. Now he wanted not the reputation of his worst enemy, but his head.

After a series of failed attempts, the goal seemed to be in sight. With the help of Lubyanka agent Mark Zborovsky, the operation to kill Trotsky's son and closest ally, Lev Sedov, had been successfully concluded. Zborovsky was born in 1907 in Russia, to a poor Jewish family. He emigrated to Lodz and joined the Polish Communist Party. Then his path took him to France, where he was recruited by the NKVD and given the code name Etienne. On instructions from Lub-yanka, he became a fervent "Trotskyite" and a friend of Sedov, who trusted him totally. In 1941, at the height of the war, Zborovsky emigrated to the United States and gradually moved away from the Lubyanka's bloody deeds, becoming a professor of anthropology. He was exposed only after Stalin's death, when the danger of falling victim to Moscow's long arm was significantly reduced. Confessing and repenting, he got a humane sentence from American courts in 1955.

A group led by two other Jews moved closer to Trotsky, who had found refuge in Mexico in a well-guarded villa. The story of his murder is too well known to bear repeating here. What is important for us is the fact that the leaders in this successful operation were major figures in the NKVD (when the NKVD introduced the rank of gen-eral, they both got it)—Naum Eitingon and Grigory Rabinovich, who received the highest decorations of the USSR for achieving the most important of Stalin's aims.

Even if Stalin's anti-Semitic campaign had not been advertised widely, the bigshots of the Lubyanka would have known about it from their own sources. And there could be no guarantees as to how these two highly sensitive agents would react, especially considering the fact that Stalin had given the assignment to Eitingon personally. There was nothing strange about this aspect of Stalin's suspiciousness. In the few years just past, agents who had justifiably been considered both important and reliable had defected to the West and revealed his deepest secrets—Valter Krivitsky (Samuil Ginzburg), Ignatii Reis (Natan Poretsky), Alexander Orlov (Lev Feldbin). And Reis, who had been involved in the preparations for the assassinations of Sedov and Trotsky, managed to warn the intended victims, but they took his information as a provocation from Lubyanka. Stalin did not have total confidence in the loyalty of his hired killers and the stakes were too high in this bloody game for the risk. Assassins sent by Stalin got Krivitsky and Reis, but this did not lessen his fear of a possible new betrayal.

So there was no point in taking the risk. Of course, Stalin's fears were not the only reason that the planned extravaganza did not take place at the start of the forties. There is never only one reason. A complex of providential factors deflected the blow from Soviet Jews as an ethnic community, though not from individual (and very numerous) representatives, for whom there was no salvation. This refers primarily to the people whom Stalin feared most. It was with their hands that he performed his blackest and vilest deeds: the high-level and lower-level bosses at the Lubyanka.

As I have already mentioned, their proportional weight in the punitive (actually execution) ministry was very great—and certainly not only because, as some naïvely believe, Genrikh Yagoda brought them in. The great majority of people holding key posts at Lubyanka had come there before Yagoda or with him, when, even if he had wanted to, he could not have called up large numbers of Jews into OGPU. And his personal power was not sufficient for appointing people to the highest and most responsible posts. The nomenklatura was already in existence, as a result of decisions of the Politburo, the Organizational Bureau, or the secretariat of the Central Committee. And the Lubyanka nomenklatura was so special that nothing could be done there without Stalin's approval.

The "architect of perestroika," Alexander Yakovlev, recently proposed in a conversation with the French historian and sociologist Lilly Marcou that Stalin had deliberately placed Jews in charge of eleven of the twelve major camp complexes of the GULAG archipelago; it could not have been sheer coincidence. This, I feel, is a very serious hypothesis that deserves attention and discussion.

Solzhenitsyn tells us that "a persistent legend lives in the Archipelago: the camps were invented by Frenkel." He probably wasn't the inventor, but it clearly suited Stalin to have the authorship, so ignoble, ascribed not to Lenin, not to Dzerzhinsky, and certainly not to himself, but to the unknown Jew Naftaly Frenkel, distinguished by inexhaustible energy, inventiveness, and organizational abilities combined with cruelty and cynicism. A businessman with many shady deals in Russia and abroad, Frenkel was arrested many times by the Cheka. And when he was still a prisoner he began overseeing other prisoners and then, upon his release, was appointed to a high NKVD post, got an Order of Lenin, and attained the rank of general. Semyon Chertok, an Israeli journalist who met with him in the fifties, maintains that Frenkel "survived thanks to a devilish gift—the ability to make prisoners on a ration of rotten bread and a bowl of stale gruel work day and night for their jailers." Clearly Stalin did not want to take credit for this devilish gift, and the rumor ascribing it to Frenkel (quite possibly spread by Lubyanka) helped preserve Stalin's image as the "marvelous Georgian." The other camp commandants were just as hated, and rightly so, and Stalin could experience pleasure in knowing that the Jewish sadists who served him elicited the disdain and loathing of their millions of slaves.

At the very head of the entire archipelago was Matvei Berman (he was also in charge of the construction of Belomor-Baltic Canal, performed by the slave labor of camp inmates), a Deputy Commissar of Internal Affairs of the USSR, executed in February 1939. He was one of the victims of the "reflex wave," when Stalin decided to destroy the majority of yesterday's executioners, who knew too much and had become too powerful. Besides which, he was directing the hatred of the tormented country into the channel he wanted. By destroying the men who effected the Great Terror, Stalin was achieving two ends. He was absolving himself of blame and transferring it to the "Jewish treacherous knot that wove its nest under the roof of the NKVD." Among the executed were Matvei Berman's brother, Commissar of Internal Affairs of Belorussia Boris Berman; Deputy Commissar of Internal Affairs of the USSR Yakov Agranov; Leonid Belsky; Semyon Zhukovsky; Leonid Zakovsky; Mikhail Frinovsky; Commissars of Internal Affairs of Union and Autonomous Republics Lev Zalin (Kazakhstan), Yukhman Zverev (Turkmenia), Izrael Leplevsky (Ukraine), Semyon Mirkin (Northern Ossetia), Mikhail Rayev-Kaminsky (Azerbaijan), and Ilya Ressin (Volga German Republic); deputy commissars Iosif Blat and Zinovy Katsnelson; executives in the Main Directorate of State Security of the NKVD USSR Yakov Aronson, Moisey Boguslavsky, Yakov Veinshtok, Zakhar Volovich, Mark Gai, Matvei Gerzon, Moisey Gorb, Ilya Grach, Yakov Deich, Grigory Rapoport, Abram Ratner, Abram Slutsky, David Sokolinsky, Solomon Stoibelman, Meer Trilisser, Semyon Firin, Vladimir Tsesarsky, Leonid Chertok (who jumped out of the window during his arrest), Isaak Shapiro, and Grigory Yakubovsky; and many other NKVD workers of the same level and the same origins.

When they lament the victims of Stalinism, today's leaders of the Lubyanka mention the number of their colleagues who suffered from repressions—approximately twenty thousand. But it wouldn't hurt to separate the sheep from the goats. Of those twenty thousand, at least a fourth and probably a third were direct participants in the repressions, drowning in blood that they shed abundantly and ruthlessly. While the deaths of millions of prisoners were carefully hidden and their relatives were informed of a mythical sentence, "ten years of confinement without the right to correspond," the reprisals against the executioners were not concealed. Guilty of unjustified repressions, persecution of honest people, etc., they were the objects of fully deserved but purposeful defamation, and no one tried to block the rumors about their fate. The names of those executed spoke eloquently.

In the vast majority of cases the people killed by the Lubyanka executioners were buried secretly (and sometimes executed) on the territory of the former dacha of Genrikh Yagoda, the NKVD chief executed in the Bukharin-Rykov case. Rumors about this had been circulating for years, but now they have been confirmed by finds in the KGB archives and recent biochemical tests on the grounds where the dacha once stood. Now it is part of the arable lands of the Kommunarka State Farm near Moscow. It is not clear if the buildings there were built for this purpose or if the suitability of these isolated and well-guarded buildings became obvious later. The bloody commissar's place was convenient for these operations—a nightmarish final chord in Stalin's mad oratorio. He managed to finish in the key he wanted. When the names were listed (in whispers then) of those who had been reached by the long arm of Nemesis and found their end at Yagoda's damned dacha, they sent a clear message to all who heard them, determining clearly against whom the people's wrath should be directed.

A parallel liquidation of other main figures of the period of the Great Terror, from adjoining ministries, was undertaken. For instance, the chief military procurator of the USSR, Naum Rozovsky, was arrested. He was charged with failing to combat the falsification of cases cooked up at Lubyanka and with not releasing the innocent people held in the NKVD cells. As if he could have done something, even if he had wanted to. The sad paradox is that he had not wanted to change anything. Even after his arrest, Rozovsky continued to maintain that no innocent people had been executed or exiled, that they had all been vicious enemies of the people, and if he was guilty of anything at all, it was only putting too few people away and not trying to get a death sentence from judges who sometimes gave terms in the GULAG. This position was appropriate to the role he would be playing in the new twist of Stalin's policy. Special lectures were read to lawyers, staffs of internal affairs offices, and party apparatchiks about "Naum Rozovsky, the vile falsifier of cases against honest Soviet people." The audiences were left to conclude who was guilty of the illegality that had shed so much blood. The classic stereotype was furthered by the concluding question, "What else could be expected from a sadist like Rozovsky?"

THERE WERE NO EXTERNAL signs of the coming anti-Semitic wave, unlike what would happen ten years later. With his usual mastery, Stalin demonstrated the opposite. For instance, on January 31, 1939, a decree was issued, which Stalin personally corrected, awarding decorations to a huge group of Soviet writers—over 170. Peretz Markish was one of the recipients of the highest Order of Lenin. Other Yiddish writers received decorations—Lev Kvitko, Samuil Galkin, David Gofshtein, Itzik Fefer. Stalin personally added three writers to the list prepared for him—M. Ilyin (Ilya Marshak, brother of the poet Samuil Marshak), author of popular science books, the prose writer Viktor Fink, and the young, as-yet-unknown poet Margarita Aliger. There had been a hitch with the poet, whose works had pleased Stalin. He thought her name was Oliger and inserted it in the alphabetical list between Novikov and Osmonov. In the decree her name was spelled correctly, but no one dared to change the position Stalin had selected for her in the list. So she is listed as "Aliger," stuck for some reason between N and P. She will appear again.

But the NKVD was not free of Jews, despite the ruthless purges. Among the sadists who came to fill the emptied slots, including very high ones, were more "of the same." Some of the old ones had survived. Spared to continue his mockery and torture of his helpless victims was one of the most feared and repulsive monsters of the Lubyanka, Andrei Sverdlov, son of Yakov Sverdlov, Lenin's right hand. Even as a boy he had worked as a secret informer for the GPU, writing denunciations of his schoolmates, the children of other Kremlin bigshots. As soon as he was old enough he joined the Cheka, evincing a special taste for the profession of investigator, which gave full scope to his pathological cruelty. He took particular pleasure in running the cases of his schoolmates and neighbors from the House on the Embankment, as the writer Yuri Trifonov had dubbed the gigantic and astonishingly dismal building across the river from the Kremlin, which was called the House of the Government at its inauguration. Incidentally, it was Andrei Sverdlov who was in charge of the case of the poet Pavel Vasilyev, accused of "counterrevolutionary anti-Semitism." There are numerous statements by victims who had their teeth knocked out, or arms, legs, and ribs broken by the son of the Soviet President. He even spent time in a cell of the Internal Prison, where he pretended to be a prisoner, and then several weeks later he interrogated his "cellmates" and beat them mercilessly. Stalin did not want to give up this fiend. He had hated Sverdlov, his "comrade" in exile in Turukhan, and this was the perfect revenge against his deceased rival. So his son was a lackey of Stalin and Beria and personally tortured his father's friends and their children. (Among his many victims was the wife of Nikolai Bukharin, Anna Larina.) And Stalin achieved his goal. The name Sverdlov, both father and son, elicits only one response in decent people—disgust.

It is popularly thought that Beria was no anti-Semite, as evidenced not only by the presence of many Jews in his close entourage but also by his initiative in promoting them to major positions in the NKVD. As examples are mentioned Generals Arkady Gertsovsky, Veniamin Gulst, Ilya Ilyushin-Edelman, Matvei Potashnik, Solomon Milshtein, Lev Novobratsky, Leonid Raikhman, and Naum Eitingon; heads of investigation groups Colonels Boris Rodos, Lev Shvartsman (more about these monsters later), Isaia Babich, Iosif Lorkish, and Mark Spektor. It is true that there is no evidence of Beria's particular anti-Semitism, and he did raise these people to high posts or kept them there as "valuable specialists." But they were all part of the Politburo nomenklatura, which in Stalin's lifetime meant Stalin's personal nomenklatura. And he needed only to lift a finger to remove them from the Lubyanka, and perhaps from this world.

He did not lift that finger. And we know why. He knew that the Great Terror was not over, that new waves were coming, followed by the Ninth Wave. And he would need scapegoats for that. He prepared them well ahead of time.

6

"BROTHER JEWS
THROUGHOUT THE
WORLD"

THE SADLY FAMOUS Molotov-Ribbentrop Pact opened up prospects of solving the "Jewish question" in Stalin's empire, but it also removed the issue from the agenda for the near future. When the long-awaited signing took place at last (Stalin had long dreamed of an alliance with Hitler and had sent out secret feelers several years earlier), when the secret protocols recarved the map of Europe, the Kremlin leader's first task was to convince the world, and his countrymen, that the ideological doctrine had not changed. In other words, it was Germany and the Soviet Union, and not Nazism and Communism, which for political and tactical reasons had moved closer. We now know that the hiatus, the freezing of anti-Semitic actions, would have ended rather quickly if not for Hitler's attack on the Soviet Union on June 22, 1941. As it developed, the "friendship, joined by blood," as Stalin had called the honeymoon between Moscow and Berlin (in a cable to Ribbentrop, congratulating him on his sixtieth birthday), would undoubtedly need more blood—the blood of Jewish victims on both sides of the new border through "abolished" Poland.

The pro-Jewish note disappeared from all the media and propaganda, but the anti-Jewish one vanished as well. The topic—in any form—became taboo. But without publicity, in a planned and organized manner, there was taking place, by mutual consent, a monstrous betrayal. Its victims were German and Polish Jews now under Soviet "jurisdiction."

Stalin had just purged—again without publicity—the apparat of the Comintern and the active cadres of the "fraternal" Communist parties who were on Soviet territory (on Party business or as political émigrés). Most were Jews—for approximately the same reasons that Russian Jews had joined the revolutionary movement, they formed, if not the majority, then a high percentage of their parties. This applied primarily to the countries where the Communist Party was banned, especially Germany. Having entered the Soviet Union illegally, usually under false passports and fictitious names, they could not seek the protection of their embassies, and no one was informed of their disappearance. These were people who truly were without homeland or tribe, who had voluntarily rejected their roots, and had taken citizenship in the "world Communist republic," only to die in its boundless expanses.

Not all were physically destroyed—thousands, mostly German Jews, were deported to Siberia and Kazakhstan or scattered throughout prisons and camps. When the two-year Hitler-Stalin honeymoon began, they agreed that these "German citizens" would be subject to repatriation. The fate that awaited them in Germany is clear. Negotiations on this point were hailed "in an atmosphere of mutual understanding and friendship," as a diplomatic document of the period reports.

Here is an unpublished archival notation in a work diary of Vladimir Potemkin, Deputy Commissar of Foreign Affairs, from November 21, 1939, on his conversation with Chargé d'Affaires Tippelskirch of the German Embassy. "Work on the transfer of German citizens to Germany has been given a good direction and the possibility of several practical decisions is not excluded . . . in the next few months. Tippelskirch expressed great satisfaction. . . . He added that the evacuees . . . should be sent in more or less large parties to Leningrad, from where they can be delivered to Germany in a ship sent from Germany."

However, German and Polish Jews, knowing nothing about this secret criminal deal between two cannibals, continued to stream into the Soviet Union, hoping to find shelter in the most democratic and most humane state in the world. Hitler was a cannibal—especially with respect to Jews—and he did not hide the fact. Stalin, however, clothed himself in the mantle of a great humanitarian and internationalist. Like moths drawn to a flame, European Jews flocked to those speeches, seeking salvation from the bloodthirsty Nazis. Taking advantage of the porous new border, not yet covered with barbed wire along its entire length (it was not even called a border between two states but "a sphere of German state interests"), Jews from western and central regions of Poland tried to cross over as quickly as possible to the areas of Soviet military units. Knowing he would be sending them to Germany and not wishing to waste time or money on this unwieldy operation, Stalin gave orders not to allow Jews onto "Soviet territory." They were shot at from both sides.

Trying to preserve his image, Stalin presented the situation as the Germans forcing German and Polish Jews into the Soviet Union only to be able to get them back. He kept up this hypocrisy even in secret diplomatic correspondence. For instance, in another notation in Potemkin's diary of December 17, 1939: "I invited Schulenburg [the German ambassador] to tell him about a number of cases of forced transfer of significant groups of the Jewish population across the border onto Soviet territory—of five thousand and more people. I noted that when we tried to return these people to German territory the German border guards open fire, and dozens of people are killed as a result. . . . And since this practice is not stopping but taking on a broader aspect, I asked the ambassador to contact Berlin about it. . . . Schulenburg, pretending extreme indignation, announced that he would get in touch with Berlin today and demand an end to the forced transfer of Jews onto the territory of the USSR."

For the time being we do not have precise figures to tell how many Jews were killed on the "Soviet-German border," how many were turned over to Hitler for certain death in the gas chambers, and how many were killed by their own countrymen, even though such statistics were definitely kept, not for historians and descendants, but for the office bureaucrats of the appropriate institutions. Many facts show that the Jewish question continued to hold Stalin's heightened attention. Let us examine just one, because it had far-reaching, truly fateful consequences.

Prewar Poland had active political and cultural Jewish organizations of various stripes. Soviet intelligence kept close watch on these organizations and their leaders and activists. They were all on the Lubyanka's lists, and whenever an opportunity presented itself, the vigilant Chekists tried to capture them. The list of "most dangerous" included Genrikh Erlich and Viktor Alter, known well in Europe and America as leaders of the Bund and members of the Polish Socialist Party, which belonged to the Second International.* Alter was even a member of the Executive Committee of the Second International and a deputy of the Polish Rada Narodowa in London, unrecognized by Moscow, that is, a member of the parliament-in-exile. Both somehow remained on territory controlled by the Red Army, were recognized, and were arrested. One was captured in Brest (October 4, 1939), the other in Kaunas (a week earlier). They were brought to Moscow and "settled" in the Internal Lubyanka Prison. They were charged with espionage, with ties with the Polish secret police, and, most important, with trying to create a united front in the struggle with fascism, and calling on the Soviet government to join them. It was quite enough that they were acting against Nazi Germany, which was friendly to the Soviet Union.

The investigation of this rather ordinary case took over eighteen months. The Lubyanka could not break their intransigent "clients" to learn of their secret ties, of whose existence they were certain (or pretended to be certain). The investigation dragged on until the Nazi invasion. But this brought no changes in the work of the Cheka and the courts, which continued mechanically. In late July 1941, Erlich and Alter were sentenced to be shot (one of the charges was agitation against the Molotov-Ribbentrop Pact). But the radically changed situation did have some influence on the hidden wheels of justice. With extraordinary speed the sentence of execution was commuted to ten years in the camps. The convicted men, however, were not even sent to the GULAG—they remained in the Lubyanka prison, waiting for further shifts in their fate.

In the West there is a persistent theory that the sharp turn in their situations (their release) came thanks to the intervention of allies, particularly the Polish government-in-exile. That is not completely true. The appeal was not only on behalf of Alter and Erlich. On August 12, 1941, the Presidium of the Supreme Soviet of the USSR

---

* In 1917, Erlich was the Bund representative at the Petrograd Soviet of Workers' and Soldiers' Deputies.

promulgated a decree on the amnesty of "all Polish citizens incarcerated on Soviet territory as war prisoners or on other sufficient bases." The last phrase is a telling one. There are no legal formulations of the "bases" on which tens and hundreds of thousands of Polish citizens, mostly Jews, ended up in prisons and camps, not even in Stalinist terminology, and this gave rise to the totally absurd phrase, "other sufficient bases."

In any case, Erlich and Alter were released in the second half of August along with other Polish (that is, citizens of Poland) victims of Stalinist terror. They immediately returned to their old idea of creating a world association of Jewish figures to combat Nazism. In view of the new political situation, that idea received a positive reaction from the Kremlin. Erlich and Alter did not deal with the Kremlin directly, but only through the NKVD officers assigned to them. But no sooner had they emerged than they turned from convicts on death row into highly visible public figures, negotiating with the top leaders on the creation of the Jewish Anti-Hitler Committee.

The idea they suggested was picked up, but transformed. Stalin gave orders for a "rally of the representatives of the Jewish people." It took place on August 24, 1941, at Moscow's largest park ("The Central Park of Culture and Rest") and was broadcast on radio. All the Soviet newspapers covered the event. Outstanding cultural figures spoke. The names of many—physicist Peter Kapitsa, film director Sergei Eisenstein, director and actor Solomon Mikhoels, writer Ilya Ehrenburg—were known far beyond the borders of the Soviet Union.

"You ancient Jewish people, persecuted and humiliated," Mikhoels exclaimed in his passionate speech. "Wherever your sons may be, no matter at what latitude of the world a Jew's heart may be beating, listen! Alongside all the citizens of our great country, our sons are fighting, with their lives and blood, in the Great Patriotic and Liberating War being waged by the entire Soviet nation. Jewish mothers! If you have even one son, bless him and send him into battle against the brown plague! Long live the liberation of all freedom-loving peoples! Into battle against fascism!"

The members of the rally appealed to "their brother Jews throughout the world," calling on them to unite in the fight against fascism. If anyone at that tragic hour had recalled the theoretical exercises of the "leader of the Soviet people" some thirty years earlier, he would have thought these words a sharp slap in their author's face. How could he talk of "brothers" who could be united on those terms? There was no such nation. Perhaps only one man's thoughts could unite those two incompatible circumstances—Stalin's. But he had other things on his mind.

Besides the people named above, the appeal was signed by the writers Samuil Marshak, Peretz Markish, David Bergelson, Samuil Galkin, and Alexei Kapler (who, as previously noted, wrote the screenplays for the extremely popular *Lenin in October* and *Lenin in 1918*); the architect Boris Iofan (creator of the unrealized project for the grandiose Palace of Soviets); the artist Alexander Tyshler; and musicians—winners of international competitions—pianists Yakov Flier, Emil Gilels, and Yakov Zak, and violinist David Oistrakh; singer Mark Reizen, who was considered a rival of Chaliapin himself; the actor Veniamin Zuskin; film director Fridrikh Ermler; chief conductor of the Bolshoi Theater Samuil Samosud, and many other "workers of the cultural front." But not a word was said about the creation of the Jewish Antifascist Committee.

Nevertheless, Stalin apparently had made a decision, at least a preliminary one. Confirmation of this is found in the information contained in the official—corrected and expanded—*Great Soviet Encyclopedic Dictionary* of 1991, which states that this committee was created in August 1941. Most likely, this discrepancy was the result of a confusion of similar names and two facts that were very close in time but diametrically opposed to each other.

In August 1941, negotiations were under way to create the Jewish Anti-Hitler Committee (JAHC), which was supposed to become an international organization, led by Erlich and Alter. It is not hard to see why Stalin soon rejected the idea. He was not at all pleased—either as an omnipotent leader or as a fervent anti-Semite—by the prospect of having at his side a powerful international organization he would not be able to control. On the other hand, he needed the support of the world Jewish diaspora—politically, morally, and financially. He sought a way to do it.

Erlich and Alter were highly respected in those circles which knew that the idea for an international Jewish committee belonged to them.

There were already discussions of creating an active army of Jewish refugees from Poland who had not yet been deported to Germany and of forming a Jewish legion in the United States that would fight as part of the Red Army. The committee would try to make contact with Jews remaining in Poland and bring them into the organized system of antifascist resistance.

By this time diplomatic relations had been renewed between the Polish government-in-exile and the Soviet Union. Alter and Erlich worked in the embassy of their country, which passed on to them the orders of General Sikorski's government established in London. They initiated a search for missing Polish officers, who were in fact buried in the ravines near Katyn, Kharkov, and other sites of extermination. Just this interest alone in the most secret and underhanded of Stalin's acts sealed their fate. And then Alter was given an assignment from London to join the inspection team of the Urals camps, where interned Polish soldiers were waiting for a chance to join the future army of General Anders. Polish Jews subordinate to London overseeing Stalin's camps! It is strange that the inconceivable, tragic absurdity of this situation was not apparent to the political figures who had spent sixteen months in the Lubyanka "school." No less strange was that they seriously expected Stalin to sanction the creation of a committee whose aim, as described in the project draft, was "the liberation of the Jewish people from persecution in every country and from Hitler's repressions in particular." The proposal stated that "the liberation of the Jewish people is possible only in a state based on the principles of social justice and national freedom." The formulation is flexible enough so that Stalin could relate it to the state he headed. But he had no desire to do so. He knew what lay behind that formulation.

Erlich and Alter's inadequate reactions to the barriers placed before them by the Chekists who never left their side can be explained only by the euphoria of their projected collaboration with the Kremlin. All the orders they received from the Lubyanka officers were given in Stalin's name. There is evidence that they discussed organizational questions on the creation of the Jewish Anti-Hitler Committee with Mikhoels, Markish, and Fefer, and that its formal announcement seemed to be a question of weeks, if not days.

In October 1941, as Nazi troops approached Moscow, the diplomatic corps and part of the Soviet government were evacuated to Kuibyshev. Alter and Erlich were sent there too, under Cheka escort, delicately called attendants, and settled in a comfortable hotel, which speaks for their official standing and a certain amount of respect. But the fact that the "respected foreigners" had not been given their Polish passports should have alerted them. It did not. They continued forming the working organs of the future committee, as if nothing were wrong. The presidium was to consist of ten people (seven representatives of the Jewry of Nazi-occupied countries, and one each from the USSR, the United States, and England). Erlich was going to be head of the committee. Alter would be the executive secretary, with Mikhoels as his deputy. Undoubtedly, this committee would carry great weight internationally and could influence American political, industrial, and financial structures.

There is nothing surprising in the fact that the NKVD put Colonel A. Volkovyssky in charge of the inchoate committee that existed only on paper. The activity of all similar organizations was under the aegis of that institution, and the circumstance should not have worried Erlich and Alter, for they had come to terms with Soviet reality. And so they foresaw nothing threatening in the urgent summons from Volkovyssky's assistant, Captain Khazanov (all the Cheka officers working with the committee were Jewish), who announced that they had received the long-awaited letter from Stalin. That was quite likely. Erlich and Alter knew that Stalin and Beria were getting reports on the basic documentation and that any decisions could be made only by them. And so Erlich and Alter left for the NKVD residence. They never returned. No one ever saw them again.

This was in early December. According to the former Polish officer Stanislas Swianewicz, who was spared execution and ended up in Kuibyshev in the fall and winter of 1941 (his Polish-language memoirs, *In the Shadow of Katyn*, were published in London in 1976), the point of the arrest was "to warn the Party elite not to enter into any contact with the leaders of the Second International or international Jewish organizations." That is unlikely. After the nightmare purges of the thirties, no one in the Party elite would dream of any contacts with any foreign organization. And an action that was kept so secret would hardly serve as a warning. It is more likely that this hasty execution at a moment when bloody battles were being fought outside Moscow was caused by the fear of leaving any important witnesses. Because Erlich and Alter were just about to leave for London.

All attempts by Polish Ambassador Stanislas Kot, Social Democrats abroad, and international and national Jewish organizations to learn something of their fate were unsuccessful. Answers were not forthcoming.

A few weeks before Erlich and Alter disappeared, another event took place, just the opposite in meaning and seemingly unrelated, but we will put them together because everything needs to be seen in a harmonic unity. As a result of the sharply changed situation, there was a brief revival in the fortunes of Maxim Litvinov. He was summoned back from evacuation, and a military plane delivered the disgraced commissar to Moscow. From the airport outside Moscow he was brought to the Kremlin, where Stalin, acting as if they had parted just the day before on friendly terms, offered him the ambassadorship to the United States—immediately. The leader's perspicacity in not liquidating "Father" (Litvinov's pre-revolutionary Party name) in the fall of 1939 saved him a valuable player for getting out of a critical situation. There was no better ambassador to America—Roosevelt hinted as much to Stalin through Harry Hopkins. Three days after that nocturnal conversation in the Kremlin, Litvinov left for the United States, taking a complicated route—Teheran, Baghdad, Calcutta, Bangkok, Singapore, the Philippines, and Hawaii. He arrived at his post almost on the same day that Erlich and Alter were killed in a Kuibyshev cellar.

He knew nothing of the fate of those two men, so popular in the West and almost unknown in the Soviet Union. But as soon as he began his ambassadorial duties, Litvinov was attacked by questions on the location of the missing Jewish activists. Litvinov passed along the queries to Moscow, but received no replies. It was only on February 23, 1943, that Vyshinsky in Moscow and then Litvinov in Washington, in response to a question from William Green, an American union leader, officially gave "to interested persons and organizations" the statement of Minister of Foreign Affairs Molotov: "After their release, Erlich and Alter renewed hostile activity, including calling on

Soviet troops to stop bloodshed and immediately sign a peace treaty with Germany." The information ended with the announcement of the death sentence for both "criminals," which had been implemented in December 1942. Five weeks later in an supplementary press release the date was corrected to 1941, and the month unchanged, which apparently corresponds to the truth.

The American journalist Maurice Hindus, author of the already-cited *Crisis in the Kremlin*, puts the action in perspective. "How Molotov could hope to convince anybody in America that Jews who were socialist labor leaders and who had always fought against fascism would suddenly transform themselves into allies of Hitler, or how any foreigners could during the war years address themselves to Soviet troops on any subject, least of all on peace with Hitler, who was still holding immense Russian territories, demonstrates the man's utter ignorance of American psychology or his contemptuous disregard for American reaction to his appallingly false explanation." Hindus also notes that Litvinov (as distinguished from Vyshinsky, of course) "was pained and incensed with 'the errand,' the most onerous one he had ever performed, that Molotov had imposed on him."

In no way wishing to whitewash Molotov, for whom no words are too strong, I must note that he was acting formally as Commissar of Foreign Affairs, whose job it is to instruct his deputies and ambassadors. The lack of logic in the explanation can be attributed to Lavrenti Beria, who, with his boss, was truly distinguished by ignorance of anyone's psychology and total disregard for what anyone might think.

THE DECISION TO CREATE the Jewish Anti-Hitler Committee (August 1941) was not rescinded, but a new decision appeared in April 1942—on the creation of the Jewish Antifascist Committee (JAC) under the Soviet Information Bureau. The latter had been constituted right after the war began to provide limited and tendentious information for Soviet citizens and the Western press on the situation at the front and in the rear. It was also an umbrella organization for various antifascist committees—the Slavic, youth, women's, and so on—whose goal was world support for resistance against the aggressor. The JAC was formally under the Sovinformburo too—yet only formally, because in fact it was under the NKVD, which directed its activities, appointed and confirmed staff, and gave permission for all events.

Stalin appointed the legal chief of the committee, its chairman, Solomon Lozovsky, who was also Deputy Commissar of Foreign Affairs and deputy chief of the Sovinformburo. Lozovsky, whose real name was Solomon Abramovich Dridzo, was in the twenties and thirties a well-known figure in the international union movement, as general secretary of the Profintern, under the aegis of Moscow, and was a member of the Executive Committee of the Comintern and of the Central Committee of the Party. In 1937 he was "elected" to the Supreme Soviet of the USSR. But then he was suddenly removed from all his state posts. At the height of the Great Terror, when bombshells were exploding all around him, he awaited arrest. However, the fact that he had not been expelled from the Central Committee or the Supreme Soviet gave him hope. He was given a modest position as director of a fiction publishing house, where his cruelty left bad memories, and then was transferred to the Commissariat of Foreign Affairs. His presence there (from 1939) refuted the fast-spreading rumor that Molotov had been brought in to purge the Foreign Affairs office of all Jews. He had found the right place. But the Jewish Antifascist Committee was no longer international, it was only a Soviet organization.

It was headed by Solomon Mikhoels. The membership of the committee (for decorative reasons) included many celebrities: the well-known aviation engineer Semyon Lavochkin, the very popular coloratura soprano Debora Pantofel-Nechetskaya, army pilot and Heroine of the Soviet Union Polina Gelman, and submarine captain and Hero of the Soviet Union Izrail Fisanovich. But the presidium, the basic working organ of the committee, was primarily composed of the most famous Yiddish writers—Peretz Markish, David Bergelson, Lev Kvitko, Itzik Fefer, David Gofshtein, and others. The "engine" of the committee, radiating inexhaustible energy, was Dr. Boris Shimeliovich, chief surgeon of the Botkin Hospital in Moscow and public health organizer. The executive secretary was the journalist Shakhno Epshtein, who was later replaced by Itzik Fefer.

But the main role in the team created by higher-ups was played by a man who was given an extremely modest position, in the classic tradition, of deputy executive secretary. The job was considered routine and bureaucratic, created especially for a colorless clerk, and the Party comrade who held it attracted no attention to himself. To the uninitiated his Jewish name meant nothing and was overshadowed by those of the luminaries on the committee. But it spoke volumes to the narrow circle of people who worked not on Kropotkinskaya Street, where the committee had its offices, but at the Lubyanka.

This man was Sergei Mikhailovich Shpigelglaz, and he was documented for the job "with a transfer from the apparat of the Central Committee of the Communist Party." In fact he had nothing to do with the apparat of the Central Committee. He was a general of the NKVD, who had been "burned" slightly, but still retained his former ammunition. His name can be found in almost every book of research and reference on the era of the Great Terror and the work of the NKVD abroad. Robert Conquest, Christopher Andrew and Oleg Gordievsky, and Dmitri Volkogonov in his monograph on Lev Trotsky all wrote about him. And they all say that Shpigelglaz was shot (liquidated, killed), and none of them writes when. But their works somehow imply that it was in the late thirties. Now we know for a fact that it was not so.

Sergei Shpigelglaz (Conquest and Andrew and Gordievsky incorrectly call him Mikhail) was deputy chief of the Foreign Department of the NKVD and after his boss, Abram Slutsky, was poisoned with cyanide-laced chocolates, he succeeded him for a short while. Shpigelglaz is known for having run the most disgusting terrorist Cheka bands who liquidated defectors in Europe. His hands were covered in the blood of Valter Krivitsky and Ignatii Reis. Through his NKVD bosses he was given Stalin's personal assignment to kill Trotsky. The operation in which he was involved failed that time. The operation on Reis was done clumsily and left unwanted traces. Shpigelglaz was recalled to Moscow and some of his colleagues (as Pavel Sudoplatov, a surviving participant in some of the dirtiest Lubyanka deeds, recalls) were accused of "criminal ties with Shpigelglaz." But the charges were not enough to kill either Sudoplatov or Shpigelglaz. Two years later we find him in his strange job at JAC.

Apparently, this position was a marked demotion for Shpigelglaz. But that does not change the essence of the work. His "human" face, his professional qualities, and his NKVD functions remained, modified only in details. Clearly, at JAC he was not a commissar but an overseer, censor, and controller. And with him as "dispatcher" JAC was called upon to fulfill the mission of the Anti-Hitler Committee, created but not realized by Erlich and Alter.

Of course, the mission (in the Stalin version) was severely narrowed and basically involved getting money from rich Jews living abroad. But even that could be done only if there were persons on the committee known in America and in the West. And for that reason, a second (and last) rally of the "Jewish community" was held in Moscow on May 24, 1942, ten months after the first, with another appeal "to brother Jews throughout the world." This was a tearful appeal for financial and material help in the fight against Nazism. New names were added to those who had signed the first appeal—Academicians Lina Shtern and Alexander Frumkin, artist Natan Altman, professor of medicine Meer Vovsi. The rally was broadcast on radio. Lion Feuchtwanger's opening remarks were given wide publicity in the certainty that they would guarantee success. A vain hope. The Soviet Union had a poor idea of the writer's influence in the circles to which they were appealing.

Sad as it may be to admit, even the most popular names (for the Soviet Union) on the steering committee had little resonance beyond the country's borders. The best-known was Mikhoels, but even his fame rested mostly on hearsay. An actor's popularity depends on the frequency of his live appearances before audiences and on his press. Even the great Mikhoels could not boast of much experience beyond the confines of his homeland.

And the books of Jewish Soviet writers had few readers abroad. Let us not forget, they were *Soviet* writers. For all their talent, their subject matter was the propaganda of Bolshevik "internationalism," and the thrust of their prose, poetry, and drama boiled down to one idea—the limitations on their rights under tsarism and the flowering of once-oppressed Jews under the sun of the Lenin-Stalin constitution. Specialists and a small circle of readers knew something of these works and a bit more about the authors. But they were not enough to accomplish Stalin's utilitarian plan, and time was short. Especially after the scandalous disappearance of two world-renowned figures of the international Jewish movement whose authority would have been invaluable to Stalin.

For almost a year the committee's activities were carried on within the country. It had collected a large sum of money for the defense fund—the campaign to collect funds had taken on enormous proportions, and various organizations and individuals competed to donate the most. The reward was a letter or telegram from Comrade Stalin with a facsimile signature. The leaders of JAC received such a telegram, which thrilled them with such attention from on high, in Kuibyshev, where the committee had its headquarters for a while.

> *Kuibyshev. To Chairman of the Jewish Antifascist Committee in the USSR People's Artist of the USSR Comrade Mikhoels copy to executive secretary Comrade Shakhno Epshtein copy to writers comrades Bergelson Fefer Kvitko Falkin copy to sculptor Comrade Scaasi copy to chief physician Botkin Hospital Comrade Shimeliovich copy chief of section of defense plant Comrade Nagler please convey to the working Jews of the Soviet Union who collected an additional 33,294,823 rubles for construction of air force squadron Stalin's Friendship of the Peoples and tank column Soviet Birobidzhan my fraternal greetings and the gratitude of the Red Army. J. Stalin.*

I cannot swear to this, but as far as I know, this telegram of thanks is unique among the thousands sent to the committee. It is impossible to imagine a single telegram from Stalin thanking "the working Armenians of the Soviet Union," or "the working Yakuts," or the "working Gypsies." To whom could such strange thanks be addressed? Who but the Jews, who unfortunately had "their own" committee?

If Stalin had known the many different texts under which his signature stamp had been placed, he probably would have winced and sworn—aloud or under his breath. But this time he did know. He has to have known. But he did it because he needed money. He needed tanks and planes, medicine, canned meat, and boots.

CONTACTS WERE NOT BEING made, time dragged slowly, and there were still no results. Stalin was irritated. Molotov kept chewing out his deputy, Lozovsky, who was responsible for JAC's activities.

Molotov demanded results. That gave rise to the idea of a trip to the United States.

It is difficult to determine with accuracy whose idea it was. I doubt that it is important. It seems (logically, at least) that it originated with Lozovsky, a man who was not so much decisive as desperate. A little longer and Stalin would demand a report on the work, and there were no results. Undoubtedly, the notion of a committee delegation going to the United States to take advantage of the wave of enormous sympathy for the Soviet Union and the mass solidarity with the victims of fascist genocide in every circle of American society, and to "attack" businessmen and financiers—undoubtedly, that notion was supported by the Soviet ambassador in Washington, Maxim Litvinov, who understood that a careful selection of visitors and a well-produced program could yield a good propaganda effect.

Litvinov's great luck lay in the fact that Stalin decided to recall him from Washington, as he did Maisky from London. Litvinov, who had done so much for the JAC activists' trip to the United States, and the delegation itself crossed paths. Recalled in early April 1943, Litvinov left on April 9 and reached Moscow on the 21st, while the JAC delegation arrived in the United States a few days later, after an arduous journey via Tashkent, Teheran, Africa, and London. If their time on American soil had coincided, Litvinov could not have escaped being charged with the general conspiracy and with contacts with all kinds of espionage centers, but primarily with JAC.

Stalin's long vacillations preceded the trip. The first shoots of state anti-Semitism, which were quite clear toward the end of the war, had just peeked through, naturally first of all in the head of the leader and teacher. Something kept him from a decisive yes. Lozovsky insisted, persuaded—and that would later be held against him.

At last, Stalin agreed—with a miserable "quota" of two people. One of them, it goes without saying, was Mikhoels—not because of his official position (chairman of the committee), not because of his talent as an actor, but because of his fame and his ability to influence minds and hearts. The second spot was a question mark. After long discussion and a backstage struggle (not in JAC, or in the Sovinformburo, but at Lubyanka), the choice was Itzik Fefer. He was not distinguished by any special qualities as a propagandist (especially as one familiar with American traditions and tastes), he was an orthodox believer and a Party member of unblemished record since 1919. But they wanted a reliable person to go with Mikhoels, someone on whom the NKVD could count during this unusual, unprecedented trip.

The formal "goal of the trip," as it was described in the decision of the appropriate "instance" (a Central Committee euphemism, sometimes for the Politburo, sometimes the secretariat, sometimes a department, and in those days, Stalin), was "the strengthening of propaganda of the achievements of the USSR and the fight against fascism." It sounds illiterate and incongruous, but in Party bureaucratese it is clear and solid-sounding.

Stalin needed this trip (it included England, Canada, and Mexico). Mikhoels, Fefer, and the JAC had to have it too, because if it was successful, it would show how useful the committee was and how fruitful their public work was. But the Kremlin literally needed it. Without an immediate financial injection and an increase in deliveries of arms, food, clothing, and medical supplies, the war-torn and pillaged country might not survive.

Mikhoels and Fefer were given the task of raising funds for at least one thousand airplanes and five hundred tanks as well as other things (uniforms, food, etc.) that seemed trifling in comparison. When they finished the seven-month tour, Mikhoels and Fefer were able to report that they had completed their task.

All Soviet citizens underwent major preparations before embarking even on an ordinary trip abroad. A trip like this required much more. The Kremlin envoys were supplied with the necessary propaganda materials that were supposed to help them work on American public opinion, particularly Jewish organizations in the United States. The organization receiving the Soviet guests was the American Committee of Jewish Writers and Scientists—that is, Albert Einstein, Sholom Asch, Lion Feuchtwanger, Howard Fast, Lillian Hellman, Albert Kahn, Jack Greenbaum, and other luminaries, known not only for their talent but also for their sympathies for the Soviet Union, and some for their unquestioning and unqualified pro-Soviet stance, which prompted them to write shameless lies praising Stalinism and Stalin that are impossible to read without revulsion. (This pertains primarily to the monstrous book *The Great Conspiracy: The Secret War Against Soviet Russia* by Michael Sayers and Albert E. Kahn, which justified the Great Terror.) The guests were in the hands of "their own people," who guaranteed the necessary contacts with individuals and organizations and who shared their interest in the success of the trip.

The propaganda materials that Mikhoels and Fefer brought with them fell into two categories. One was data on the enormous losses of the Soviet Union during the war, destroyed factories and plants, mines and fields, human losses, decline in production, and defense production in the rear. The other consisted of material on the life of Soviet Jews— not so much about genocide as about their idyll "in the family of free peoples," their success in the new homeland in the Far East created for them by Stalin's genius, in the provincial town of Birobidzhan, suddenly known all over the world. This "information" contained statistics on the area's natural resources, agricultural potential, and prospects for development after victory in the war. Naturally, all the information was prepared, filtered, and approved by numerous experts and controllers, signed and stamped all the way. There can be no doubt that Sergei Shpigelglaz was among those who approved the materials, since he had been brought in especially for this work. No one in JAC had any misapprehensions about his functions and responsibilities. Neither Mikhoels nor Fefer understood economic and geographic issues. Their interests lay elsewhere. The files they took with them were just background material and factual support for their appearances at rallies, discussions and conferences, and meetings with the business community.

The trip was a success in more than fundraising. There was the dazzling reception for the Soviet guests by Mayor Edward Kelly of Chicago. And there is a tragicomic story about the ovation for Mikhoels at Carnegie Hall. A large crowd stormed onto the stage to embrace Mikhoels and the floor gave out beneath them. Mikhoels was one of the injured. He broke his leg and had to continue the tour on crutches, which did not in the least detract from his triumph.

"Stalin's couriers," as some American journalists called them without negative intent, brought back thousands of clippings to Moscow. Newspapers responded enthusiastically to their trip. Fefer also brought back a luxurious fur coat, a gift from a millionaire touched by their mission. And he asked Fefer to take back a second one to Stalin.

He had the best furriers in New York make one, guessing at Stalin's height, which was a well-kept secret. The apocryphal version of the story is that Fefer, who for all his gifts was not very bright, had no more sense than to wear his own fur coat to the meeting with Stalin and casually sling its twin over the shoulders of the Leader and Teacher. Perhaps this striking scene never took place. There is no evidence that Stalin ever received Fefer (alone or with the limping Mikhoels) upon their return. But the fur coat was delivered to him. And it is not hard to imagine his furious reaction.

LATE 1943 (when the JAC delegation returned from abroad) marked the beginning of a very brief but event-filled period in the committee's activity, which could be described as euphoric. It seemed that success went to some people's heads, while the tragedy of European Jewry, which later came to be called the Holocaust, presented a quick solution to questions that had seemed unresolvable and perhaps unreal. The most important was the creation of a national Jewish hearth on the territory of the Soviet Union to serve as a center of attraction for the Diaspora abroad.

The idea of gathering Jews scattered all over the world in their historical homeland, in Palestine, had been widespread in varying degrees of intensity in Russia, America, and Europe. The activists of Soviet Jewish culture, concentrated in JAC, countered with the idea of creating a Jewish republic on the territory of the USSR. They thought—not without some justification, I believe—that this notion would meet with complete sympathy and understanding in the Kremlin (primarily out of political considerations). By that time the preparations for the founding of Israel were in the final, decisive phase, and negotiations that had been going on behind the political stage were moving successfully. The concept was realized less than five years after the U.S. trip of Mikhoels and Fefer, during which they naturally discussed the issue and learned many things. Fefer wrote a report to the Central Committee about their trip, giving detailed information on what they heard in the United States and England on that topic, which concerned Stalin greatly. It was not merely a question of the fate of the Jews but of spheres of influence in the Near East.

Fefer's report, copies of which had been sent to Molotov and Beria, evoked a good response. It satisfied the Lubyanka, as did his behavior in the role of Party commissar accompanying Mikhoels, who was not a Party member. The success of the mission and his thorough report raised Fefer's standing in the offices of the Lubyanka, and led to a promotion. Fefer agreed to become a secret informer, taking the offer as a demonstration of great trust in him. He was given the pseudonym "Zorin."

Not long afterward came an event that was to be the most dramatic page in the history preceding the devastation of the JAC and of Soviet Jewish culture and the start of state anti-Semitism in the USSR, which lasted almost half a century. This event is tied to the attempt to realize a Jewish national center in the USSR. By then no one hid the fact—it was almost official—that the formation of the Jewish Autonomous Oblast in the taiga near the border in the east had yielded no results. The artificiality of that "national-territorial" formation, its great distance from the areas where Jews had lived historically, and its harsh climate did not give hope that the situation would improve.

Another site was required, one more realistic and more attractive. Most likely, Mikhoels and Fefer discussed the question of which territory should be requested for a "national hearth" with their American Jewish colleagues—with friends, leftists who were very kindly disposed to Stalin's Soviet Union, as Fefer must have reported to the Kremlin and the Lubyanka. Neither he nor Mikhoels could have seen the slightest craftiness about these conversations or in the idea itself—on the contrary, they were acting out of purely patriotic considerations and had no doubts that this idea would be fully supported higher up. The bankrupt country as a whole, and the future Jewish Republic (as a Union republic? an autonomous one?) in particular could not stand on its feet without foreign aid. At least that is how things seemed to them then—after all, they had been sent to America to ask for help. And since that was the case, they might as well get preliminary support from their partners across the ocean. And finally, there were various tendencies within the Jewish national movement abroad, especially in the United States, and by no means were all of them proponents of creating a state in Palestine or of mass settlement by *aliyah*, that is, immigration from other countries, if only because that presumed a long and difficult conflict with the Arab population of the region and the resistance of the great powers, who had their own interests in the area. So the creation of a "parallel" national hearth in an international country (in the "socialist homeland of the workers of the world") could find support even in foreign Jewish circles, and was certainly worth discussing with them. No one on either side saw anything the least seditious in such discussions.

As far as can be determined from the fragmentary testimony of eyewitnesses, the question was first discussed somewhere on high and it was hinted to the JAC leadership, which was intended to be the initiator of the project, that it was acceptable and had good prospects. The intermediary in the preliminary negotiations was Lozovsky—a truly official personage, deputy to Molotov, who saw his boss almost daily and had access to Stalin.

This, then, was the atmosphere in which the collective letter was addressed to Stalin with a request to allow the Crimea to be settled by Jews and subsequently to form there a Jewish Republic. A draft of the letter was located by Alexander Yakovlev, who refers to it in his interview (see "Ce que nous voulons faire de l'union Soviétique," Paris, Editions du Seuil, 1991, p. 143). My search in the archives revealed a registered copy of the final draft of the letter, which allows us to determine the date, restore the text, and picture the subsequent events that were to be so far-reaching and so fateful.

The letter originally had five typed pages, signed by Solomon Mikhoels, Shakhno Epshtein, and Itzik Fefer, and was addressed to Stalin. Lozovsky showed a draft of the letter to Molotov, who made a few corrections and suggested addressing it to him. So the salutation "Dear Josif Vissarionovich!" was replaced by "Dear Vyacheslav Mikhailovich!" and sent "upstairs." It was dated February 21 and had only four pages in the final version. On February 24 it was registered as number 2314 in Molotov's office, and he marked it, "To Comrades Malenkov, Mikoyan, Shcherbakov, Voznesensky."

The argumentation of the letter is sound and corresponds exactly to the basic tenets of the JAC's work for the preceding year (this is confirmed by an analysis of the minutes of their meetings and correspondence with various official organs). Jews are scattered all over the territory of the Soviet Union, the letter said, and under these conditions they cannot create their national culture (this coincides with Stalin's concept of the "nonexistent" Jewish nation). It will be difficult for them to return to their former homes once cities and villages are liberated from the Nazi occupiers. Ashes and the graves of their tortured families are all that await them. Besides which, the apartments and houses are now occupied by people who survived the horrors of occupation and lost their own homes. An attempt to resettle them in their former domiciles will merely heighten conflicts. The letter reminds Molotov that the anti-Semitic feelings awakened by the Nazis will not vanish with the occupiers. Jews can create their own statehood, as evinced by the experiment in the Far East, but Birobidzhan is far away and cannot attract a large number of settlers. A much more suitable place is the Crimea—in terms of geography, climate, and space. And as a final argument, Jewish collective farms are already functioning well there.

"The creation of a Jewish Soviet republic," the letter went on, "would solve once and for all in a Bolshevik way, in the spirit of Lenin-Stalin national policy, the problem of the state and legal status of the Jewish nation and the future development of its age-old culture. No one has been able to solve this problem for many centuries and it can be solved only in our great socialist country."

The proposal consisted of two points: (1) create a Jewish Soviet Socialist Republic on the territory of the Crimea, and (2) create in a timely fashion, without waiting for the Crimea to be vacated (which was two months away), a government commission to develop all the necessary organizational measures.

Subsequently this very letter was declared "a subversive action of international Zionism," allegedly inspired by "the Zionist leader Chaim Weizmann, the millionaire Rozenberg, a certain Budish,* and other Jewish nationalists with whom Mikhoels and Fefer met in the USA" (I am quoting from the indictment in the JAC case) and who allegedly demanded "making the Soviet government settle Jews in the

---

* "A certain Budish" is J. M. Budish, chairman of the Ambidjan Committee (American Committee for the Settlement of Foreign Jews in Birobidjan), uniting the most left-wing pro-Communist Jewish organizations of the United States. It was headed by the polar explorer Stephenson. They knew very well who this "certain Budish" was at the Central Committee and at the Lubyanka, because his letters, addressed to the JAC, were immediately sent there. And this "certain Budish" helped raise one million dollars for the orphans of Stalingrad.

Crimea and create there a Jewish republic," which in Rozenberg's apocryphal statement "is of interest to American Jews not only as Jews but as Americans." Of course, this ridiculous accusation could only be made secretly. Made public, it would be the bitter laughingstock of the world because the people named with their colleagues had fought all their lives against any attempt to create a place for Jews outside Palestine, and had even fought against the abstract idea of the existence of such a hypothetical possibility. The JAC project could have found support only with the left-wing part of the Diaspora, which was negative or at least skeptical about Zionism.

Researchers today of that grim page of recent history consider the encouragement to send the letter on the Crimean Jewish Republic as an open provocation from Stalin, Beria, and others, so as to have a "base" for unfolding a broad anti-Semitic campaign. I doubt very much that is so. In fact, I am certain it is not.*

Support for this provocation comes from only one fact. How would the JAC leaders know, without highly placed prompting, that a barbaric deportation of the Crimean Tatars was planned and that the enormous territory of the emptied peninsula would suddenly become available for colonization? There were two months left before the Crimea was to be vacated and there was no experience then in deporting repressed peoples. In 1943 only the Kalmyks had been banished from their land (and under top secrecy, of course) and that took place while Mikhoels and Fefer were in the United Sates. The eviction of the Chechens, Ingush, Balkarts, and other peoples of the Northern Caucasus would happen later, in 1944, simultaneously with that of the Crimean Tatars. But somewhere in the Lubyanka-Kremlin, preparation was under way, and a very few highly trusted people knew about it.

Lozovsky was certainly one of them, and he could have confided the information to Mikhoels and Fefer. And Shpigelglaz was not ignorant

---

* A few years ago the memoirs of Ester Markish, *Such a Long Return*, were published in Israel. In them she recounts that at the end of 1947 Molotov and Kaganovich summoned a group of JAC leaders and suggested that they propose to the Politburo the creation of a Jewish Autonomous Republic in the Crimea. But archival documents make it unmistakably clear that this proposal was made several years earlier. In late 1947 events were such that there was neither need nor time for a multi-step provocation with a letter to the Politburo. As for Peretz Markish, he thought it "historically most just" to create a Jewish autonomous area on the lands of the former republic of the Volga Germans. I will not comment on the "justice," which, is self-evident. But any such proposal was nevertheless doomed.

either. Who today can say with certainty whose idea it was to take
advantage of the opportunity? Naturally, there had to have been an
active and promising (as it then seemed) intention of support from
above. But who needed, especially then, a complex, unwieldy provocation with far-reaching goals? The question of liquidating JAC was
not an issue then, but if it had been, JAC could have easily been
disbanded simply because the war was over and therefore it had outlived its usefulness.

Today's discussions of the subject involve a small time shift that is
psychologically understandable and not very noticeable. The first half
of 1944 was not 1947 or even 1946 by any means. There was no need
for a long-range, multi-step plan to prepare reprisals against JAC, its
leaders, and all Soviet Jewry. Besides which, Stalin did not need any
"justification" to mete out reprisals to people who did not suit him.
Justifications might be necessary for public trials, but not for secret
ones. And the era of public bloody shows was in the past. At that time
Stalin had no desire to argue with wealthy Americans even if they were
of Jewish origin.

It is quite possible that no one discussed the question with Molotov
first. That may be why he suggested addressing the letter to himself
first, and not to Stalin. After all, they were discussing only a proposal,
not a decision. Lozovsky needed only to confer with Molotov. I will
risk suggesting something that might outrage those who have as little
tenderness for the "stone arse" as I do. Molotov suggested addressing
the letter to himself because he wanted to help the project, which did
not seem utopian or dangerous. If the letter had been sent right to
Stalin, Molotov could not have presented it to him. Then he would
not have been allowed to have an opinion on the matter, unless Stalin
asked for it. And Stalin asked for an opinion only after he had formed
his own and wanted to preserve the image of "collective leadership."
Molotov would have been able only to support the leader's wise and
correct decision.

I remind the reader of the foursome to whom Molotov sent copies
of the letter for consultation. Malenkov was the number-two man in
the hierarchy on Party affairs, Shcherbakov was in charge of ideology,
and Voznesensky, then secretary of the Central Committee, was responsible for the recovery of occupied territories. Their positive re-

sponse could have given the proposal added weight and prospects. But the most interesting name on the list is Mikoyan's. Officially, Mikoyan had nothing to do with this project. But he was closer to Molotov than the others and probably would have supported the project. It is worth noting that Molotov did not approach Kaganovich (his support in this case might have lowered its chances of success), or Khrushchev (even though most of the potential residents of Jewish Crimea were from Ukraine), or Beria (without whom such a question could not be decided). By having the letter addressed to him, Molotov gained the opportunity to report personally on it to Stalin and then react in accordance with the leader's reaction. And he had an alibi—the letter was addressed to him and he had followed channels.

Summarizing the information to which we have access, we can say that, armed with the support of certain circles in America on the one hand and encouraged by the predisposition of the Soviet leadership and Lozovsky's optimism on the other hand, the JAC activists decided to take advantage of a unique situation to open the doors to a heavenly spot for their long-suffering people, one that, unlike Birobidzhan, would definitely attract thousands and thousands of persecuted, injured, and homeless people. In that political situation, especially in their unjustified euphoria, it seemed logical to them that the "helpers of the occupiers" would be punished and the victims of genocide would receive a just compensation.

Thus, the reanimated idea of a Crimean "colonizing" did not contain anything daringly new, first of all, and certainly nothing criminal, secondly. The worst that could happen to it (and I am convinced that it had to happen) was that it could be rejected. Yet the authors of the letter had no doubts about a positive and speedy reply, for the fate of Crimea did have to be decided quickly. They did not make a secret of their idea. By March 1944 "all Moscow" knew about it—not the letter, but the imminent creation of a Jewish SSR in the Crimea. I remember one morning as I came to school, I saw that someone had chalked on the blackboard, "We nominate Arkady Vaksberg as People's Commissar of Foreign Affairs of Jewish Crimea." My response was, "I accept, but only on the condition that chairman of the Council of Commissars is Volodya Segal" (a school friend who now lives in the

United States). We had a good laugh over it and jokingly distributed the ministerial portfolios more than once. I sensed no anti-Semitism in these jokes. I bring this up only to emphasize how widely known the Jewish Crimea plan was in those days.

This plan met with resistance not only in Party circles. It frightened those representatives of the Jewish intelligentsia who were sober-minded politicians capable of foreseeing the consequences of irrational behavior. There is reliable evidence that Ilya Ehrenburg and Maxim Litvinov spoke out against the Crimean project, but their voices were not heard. Probably two circumstances contributed to that. First, both "opponents" were well-known proponents of assimilation, and second, Lozovsky's position was perceived as being the Kremlin position.

This incongruous, dangerous, and foredoomed notion seemed so realizable that the leaders of JAC began preparing for practical steps without waiting for an answer. Leib Kvitko, author of poems known by millions of Soviet children of all nationalities, thanks to masterful translation by Russian poets, set aside poetry and went to the Crimea to "study the situation on location." He wanted to examine the practical problems that would arise in resettling "compact masses" onto ravaged land and to give his suggestions. A few years later this fruitless but innocent action, dictated by the loftiest of intentions, would be described by the MGB as: "Executing the criminal orders of the leadership of JAC, he traveled to the Crimea to gather information about the region's economic situation."

The seemingly smooth-running machine broke down. The proposal in the letter was not rejected, but it was not supported either. But JAC did not lose hope. Nothing seemed to foretell the coming events. The committee, Mikhoels's daughter, Natalya Vovsi-Mikhoels, recalls, "created a special commission on locating lost persons . . . occasionally partisans appeared and told of the fighting of partisan units with the fascists. . . . Information on deaths in the camps was collected. An Information Bureau was created, and crowds came to learn about their loved ones. The first miraculously surviving refugees appeared." In addition, the JAC staff was preparing *The Black Book*, a collection of documents and eyewitness accounts of Nazi genocide of the Jews. The basic work was done by early 1944. The book had been compiled by Vassily Grossman and Ilya Ehrenburg, and the witnesses' accounts were edited by such writers as Andrei Platonov, Vsevolod Ivanov, Pavel Antokolsky, Lidia Sifullina, Vera Inber, Veniamin Kaverin, and Margarita Aliger. A joint Soviet-American edition of *The Black Book*, with a foreword by Albert Einstein, was planned, and JAC was in constant telephone and mail contact with America. Each spoken and written word was monitored by the Lubyanka.

The American edition of the book—alas, far from complete—came out quickly, and it was also set to be published in Paris, Bucharest, and Sofia, but the Central Committee kept holding up the Russian edition and then had Glavlit (the censors) ban its publication, with no explanation. The very action of sending materials to the United States about Nazi atrocities toward Soviet Jews was declared a crime. It would soon become an official charge against the JAC activists.

In the meantime, more and more letters were coming in to the committee from Jews who had returned home from evacuation, letters that described the repressions they had experienced in trying to secure employment and housing. It was a natural reaction of people who were encountering, to their great surprise, the first and probably not very intense manifestations of official anti-Semitism, if only on the regional level. Grown unaccustomed to it over the last twenty years before the war, and especially after having been the victims of the Nazis in the antifascist war the Soviet Union had waged, they could not believe the initiative for anti-Semitism could be coming from above. They thought that these were discrete actions of "fascist remnants" or "enemies of the people," about whom JAC should immediately inform the authorities so appropriate measures could be taken. And this was exactly what the committee (i.e., its respected leaders) did. Not only to the top, but to various republic, regional, and city organizations they sent queries, complaints, and protests—soon the "competent organs" (i.e., the Central Committee and the MGB) had enormous collections.

Here are only a few typical letters sent to the very top by the Jewish Committee.

One has no date, but it appears to have been sent in the latter half of 1944 and is addressed to Andrei Andreyevich Andreyev, member of the Politburo of the Central Committee and Commissar of Agriculture.

Dear Andrei Andreyevich!
In view of the growing abnormal situation for Jewish kolkhozes in the Crimea and Ukraine we ask that you receive us, if possible, in the next few days. S. Mikhoels (People's Artist of the USSR), L. Kvitko (writer), B. Shimeliovich (chief surgeon), M. Gubelman* (Chairman Central Committee of Trade Workers).

Here is another letter, dated May 26, 1944, addressed to Beria.

Dear Lavrenti Pavlovich!
I am sending you copies of several letters received by the Jewish Antifascist Committee, evidence of a series of abnormal manifestations toward Jews in the provinces. S. Mikhoels, Sh. Epshtein.

An explanation of the "series of abnormal manifestations" can be found in a third letter signed by the same people and addressed to Secretary of the Central Committee Shcherbakov. It was sent in October 1944 (the exact date is illegible in the archival original).

In our previous letters to you [this suggests that the correspondence on this topic was voluminous], *we indicated a number of unacceptable phenomena in the distribution of gifts received by the Red Cross from abroad. The Jewish population, with a few rare exceptions, is completely ignored by local organs of power in the distribution of this type of aid. Even the Jewish partisans of Belorussia, Ukraine, and other republics are not getting anything.*

This is a reference to the aid packages sent to the Soviet Union from the United States by air, sea, and land (via Iran). One of the main donors was JAC, which tried to aid the victims of Nazi genocide, Jewish refugees and orphans.

There is a notation on the JAC letter, probably by Shcherbakov, "Com. Mikhoels ordered an investigation by the Commissariat of State Control." The Commissar of State Control then was the vile and vicious Lev Mekhlis. This was a Jew who would never confirm what Mikhoels and Epshtein claimed—if only because he wanted to avoid suspicion of helping his own. Naturally, he did not support them.

---

* Moisey Gubelman (1914–1968), brother of the country's "chief atheist," Emelyan Yaroslavsky (Minei Gubelman). He survived all the phases of the Great Terror and remained in rather mid-level posts in the Stalinist unions.

The contents of the letters sent to dear Lavrenti Pavlovich, and the circumstances dictating them, are perfectly obvious without the attached correspondence or the sad report brought back from the Crimea by Lev Kvitko. The Jewish collective farms (on orders from above) were not restored, the Jews returning from evacuation were not given jobs, and their living quarters were not recovered, nor were they compensated for their loss. For many of them, it was the first time in their lives that they were to hear—and not on the street, or on the bus, or in the marketplace, but in a Party or other official office—the soon-to-be-familiar "Why don't you go back to your Birobidzhan!" "Your Tel Aviv" did not yet exist, and so instead of the Near East, it was to the Far East that they were sent.

Recalling those times, Boris Slutsky later wrote a bitter poem that captured the popular mood at the time.

> Jews don't sow grain,
> Jews sell in a shop,
> Jews grow bald sooner,
> Jews steal more.
> Jews are clever people,
> They make bad soldiers:
> Ivan fights in the trenches,
> Abram trades in the store,
> I heard all that from childhood,
> And soon I will be gray.
> And there's no getting away
> From the cry of "Jew! Jew!"
> Bullets spared me
> So that it could truthfully be said,
> "The Jews weren't killed,
> They all came back alive."

The poem was published only in the Gorbachev perestroika years. And at the same time it was revealed—not in a statistical handbook but in the mass media—that 103 "Jews who did not see combat" were awarded the title of Hero of the Soviet Union and hundreds of thousands who were not in combat received medals.

Perhaps no documents or letters can convey the emotional immediacy of the changed attitude toward the national question as can the contemporary poets, stunned by their new misfortune. Margarita Aliger, the one whose name Stalin had personally inserted in the list of prize winners five years earlier, wrote:

> *I will ask Marx and Einstein,*
> *Who are deeply wise.*
> *Maybe they have solved*
> *The mystery of our eternal guilt.*
> *The sweet canvasses of Levitan,* *
> *The kind light through birches . . .*
> *Charlie Chaplin on the white screen—*
> *Answer my question.*
> *Haven't we shared everything*
> *With which we were rich?*
> *Why do millions think we're guilty,*
> *Tell me, Ehrenburg, Bagritsky,† and Svetlov?‡*

These lines were banned by the censors, who deleted them from Aliger's narrative poem "Your Victory," which was published as a separate volume. But the lines were circulated widely in manuscript, and I have one copy on thin cigarette paper in my archives. But the other lines from her poem did make it into print. Refuting the slander viciously spread about her people, Aliger wrote that the people she knew were not deserters or loafers, but

> *. . . poets and scholars*
> *Of various countries, languages, and ages . . .*
> *Enthusiastic like children about life,*
> *Noble and sorrowful jokers.*
> *Generous, unstinting of their talents,*
> *Not hiding the best strengths of their souls,*

* Isaak Levitan (1860–1900), a Russian landscape painter, a master of lyric mood paintings of the Russian countryside, a close friend of Chekhov.
† Eduard Bagritsky (Dzubin; 1895–1934), Russian poet of Jewish descent from Odessa. Author of very popular revolutionary-romantic poetry. His narrative poems "Thoughts on Opanas" and "Death of a Pioneer Girl" were memorized by schoolchildren.
‡ Mikhail Svetlov (1903–1964), Russian poet of Jewish descent from Ukraine. Author of lyric poems and songs that were popular all over the Soviet Union, like "Grenada," "Kakhovka," and "Lamplights."

I know doctors and musicians,
Workers small and big,
Descendants of the brave Maccabees,
Sons of their fathers,
Thousands of fighting Jews—
Russian commanders and soldiers.

These feelings—of hurt, disbelief, indignation, and rebuttal—came in the hundreds and thousands of letters that poured into JAC, and Mikhoels and his friends could not disregard them. The JAC complaints about "individual" manifestations of anti-Semitism challenged and infuriated the apparatchiks who received them, because they knew the true situation, and these complaints hastened the inevitable end of that strange "sociopolitical" institution that lingered too long on the political horizon of the forties. The Jewish Antifascist (i.e., openly propagandistic, openly political) Committee was turning into the Jewish Committee, and for that reason alone was doomed, but its aggressive activists, who were not reacting appropriately to the changes, were like a red flag for Stalin, angering and irritating him.

The latest archival discoveries lead to the conclusion that the displeasure for JAC began to appear (not in conversation but in official correspondence) not in 1944, but much earlier, even as the committee leaders were bathing in the radiance of glory and success and dreaming the impossible. For instance, on May 11, 1943 (Mikhoels and Fefer had left for the United States a month earlier), V. Kruzhkov, the executive secretary of the Sovinformburo (a job created by the Central Committee and the NKVD to supervise the activities of all the organizations under Sovinformburo's umbrella), wrote to the head of Sovinformburo (and secretary of the Central Committee) Alexander Shcherbakov, whose rabid anti-Semitism was well-known, "I feel that the JAC leadership is getting involved in things that are not its business. I feel it is politically harmful that the JAC leaders, upon receipt of letters of complaint and appeals of material and housing questions [this is his description of the cries of the humiliated and persecuted] from Jewish Soviet citizens, take it upon themselves to satisfy these requests and initiate correspondence with Soviet and Party organs." At the end of his denunciation Kruzhkov asks his boss to give JAC the "appropriate instructions to cease their activity immediately."

Those instructions were not given (it was not yet time), but the report was remembered. At any rate, the archives have many later complaints and tearful reminders from JAC about cases that were not their business. For instance, Mikhoels asked General Procurator Gorzhenin to defend Jewish artists who were being evicted from their apartments, and the Kiev City Executive Committee to help Jewish physicians find work. If he had been given the "appropriate instructions" that Kruzhkov had requested, he would not have signed such letters. On April 21, 1944, N. Kondakov, an official of the Central Committee, approached Shcherbakov with an analogous suggestion. He also noted that JAC "was involved in cases having nothing to do with their responsibilities." And it was just then that JAC, its hopes at their peak, was awaiting the resolution of the Crimean-Jewish question.

One letter speaks eloquently about the drama unfolding within JAC and outside its walls. Strictly speaking, it is not a letter, but a denunciation of one member of the JAC presidium by another member, dated November 27, 1944. The author is the Deputy Minister of State Control of the RSFSR, Solomon Bregman. The "statement" is addressed to Solomon Lozovsky. Here is the text.

> *In addition to my oral information, I relate:*
>
> *Peretz-Markish spoke at the presidium of the Jewish Antifascist Committee on 12.XI.44. In his speech he permitted politically incorrect and even dangerous statements. The character of his utterances was something like this: He considered the renaming of the village areas in the Dnepropetrovsk Region as Stalinsky and Kalininsky (instead of "Stalinodorf" and "Kalininodorf") an annulment of the Stalin Constitution. On the question of not giving housing registration to Jewish families, Peretz-Markish antagonistically declared that "Jews were in the ghetto once more." After such an outrageous speech I harshly judged such an evaluation of the facts.*
>
> *Peretz-Markish's speech created panic and was politically dangerous. Unfortunately, Chairman S. M. Mikhoels did not utter a word on the issue.*
>
> *Since such statements by Peretz-Markish are not accidental, he must be called to order even with expulsion from the Committee.*

Let us forgive Bregman, "a leading Jewish activist," for not knowing the name of the outstanding Soviet Jewish poet of the time. In hyphenating his given name and surname, he must have thought they were both his surname. But that doesn't matter. However, this denunciation reveals something that was never publicized—the removal of Yiddish names of Ukrainian towns and villages (in those regions the prewar population was 80 percent Jewish, which is why they were given Yiddish names in the twenties). And it also reveals the stratification of JAC—seemingly a single organism united by the ethnic and national origins of its members. But there was no unity, nor could there have been. What did Jewish Shpigelglaz have in common with Jewish Mikhoels? Or Bregman and Markish? Actually, there was one thing. No matter which God some served and which Caesar others served, they were all burning in the flames of the same bonfire.

At Party headquarters on Staraya Square and at the Lubyanka, the struggle for influence, position, and career advancement was at its height among various forces. The Jewish card came into play. The Party apparatchiks and the Chekists caught Stalin's almost undisguised turn to anti-Semitism.

Usually the start of the official anti-Semitism campaign in the USSR is considered the late forties, but the most recent archival discoveries make it possible to date it back with certainty to at least mid-1942. The documents are implacable witnesses. On August 17, 1942, when German troops were approaching Stalingrad, the fateful battle on the Volga that could have brought about the fall of the regime, the Department of Propaganda and Agitation of the Party Central Committee had nothing more important to do than appeal to Central Committee secretaries Malenkov, Shcherbakov, and Andreyev with a memorandum on the fact that "the heads of the institutions of Russian art are not Russian (primarily Jews)."* Then came a long list of "not Russians," with special attention paid to the "unacceptable clogging" of the Bolshoi Theater, where "management of administrative and creative work were the Jews Leontyev (chief director), Samosud (chief conductor), Shteinberg, Melik-Pashaev (Armenian), Gabovich (head of the troupe), Messerer (choreographer), Zhuk (concert master), and others." The authors of the memorandum discovered the same sins in

---

* This document was found in the former Central Party Archives by historian Gennady Kostyrchenko.

the Moscow and Leningrad Conservatories and in the theater and music press and criticism. The department heads at the Moscow Conservatory, noted the as-yet-undeclared proponents of racial purity, "are the Jews Tseitlin,* Yampolsky,† Dorliak,‡ Gedike,§ Pekelis, and others." The situation was just as grim at the Leningrad Conservatory—there "the leading spots were captured by the Jews Ostrovsky, Shteinberg, Eidlin, Ginzburg." The most active writers in the musical press, they went on, were Rabinovich, Grinberg, Kogan, Shlifshtein, Zhitomirsky and Tsukerman, who "hush up the concerts of the Russian pianist Sofronitsky** and produce extended articles on E. Gilels, D. Oistrakh, and others." And in conclusion, the management positions in the Committee on the Arts "were taken by Galkovsky, Vladimirsky, Plotkin, Shlifshtein, Goltsman, and their like."

This was not written in 1949 or 1952, but in August 1942. What a pleasant find this official Soviet document would have been for Goebbels. The young head of the Propaganda and Agitation Department of the Central Committee, Georgy Alexandrov,†† was just starting out in his Party career and would not have dared to use such turns of phrase and such an aggressively prosecutorial tone if he had

---

* Lev Tseitlin (1881–1952), professor, doctor of arts, Honored Worker in the Arts, one of the founders of the Soviet school of violin instruction.

† Abram Yampolsky (1890–1956), professor, doctor of arts, Honored Worker in the Arts, creator of one of the major Soviet violin schools (his students include Leonid Kogan, Elizaveta Gilels, and Igor Bezrodny).

‡ Nina Dorliak, professor, doctor of art, outstanding vocalist and teacher, the wife of the great pianist Svyatoslav Richter. She was in this "shameful" list by accident because of her un-Russian-sounding name. She was not Jewish.

§ Alexander Gedike (1877–1957), professor, doctor of art history, founder and head of the Soviet organ school.

** Vladimir Sofronitsky (1901–1961), romantic pianist with an active concert career who always enjoyed good press. He received the award of Honored Worker in the Arts and the Stalin Prize. It would have been both absurd and impossible to "hush up" his concerts, which always attracted enormous crowds.

†† Georgy Alexandrov (1908–1961), a typical illiterate Marxist "philosopher." In the late thirties people like him replaced Bukharin and his students, killed on Stalin's orders. In 1941, Stalin, who liked this energetic and loyal careerist, made him candidate member of the Central Committee and in 1946 elevated him to the rank of academician and bestowed his prize on him twice. Initially as the right hand of pogrom leader Shcherbakov and then the obscurantist Zhdanov, Alexandrov took an active part in the persecution of the poet Akhmatova, the writer Zoshchenko, the composers Shostakovich and Prokofiev, geneticists, cyberneticists, and other representatives of "reactionary Western ideology." Under Khrushchev, in 1955, he was fired from all his posts, including the Supreme Soviet of the USSR (without a discussion in the Soviet "parliament"), for establishing a bordello for the Party and intellectual elite, where many prominent Muscovites whiled away their free time.

not had firm if oblique instructions from his superiors to do so, from Stalin directly or through intermediaries.

In the Party archives for 1942–1944 there are many documents of similar content listing dozens of names of Jewish cultural figures to be "replaced by persons of Russian nationality." Among them is the film director Sergei Yutkevich,* friend of Leo Tolstoy, and the pianist Alexander Goldenveizer, who was then head of the Moscow Conservatory. The direct target of these denunciations was undoubtedly the Chairman of the Committee on the Arts, Mikhail Khrapchenko, an unacknowledged Jew who had replaced the "pure-blooded" Platon Kerzhentsev, shot in 1940. By November 19, 1942, the badgered Khrapchenko reported to the Party that Goldenveizer, "advanced in age," was replaced as head of the Conservatory by the "Russian composer Vissarion Shebalin" (whose Aryan origins did not save him from charges of formalism six years later). It was in the field of culture that the expulsion of Jews from management and administrative posts began, for the moment camouflaged each time (out of a desire to maintain good relations with their allies, the Americans and British) with some decent excuse (age, illness, "transfer to other work," "necessity," etc.). But the real reasons for the firings were not a secret. Evidence of this is a letter recently discovered in the archives. Besides its unambivalent content, it is noteworthy because it had been read by Stalin, Andreyev, and Shcherbakov, as indicated by their signatures and notes on the original.

It was written by Yakov Abramovich Grinberg of the Moscow Department of the Arts and a Party member since 1919. Here are just a few of the eloquent passages from his letter of May 13, 1943.

> Dear leader and teacher J. V. Stalin!
> How can it be explained that in our Soviet land in such harsh times the murky wave of repulsive anti-Semitism has been reborn and has penetrated into individual Soviet apparats and even Party organizations? What is this? The criminal stupidity of conceited people who are involuntarily aiding fascist aggression, or is it something else?
> . . . In the organs supervising the arts, people whisper about it with

---

* Sergei Yutkevich was best known for his films about Lenin. The first in the cycle, *The Man with the Gun* (1938), was praised by Stalin himself.

enigmatic expressions. This then breeds hostility toward Jews working in that field. . . . Any qualified Jew can no longer count on getting independent work even of the most modest scope. This policy has loosened the tongues of many ignorant and unstable elements, and the mood of many Communist and non-Party Jews is very bleak. . . . I know that People's Artist of the USSR Comrade Mikhoels, People's Artist of the RSFSR Tairov,* and many rank-and-file workers have spoken of this with great anxiety. We know that a number of representatives of the artistic intelligentsia (Jews) appealed to writer Ehrenburg to raise this issue. The writer Boris Gorbatov† has spoken to me about these phenomena.

. . . It is becoming unbearable! It is no longer random, it is planned. Once again the terrible Jewish question has arisen. Our generation of Jewish people has suffered much—from the times of the "Union of the Russian People" to the frenzy of bloody fascism. My comrades assure me that much is known in the leading party organs. Your personal intervention could change the situation radically, which is why I have appealed to you directly.

The personal intervention of the "dear leader and teacher" was not slow in coming. The expulsion of Jews from all levels of administrative jobs increased. Stalin read the letter, but he did not express any indignation about its facts. Or approbation. His silence, however, was tantamount to approval. Everyone who knew the rules of the Kremlin game recognized it as his reaction, the equivalent of a resolution. And in order not to appear an anti-Semite in the eyes of his contemporaries and posterity, to distance himself from the pogroms that he himself authorized, the crafty "Kremlin mountain dweller" (as Osip Mandelstam called him) found a simple method that worked on the gullible. He handed out the Stalin Prize generously to Jewish scientists, scholars, and cultural figures. The Stalin Prize—the state's highest and most desirable award—served as a shield, guaranteeing the safety of the laureate, and the number (quite high) of Jews in the list of recipients lulled naïve simpletons, desperate for a ray of hope, into

---

* Alexander Tairov (1885–1950), creator and irreplaceable director of the Moscow Chamber Theater until it was shut down in 1949, outstanding theatrical innovator.
† Boris Gorbatov (1908–1954), a mediocre writer of Jewish descent, who held administrative positions in the Soviet Writers' Union. He "voluntarily" quit these positions after his wife—the popular film actress Tatyana Okunevskaya—was arrested for ties with foreign intelligence services.

thinking that there would be no further persecutions. At least this gesture removed the dear leader and teacher from the taint of the outrages of the local authorities.

In that respect the fate of the people who were named in the memorandum as "clogging up Soviet culture" was sealed. Conductor Samuil Samosud, given the Stalin Prize back in 1941 and then fired from the "government" Bolshoi Theater in 1943, received two more Stalin Prizes after that—both from the hands of the tyrant. Conductor Yuri Fayer had four bestowed upon him; ballet soloists Asaf Messerer and Mikhail Gabovich, two each; Alexander Goldenveizer, David Oistrakh, and Emil Gilels, one. So there was no need to rebut the rumors of sanctions against people of Jewish descent. The resolutions on conferring the Stalin Prize, signed by Stalin and published in all the newspapers and solemnly read over the radio, were visible, weighty, and irrefutable rebuttals. Any foreign slanderer who would dare mention signs of anti-Semitism in the USSR could be shut up with a look at the lists of recipients.

That was the public facade—on stage, in front of the footlights, in view of the honored audience. But backstage, a parallel game was being played. At the same time, in 1943, Ivan Bolshakov, head of Soviet cinematography, reported to Central Committee Secretary Shcherbakov on the preparations for the filming of *Ivan the Terrible* (the film was under Stalin's personal supervision) and felt it necessary to note that the "director Sergei Eisenstein is testing for the role of Efrosinia the actress Faina Tanevskaya, whose Semitic features are blatantly obvious in the close-ups. . . . It would be good with your help to force Eisenstein not to accept this actress for that part."

In going through the voluminous exchange of memos marked "secret," it is impossible not to conclude that 1942 marked the start of the sharp change in Stalin's already revealed policy toward Soviet Jews. The subtle signals he sent out were picked up by the sensitive radar of the apparatchiks and influenced the position of the major and minor nomenklatura, which shamelessly began a hue and cry about Jewish preponderance, without bothering to find euphemisms for their vicious anti-Semitism.

Let us look at some other facts, known from absolutely reliable sources. It was in 1942 that young Svetlana Allilueva had her brief affair with the screenwriter Alexei Kapler. Stalin gave full rein to his anti-Semitism, crudely interfering in his daughter's private life, and sending the Jew he hated so much to the GULAG on trumped-up charges of being a British spy. A little over two years later Svetlana married a Jew, a law student named Grigory Morozov (Moroz), and Stalin destroyed that marriage unceremoniously, never having seen his son-in-law, or his grandson, called Iosif after both grandfathers. (A celebrated lawyer and professor of international law, Grigory Iosifovich Morozov is hale and hearty to this day. Kapler, rehabilitated only after Stalin's death, died in 1979.) Around that same time, Stalin forced the faithful and fearful Malenkov to get his daughter a divorce, for she was married to Vladimir Shamberg, a Jew. And he was driven to a frenzy by the reports of his secret agents that Anna Akhmatova's meeting with Isaiah Berlin, of the British Embassy, lasted until morning. Randolph Churchill was with Berlin on this trip to Russia, but Stalin did not care about the Prime Minister's son—he was interested in "that Riga Jew"—interested in the sense that he drove Stalin crazy. "He will not become my dear husband," Akhmatova would later write, "but he and I will be punished so that the Twentieth Century will be upset." Alas, it was not upset. Publicly declared a spy, the diplomat was forced to leave Moscow—Sir Isaiah has told this story better. Akhmatova was punished with the infamous Central Committee resolution that led to her expulsion from the Writers' Union. The leader's jealousy was so specific that we might call Akhmatova a victim of his anti-Semitism too.

To bring together facts from diverse areas for that period, let us not forget that in 1943 ambassadors Maxim Litvinov and Ivan Maisky, men who had personified professionalism and adherence to democratic principles, culture, and intelligence, were recalled almost simultaneously from Washington and London. Since which time the Soviet Union has never again had a Jewish ambassador in a single world capital. Stalin had drawn the line.

IN FEBRUARY 1945, at the Yalta Conference, when the conversation turned to the responsibility of the Nazis for their villainy, including the destruction of Jews, Roosevelt told Stalin, "I am a

Zionist." Without blinking, Stalin replied, "So am I." I have no doubt that if Zionists were being executed on Red Square, Stalin would watch through binoculars and puff on his pipe and say, "I have great respect for working Jews and treasure their love." And that those words would mean much more to "all of progressive humanity" than the innocent blood shed by that love-filled tyrant on the red Golgotha.

The world hears only what it wants to hear.

7

THE CALM
BEFORE THE STORM

ON MAY 24, 1945, weeks after the victorious end of the war, Stalin gathered the officers at the Kremlin to bestow the honors they deserved and to celebrate in an elite Party-military circle. At this event he gave a toast that was intended to, and in fact did, herald a new stage in domestic policy, moving into a rather official channel what had been occurring secretly and almost shamefully. The text of this final toast (which means there were others that remain unknown) was published in the newspapers on the next day and took on the status of a classic work of Marxism-Leninism to be studied in all schools and all universities, and in the network of Party courses. Because of its fateful role, brevity, and expressivity, I will quote it in full.

I would like to raise this toast to the health of the Soviet people, and first of all, of the Russian people.

I drink, first of all, to the health of the Russian people because it is the most outstanding nation of all the nations who belong to the Soviet Union.

I raise this toast to the health of the Russian people because it earned in this war general recognition as the leading force of the Soviet Union among all the peoples of our country.

I raise this toast to the health of the Russian people not only because it is the leading people but also because it has clear mind, steadfast character, and patience.

Our government made many mistakes, we had moments of being in a desperate situation when our army retreated . . . because there was no other way. Another nation could have said to the Government: you did not justify our expectations, go away, we will put in a different government, which will make peace with Germany and guarantee our tranquillity. But the Russian people did not do that because it believed in the correctness of the policies of its government and it accepted the sacrifices necessary to destroy Germany. And that trust of the Russian people in the Soviet Government turned out to be the decisive force that guaranteed the historic victory over the enemy of humanity—fascism.

Thanks to the Russian people for that trust!

To the health of the Russian people!

At the time, in the euphoria of the early postwar weeks, few people caught the evil meaning of Stalin's toast, all the more evil for having been spoken on the occasion of the event that put an end to the bloodiest page of the long-suffering country's history and started a fresh page. Clearly intended for the "broad popular masses" and the obedient Party propagandists, rather than for professional politicians, this toast seemed to be merely what was due to those who brought the greatest sacrifices to the altar of victory. People were not alerted even by the concept of "leading people," more than bizarre for a Marxist theoretician, and the division of nations into "most outstanding," simply outstanding, and apparently not outstanding, but mediocre. And since there were mediocre ones, it necessarily followed that there had to be others that were not even good enough to be mediocre, straggling along at the tail of humanity. No, this blatant nonsense did not call attention to itself, did not frighten people with its absurdity and its frank *épatage*. The marked flattery of the Russians by the Georgian Stalin did not offend the equally long-suffering other nations of the multinational empire who had also endured gigantic losses in the war. Even the most perspicacious saw in that toast only an unexpected and rather touchingly sincere admission on the part of Stalin. He had feared being overthrown, was now honestly revealing it and thanking the Russian people for their faith in their ruler.

Even more significant, the numerous propaganda albums and booklets published soon after the event added another quotation that was not in the text published on May 25, 1945: "Comrade Stalin also said that in the USSR 'for the first time in history the national question was justly solved.' " This was a belated correction to deflect accusations of great-power chauvinism. But who read the albums and booklets? Only the canonical text counted.

The true meaning of this toast which immediately became historic (I mean that without any irony) soon became apparent for all. It heralded a sharp turn to official great-power politics, to chauvinism, and to an almost complete rejection of feigned "proletarian internationalism." It was a natural continuation of the genocide to which the "traitor" peoples had been subjected: the Crimean Tatars and Balkars, Chechens and Ingush, Kalmyks and Volga·Germans, all expelled from their native lands down to the last child. And juxtaposed to the "traitors" were the ones they had "betrayed"—the Russian people. Stalin, who had killed millions of Russians during the terror, hypocritically called them great. The rest, it now appeared, were of a lower rank, but this did not worry the leader. Now, after the victory, after what he had survived, he could deal with any dissatisfaction, be it from an individual or from an entire nation.

And still, the main thrust of this toast was aimed at Jews; from long Russian tradition they were not named openly, but this has been presumed and understood silently and unanimously whenever rulers have spouted patriotic terminology. All the Party and government officials of various levels instantly grasped the program in the leader's speech (which was made mandatory study in Party courses, universities, and even high schools) as an official instruction to limit (at least for the time being) the promotion of Jews in work and to close access to higher education, if not completely, then significantly. The famous "percentage quota" of tsarist times, often and justly called criminal in Lenin's works and Bolshevik party documents, now appeared almost a model of tolerance and democracy by comparison. It kept the number of Jews in every entering class down to 5 percent of the total accepted students, while after 1945 only a few Jewish individuals who had outstanding grades (and super-persistent parents) managed to get past all the barricades into college.

Probably the first postwar summer should be considered the start of official state anti-Semitism in the USSR, no longer covered by a fig leaf of internationalist declarations. Not so long ago, the Soviet press, even if only for propaganda purposes, fiercely exposed the Nazi atrocities against Jews in occupied territories. Now there could be no mention of "the propaganda of alleged Jewish martyrdom." I put those words in quotation marks for a reason. In my mother's files I found a letter from Sofia Kuperman of Kiev, dated February 22, 1946. Appealing to my mother for legal assistance, she described her suffering, going from office to office for action on the court decision that allowed her to move back into the apartment that once belonged to her. Using not only legal arguments but emotional ones, Kuperman wrote that eleven members of her family were killed by the Nazis during the occupation. The first secretary of the Party in their region, whom she finally got to see (she does not give his name), replied, "Who supplies you with hostile disinformation on the alleged martyrdom of Jews? Why don't you look for your tortured relatives in Tashkent somewhere? They just changed their names and are living happily ever after. And where did you hide? Not in partisan trenches, I'll bet. You fed your face in the rear of the front and now you want an apartment too. I'll pass your complaint on to the NKVD, they'll take care of it for sure."

By then the already extremely small number of Jews in the higher echelons of power was reduced even more. Besides Lazař Kaganovich, a person very close to Stalin was the unsinkable Lev Mekhlis—an ignorant, obnoxious, arbitrary boss who almost destroyed the 40th Rifle Division of the Red Army before World War II during a Soviet armed provocation near Lake Khasan in the Far East. (Vassily Blukher, who rescinded Mekhlis's orders and thereby saved the army from being routed, was executed soon after.) In 1941–1942 hundreds of thousands of Soviet soldiers died at Kerch (Crimea) because of Mekhlis's incompetence and heedlessness. Stalin knew full well his toady's "work qualities," but he also knew that he was as loyal as a dog. Mekhlis along with Kaganovich were the Jews whose presence in Stalin's retinue was supposed to refute any "gossip" of anti-Semitism. After the war Stalin made Mekhlis Minister of State Control of the USSR.

Another Jew in the government was Semyon Ginzburg, Minister of Construction. As opposed to Mekhlis, he had more than a decorative role in the Kremlin, as a highly competent manager and organizer of production. In 1950 he was "reduced" to a deputy union minister. Now, as these lines are written (early 1993), Ginzburg is in his ninety-sixth year. And there were a few specialists in very modest posts as deputy ministers. Naum Antselovich (1881–1952), an Old

Bolshevik who miraculously survived the terror, continued on as a member of the Central Committee and worked as Deputy Minister of Trade of the USSR. As Deputy Minister of State Control of the RSFSR, Solomon Bregman held an even more modest post. The situation was comparable in the other Union republics. For instance, one of the leaders of the partisan movement in Belorussia and secretary of the Belorussian Central Committee, Grigory Eidinov (1908–1977) was still vice premier of the republic's government, where he remained until 1948. A few more such individuals could be listed. They were all remnants of the past (no Jew of a younger generation had the slightest chance to get a middle or even lower position in the power structure) and no more than a silent refutation of any potential accusations of anti-Semitism against Stalin.

The most ardent apologists for Stalin today are divided into two kinds—those who avoid the whole question of his anti-Semitism, which suits them very well but which for tactical reasons they are not yet ready to hail out loud, and those who furiously deny that "unjust accusation." The latter include the still-living former bodyguard of Stalin, KGB Major Rybin. In particular, he produces as evidence the fact that his friend, a certain Nisson Altshuler, played skittles with Stalin, which is clearly proof that the leader did not suffer from anti-Semitism. "Do you think he couldn't see Nisson's face?" Rybin heatedly told a television interviewer. "You could tell he was a Jew a mile away. Stalin could have told Vlasik [General Vlasik, chief of the bodyguards]: 'Listen, what are you bringing a Jew in here for?' But he didn't say that." I don't know if this Nisson ever existed, but the level of argumentation of the pro-Stalin group speaks for itself.

In a recent interview the columnist on international affairs Valentin Zorin stated, "When I started at the Institute of Foreign Relations, state anti-Semitism was almost imperceptible, but it grew very strong in a few years." I think that my respected colleague is fudging a bit. There was no one in those days who did not know that the Institute of Foreign Relations was closed completely to Jews. Zorin, like Georgy Arbatov and Nikolai Inozemtsev and a few other famous political figures and scholars, was admitted to the institute then because he had a Russian surname and was listed as Russian in his passport. (Strictly speaking, they had the right to do so, since most of them were "half-bloods.") Shortly thereafter, the Lubyanka stopped accepting what people put in their applications, and they traced people's origins through generations, ruthlessly pulling out the "weeds."

The situation was a bit better in the arts, but only for a few individuals, primarily in areas that had nothing to do with ideology. For instance, in ballet Maya Plisetskaya, just starting her career, danced with exceptional triumph on the stage of the Bolshoi Theater. And in music, Stalin still needed world records, and what could he do if Jews got the prizes at the most prestigious competitions? So it was in this period, with great resistance from the arts bureaucrats, that the stars of Bella Davidovich, Leonid Kogan, Yulian Sitkovetsky, Igor Bezrodny, Eduard Grach, Naum Shtarman, and Igor Oistrakh ascended. But the ones who were not supported by international prizes, despite their talent, could be tossed by the wayside. In 1944 the brilliant violinist Gita Atlasman graduated from the Moscow Conservatory and her name was placed in gold letters on the marble honor board. (The graduation commission, chaired by Shostakovich, gave her the highest grade.) But she was not allowed to enter international competitions, and that determined her fate, depriving her of any protection.

"You have a horrible surname," a ministry clerk explained frankly when the violinist tried to find out why she was being refused and denied everything. "Let me give you some friendly advice. Don't go anywhere and don't ask for anything," the kind man concluded.

The whole country continued singing songs written by Jewish composers, and every morning began with the radio playing the famous (and still remembered) "Song About the Homeland" ("I know no other country where a man breathes so free"), written by Isaak Dunaevsky and recorded by Stalin's favorite singer, Mark Reizen. This began to annoy Stalin, and he made efforts to push aside the Jewish composers he was sick of and to replace them with "expressors of the Russian national spirit." He said that Dunaevsky's latest "Song About Stalin" "did not work." ("From shore to shore, along mountain peaks, Where the proud eagle flew, The people put together a song / About wise, dear, and beloved Stalin.") "Comrade Dunaevsky," he stated publicly, "has put his marvelous talent to making sure no one sings this song about Comrade Stalin." And he personally ordered a "Cantata About the Great Stalin" to the same text from the Kremlin court composer, Alexander Alexandrov, creator of the Soviet anthem.

The public slap in the face from the leader did not strip the composer of his loyal, toadying feelings. Even in a private letter not meant for publication, written in 1949 and recently discovered in his archive, Dunaevsky wrote, "Coexisting with Stalin demands unbounded purity and loyalty, faith and will, moral and social exploits from his contemporaries. Stalin's life is an example of such exploits in the name of a better life for the whole planet." Even as these ecstatic lines were being put to paper, Stalin was planning a Holocaust whose flames would have destroyed the composer. He remained faithful to his master to the end and committed suicide in 1955, after Stalin's death.

Quite a few commanders of Jewish descent distinguished themselves during the war. Dozens (perhaps hundreds) were generals. After the war they were all shunted aside to out-of-the-way posts. Most were forced to retire, others sent to remote districts with no hope of promotion. In an interview published posthumously, General David Dragunsky of the tank corps, twice Hero of the Soviet Union, who tarnished his combat glory by participating in the work of the KGB "anti-Zionist" committee, makes this confession: "After I graduated from the Academy of the General Staff (1946), I was a colonel then, everyone was given an assignment, except me, I was held up, not even given a post. But Marshals Rybalko and Vasilyevsky were still alive, they were real internationalists. And they helped me. And where do you think I was sent? Beyond Lake Baikal. . . . And how long did I wait for promotion to general? I got it only six months after Stalin died."

For the majority of Jews who had already felt the changes in Stalin's policy, moral support of the heroic commanders—those "descendants of the brave Maccabees" Margarita Aliger described—offered an illusory ray of hope or at least an argument in any naïve attempt to refute charges of lack of patriotism. But even that was being suppressed.

In my mother's legal files I found scattered pages from her dossier on the case of Abram Noevich Broido, a photographer charged in 1947 under Article 58 ("counterrevolutionary agitation and propaganda"). The main point in the indictment was the photo studio where he worked, which had placed in its window his picture of a military man with all his medals and ribbons and captioned it: "Hero of the Soviet Union Lieutenant General Izrail Solomonovich Beskin." The investigator asked why none of the other pictures in the window had explanatory captions, and poor Broido explained that the others "were not so famous" and that he "was giving its due to the Red Army that had saved the world from fascism." This answer cost him an additional charge of a "condescending and scornful attitude toward simple Soviet people, who allegedly do not deserve any attention." The Moscow city court which heard his case behind closed doors found Broido guilty of "malicious nationalistic propaganda" and of "infringements on Stalin's friendship of peoples." He was sentenced to eight years in the camps and was rehabilitated only in 1955—whether posthumously or in his lifetime, I cannot tell from the materials available to me. Pride in one's heroes was for everyone except Jews. Their pride was considered an infringement on the friendship of peoples—naturally, Stalin's friendship, for there could be no other kind.

I do not know whether Broido himself or his family had applied to the Jewish Antifascist Committee for help, but logically they should have done so. Where else? For people who were not subject to the pathological twists of Party bureaucracy, the committee was founded for just that reason, to fight fascism in all its manifestations, and in particular the form of fascism directed against the Jewish people. That was apparent from its name. And it was their firm conviction that only the committee would give them understanding and protection that made so many people appeal to the great defender Mikhoels and his colleagues. JAC sent inquiries and asked the appropriate comrades to pay attention and take measures. Earlier informational reports had not moved them. The need for stronger measures was apparent—not for reports but for screams.

BOTH IN THE KREMLIN and in the Lubyanka, forces were at war, struggling for command positions closer to Stalin and eventually planning for a takeover after his death. Alexander Shcherbakov, the chief anti-Semite in Stalin's entourage, was gone (he died the day after May 9, VE-Day) and ideology was now in the hands of Andrei

Zhdanov and Mikhail Suslov, whose careers were rising as if they were yeast-fed. JAC formally belonged in the sphere of ideology. Memos from various Party apparatchiks and Lubyanka big shots went to Zhdanov and Suslov, reporting that JAC was still involved in things that were "not their business." Proposals to disband the committee were made without any ornamental cover, especially since the change in relations with former allies—the United States, Britain, and France—no longer made it necessary to care about public opinion in those countries.

A letter found in the archives from Mikhoels to Suslov, dated June 21, 1945, shows how much discussion surrounded the committee at the Kremlin. Obviously not on his own initiative but in response to a request from above, Mikhoels patiently and persuasively relates the history of the creation of JAC, its not very long history (just five years), which Suslov in his official position as a department head in the Central Committee should have known. Mikhoels informs him that the committee has seventy members and nineteen in the presidium, stresses that the deputy executive secretary "is Comrade Shpigelglaz, S.M., member of the Party since 1919, formerly a Party worker." It is clear that Mikhoels assumes this "former Party worker" is well known and that his name is a guarantee of the entire committee's reliability.

The knife was already aimed for a blow against the committee, but Mikhoels heroically tried to avert danger. Perhaps he might not have succeeded, but aid came from within the Central Committee. Two executives—L. Baranov, deputy chief of the International Department, and V. Grigoryan, deputy chief of the Agitation and Propaganda Department, wrote a general conclusion (June 19, 1947), "On the Mistakes in the Work of JAC." The heading was the committee's salvation. Listing the familiar "inadequacies in work" (interference in the activity of Party, soviet, and procuratorial organs in defending Jews), the authors in conclusion proposed not disbanding the committee but "improving it, showing the leadership that work with the Jewish population of the Soviet Union is not part of its functions." Their poor information on the internal workings of the Lubyanka is evident from the fact that they suggest dismissing "Comrade Fefer,

I. S., a former Bundist," when that comrade was on the nomenklatura list of the Lubyanka. He tendered his resignation from the committee only when his masters permitted it (October 21, 1948).

At the same time other forces (Zhdanov, Alexandrov, and then Suslov) wanted JAC disbanded. Alexandrov, returning to *The Black Book*, wrote a mocking and silly summary. "It presents the idea," he wrote to Zhdanov on February 3, 1947, "that Germany fought the USSR in order to destroy the Jews, whereas the Hitlerites killed Russians, Jews, and Ukrainians, and representatives of other peoples of our country in equal measure. . . . Some of the accounts maintain that it was enough to get a 'Russian passport' during the occupation to be saved. That is a vile slander on the great Russian people."

Upon learning that Glavlit had banned the publication of *The Black Book*, Mikhoels wrote a restrained but indignant letter to Zhdanov. His argument is directed more at saving the committee than the book. There was no written reply. The Kremlin followed the rules of all experienced criminals and did not leave evidence.

Confirmation of the fact that there was a struggle in the offices of the Cheka and that Stalin's entourage was not unified is a letter signed by Mikhail Suslov and Georgy Alexandrov, dated November 7, 1947. (Did they really work on that great holiday, the anniversary of the October Revolution? It's quite possible. Suslov was a workaholic and his asceticism when it came to drinking was well known.) This time the letter was addressed not simply to the Politburo but personally to Vyacheslav Molotov and Central Committee Secretary Alexei Kuznetsov, and the authors called on them to become their allies in the struggle to disband the villainous committee.

There was no reply. Stalin was still waiting. However, he did not hide which way the wind was blowing from the Kremlin. People who knew the wind direction because they were so close to the leader could understand his wishes before he expressed them and did everything to make sure the wind reached its destination.

In the fall of 1946 in Paris at an international conference, Foreign Minister Molotov noted a man with clearly Semitic features in the Czech delegation. The minister's people must surely have told him who the man was, but he felt the need to play out a little scene.

"Who is that man?" he asked disdainfully of Rudolf Slansky, the

General Secretary of the Czech Communist Party, in the presence of the Czech Foreign Minister, Vladimir Klementis.

"That's the editor-in-chief of *Rude pravo* [the Central Committee organ], André Simon," Slansky replied.

"And what's that cosmopolite doing here?" Molotov muttered, and turned without waiting for a reply.

Stunned, Slansky immediately reported this "dialogue" to Prague and the rest of the Politburo members. Simon was fired soon after. And six years later, Slansky, Klementis, and Simon were co-defendants in an anti-Semitic trial in Prague and all three were executed.

No one, however, could say that a real threat of genocide hung over the Jews of the Soviet Union or that they were subjected to discrimination spearheaded by the government. Stalin's new and brilliant move mixed up all the cards.

Freilekhs, a play directed by Solomon Mikhoels at the very end of the war at the Jewish Theater, was nominated for the Stalin Prize. This vivid, festive, happy, and sad musical, attended by thousands of every nationality, was the hit of Moscow's theatrical season. Every night the play was on, the invited celebrities could barely make their way through the crowd besieging the theater. Dozens of seats were reserved for the diplomatic corps and foreign guests, but they were not enough—people were willing to watch it in standing room. Contemporaries recorded the enormous impression the play had made on them because it was so different from the ideology-bound officious claptrap dedicated to the Year of Victory on all the other stages.*

The nomination of the best play of the season, so highly praised and popular, for the Stalin Prize seemed not only proper but indisputable. However, the Committee on the Arts, whose leaders were well versed in the moods up above, did everything possible to cut the play out in the early rounds of the competition, thereby demonstrating vigilance

---

* As just one example I quote the outstanding pianist ("the genius of the forte-piano," as she was called in her lifetime) Marina Yudina. Her letter to Mikhoels is in a private archive. Calling *Freilekhs* a play "worthy of admiration," "a great and true manifestation of art," she explains her reasons. "I am in despair by everything I come into contact with, its tastelessness, ignorance, dilettantism, bowing and scraping and other moral degradation. . . . In your theater I felt I was in another world, where everything was real." Yudina's flawless taste gives greater weight to her review. I remember that marvelous woman when she played at Pasternak's dacha in Peredelkino, seeing her great friend off on his final journey.

and loyalty. They organized "closed" (that is, anonymous) negative reviews of the play, their main conclusion being accusations of nationalism, and also faked "letters from workers" with similar content. These reviews and letters were handed over to the Committee on Stalin Prizes, that is, to Stalin personally, because he did not stint on time and delved personally into all the details of the discussions and made the decisions himself.

But Comrade Stalin was much more cunning, and smarter, than his toadying lackeys. He knew how to blow smoke into people's eyes. Stalin supported the play, which he had not even seen. The Stalin Prize for 1946 went to Solomon Mikhoels, Veniamin Zuskin, the artist Alexander Tyshler, and other members of the production team of *Freilekhs*. No one doubted that the prize was totally deserved. But it had nothing to do with art. Its aim was to serve as ammunition against any spoken or unspoken accusations of anti-Semitism.

IN THE MEANTIME IN the offices on Staraya Square, home of the Central Committee, and at Lubyanka, where Beria was no longer in power, having been replaced by Stalin's new favorite, Viktor Abakumov, work went on. Everyone knew very well that the Stalin Prize for *Freilekhs* was a smoke screen and what was behind it. By that time Stalin, Malenkov, Zhdanov, and Suslov had a large collection of memoranda marked "Top Secret." They all said the same thing, presenting "additional facts" on the nationalist, hostile, and espionage activity of the Jewish Antifascist Committee. Without a doubt this flood of tendentious and lying "information" could not have been sent that high up unless its fabricators knew that these materials were welcome.

The scenario hastily put together by the Cheka had as its protagonists two American Jews who were considered "extreme leftists" in the United States and were suspected of ties with Soviet intelligence—the journalists P. Novik and B. Goldberg. Novik was a veteran of the labor movement in the United States. He joined the Communist Party in 1921, in its most pro-Soviet wing, and was editor of *Morning Freiheit*, the newspaper of American Jewish Communists that published articles praising "Stalin's nationality policies." Goldberg was the author of such articles. Upon his return from the Soviet Union, Goldberg wrote not only for *Morning Freiheit*, but for other American left-wing newspapers, using Moscow propaganda to praise Stalin, the Soviet "friendship of peoples," and everything that was called the "Soviet way of life." The materials, which would soon be used against them, had been given to him by JAC, and were classified as espionage. Both Goldberg and Novik were leaders of the Committee of Jewish Writers, Artists, and Scientists—JAC's main partner during the war years, which helped Mikhoels on his trip and collected money for the Red Army.

And it was these men (suspected by American counterintelligence of ties with the Soviet secret service) that the Lubyanka served up to the Kremlin as CIA agents. They had to use them because no other American emissaries had come to Moscow for contacts with JAC. Abakumov took Stalin's new policy twist very seriously, and he employed what was at hand to prepare materials that would find a sympathetic reading from his leader.

The Jewish topic had taken stage front in Stalin's thoughts. Three weeks after Suslov and Alexandrov had called on Molotov and Kuznetsov to strike a "blow against Zionism," the UN General Assembly passed a resolution (November 29, 1947) to establish the state of Israel on the land of Palestine ("mandate" territory of Britain since 1920). Stalin felt no sympathy for this new state, but Britain supported the Arabs, and for that alone Moscow warmly hailed the return of their historical homeland to the Jews. Some of JAC's members took this warm response as genuine. A complex political intrigue was being planned, and the members of the dying committee, incapable of figuring out the Kremlin games and in the thrall of ideas that were soon to be branded "nationalistic," were doomed to be its victims. They clearly did not understand this.

IT DOES NOT TAKE much time to organize a murder from above. Nevertheless, a decision must precede its execution. That means that Stalin must have decided to get rid of Mikhoels no later than December 1947—no later and probably not much sooner. The strategy that came to Stalin after the UN decision did not allow for the presence in the USSR of a recognized leader of the Jewish national movement, and one with worldwide fame and respect. One would not think that he was a state figure, with influence on politics, but his personality—and that meant his opinion, and that meant his position, and that meant his words—carried weight. He was as superfluous as in another period and for other reasons Gorky had been superfluous. There are people who are not acceptable for a trial, neither secret nor open. Or even for murder in a prison cellar. It is better to help them leave the scene.

Evidence of how correct Stalin's bloody decision was is the fact that there has never since been a spiritual leader of Russian Jewry. And most likely, there never will be. There are many reasons for that, and this is not the place for an analysis or a listing of them. We must merely recognize this sad reality as we reconstruct the thought processes of the greatest criminal of all time, whose unbounded cruelty coexisted with amazing perspicacity and planning. He made only one major mistake—his trust of Hitler—but that is a different story.

There is another confirmation that December 1947 was a fateful month. On December 19, on the orders of Minister of State Security Abakumov, without a procurator's sanction (though what procurator would have denied it then? and in fact Procurator of the USSR Safonov signed on January 8), Isaak Goldshtein, doctor of economics, senior researcher at the Economics Institute of the Academy of Sciences, was arrested. It is impossible to learn what served as the formal excuse for his arrest, but the hidden agenda is clear—not only from the questions of the investigator but from Goldshtein's explanation, given on October 2, 1953. The progenitor of the gigantic scenario, chosen at the Lubyanka as the first victim to bring the others down, did not lose his life. On October 29, 1949, without a trial but by summary court, he was given twenty-five years in the camps, most likely because he might come in handy later.

But we are running ahead of ourselves. The transcript of Goldshtein's first interrogation is dated only January 9, 1948, even though there is a notation in his dossier that between December 19, 1947, and January 8, 1948, he was summoned for interrogation seventeen times and "gave evidence" for a total of sixty-nine hours. The details we can learn from two other documents—the conclusion of the military procurator, Lieutenant Colonel of Justice Zhukov (1955), the basis for the rehabilitation of JAC, and the written explanations of Goldshtein, who survived the camps and was freed on October 2, 1953.

The conclusion states: "After [Goldshtein's] arrest Investigator Sorokin and former deputies of the Investigation Department for especially important affairs of the MGB USSR Likhachev and Komarov, on orders from Abakumov, began trying to get from Goldshtein testimony on his alleged espionage and nationalistic activity, despite the fact that *there were no data on that account in the organs of state security* [italics mine]. . . . Goldshtein was beaten, forced to sign a transcript of the interrogation, fabricated with the participation of Broverman* from Abakumov's secretariat, in which he declared that Lozovsky, Fefer, Markish, and others were using JAC as a cover for alleged anti-Soviet nationalistic activity . . . and espionage work."

And here is what Goldshtein himself wrote after his release: "On December 19, 1947, I was arrested in Moscow, brought to the Lubyanka, and then to the investigation person in Lefortovo [that meant that he did not give the evidence they wanted and was sent there to be worked over]. I was beaten cruelly and at length with a rubber truncheon on my soft parts and the bare soles of my feet. They beat me until I could no longer sit or stand. . . . Sorokin and another colonel [a comparison of Goldshtein's account with others suggests that it was Komarov] began beating me so hard that my face was swollen terribly for several weeks and my hearing was affected for several months. . . . I was forced to sign that transcript. . . . I was beaten eight times as they demanded new admissions. Exhausted by day and nighttime interrogations, terrorized by the beatings, curses, and threats, I fell into a deep depression, a total moral confusion, and began to give evidence against myself and others for committing serious crimes."

Investigator Georgy Sorokin corroborated Goldshtein's statement. In the course of the investigation, he was given a chance to write his

---

* This name occurs in various materials of the investigations that were done many times, beginning in 1953. Yakov Broverman was considered the best, if not the only, grammar whiz at Lubyanka. Without taking part in the interrogations or beatings, he turned their illiterate gabble into acceptably literate form. He was later arrested and tried along with Abakumov, Leonov, Likhachev, and Komarov in December 1954. At the trial he testified against the other defendants but not himself. He was sentenced to twenty-five years in the camps, but was released long before his term ended. He eventually disappeared from sight.

version. This is what he said (dated January 3, 1954): "Abakumov's orders on using methods of persuasion on Goldshtein were executed that same evening by Komarov with my participation. . . . When he read the transcript of the interrogation, Abakumov told me that I had interrogated Goldshtein badly and written the transcript clumsily, and therefore it had to be corrected by Broverman, who worked on it with some deputy of the Investigation Department . . . in my presence and then it was sent to the Instance."

We know what was meant by "Instance" (usually capitalized)—up the chain of command to Stalin. By comparing the dates, we can reconstruct the sequence of events. There was no decision yet on how to deal with JAC and its leader, for two reasons—"domestic" and "foreign." And no one knows which was the more important. Both were intertwined tightly, and dividing them into more and less important is probably impossible.

IN SAYING THAT GOLDSHTEIN was the Lubyanka's first victim in its monstrous conspiracy against an entire nation, I consciously permitted myself an inaccuracy, following the outline sketched by the Chief Military Procuracy in 1953–1955 as they exposed the conspiracy. (In passing, let us note that the procuracy was merely following orders. The authors of the exposés, which were done in great secrecy, were in Staraya Square, in Party headquarters.) In fact the *first* victims were others, but this was not publicized even after Stalin's death and even in secret documents. So now we will combine into one stream (as it was in reality) two seemingly parallel and unconnected currents.

Nine days before Goldshtein's arrest, the MGB took into custody a relative of Nadezhda Allilueva, Stalin's wife. Yevgenia Alexandrovna Allilueva was the widow of Nadezhda's brother, Pavel, who died in mysterious circumstances. She must be considered the very first victim, even though she had no connection to JAC and no one interrogated her about the committee. She was accused of "convening anti-Soviet meetings for many years at her apartment, where she spread vile slander against the head of the Soviet government" (that is, her relative by marriage, Josif Stalin). The same charges were brought against her second husband, Nikolai Molochnikov,* and her daughter, Kira Allilueva, an actress at the Maly Theater, arrested on January 6, 1948. The same charges were also brought against Nadezhda's sister, Anna Allilueva, a member of the Writers' Union (arrested January 30, 1948); against their friend Lidia Shatunovskaya,† a graduate of the State Institute of Theater Arts, a student of avant-garde director Meyerhold, and a theater historian; and against Shatunovskaya's second husband, physics professor Leonid Tumerman (we have come across his name before), arrested on December 27, 1947. These details, especially the dates, are extremely important for keeping track of the development of events.

But what do the arrests of the Alliluev family and their friends have to do with anti-Semitism? Stalin's "love" of his wife's family was well known. And the story of the eradication of Anna Allilueva's husband, Stanislav Redens, executed in 1938, has been described at length (interested readers should turn to Svetlana Allilueva's *Twenty Letters to a Friend*). Stalin's pathological desire to eradicate the family was not kept from Beria or Abakumov or the rest of the secret police. A decision was made to tie up these loose ends, to create an incredible plot that only the Lubyanka masters could handle.

Shatunovskaya was good friends with Mikhoels, helped him in his literary work, and often saw him. A memorandum to the Kremlin from the MGB maintained that she was the link, bringing slanderous information to Mikhoels, which then went to the JAC, and from there to the American spies, who then had information on the "head of the Soviet government" (even in top-secret documents the idol's name

---

* Even though engineer Molochnikov was arrested, Yevgenia Allilueva came to understand from her interrogation that he was an MGB agent who had for many years supplied information on the life of the Alliluev clan so hated by Stalin. After her rehabilitation and release, she divorced him.

† L. A. Shatunovskaya was an adopted daughter of Petr Krasikov, an Old Bolshevik, member of the Central Executive Committee, and Deputy Chairman of the Supreme Court. Her closeness to this family and her marriage to an important Soviet administrator who died in 1932 made it possible for her to move into the Government House, where she met many members of the Party, state, and military elite. After her release from prison camp she lived and worked in Moscow. She emigrated with her husband to Israel in the seventies. Her memoirs, *Life in the Kremlin*, were published in Russian in 1982 (Chalidze Publications, New York).

could not be used). The information was slanderous, naturally, for what else could interest foreign spies? This was a hobbyhorse of Stalin's, which could be used with guaranteed success. Remember, just a few years before these events, young Svetlana Allilueva's first love, film writer Alexei Kapler, was accused of trying to worm his way into the "royal" family on assignment from British intelligence to discover secrets about the leaders of the people and sell them to the enemy.

And so plotline number one developed like this. The hired flunkies of international Zionism, led by Mikhoels, centered in JAC, received "slanderous information" about intimate secrets of the great Stalin through Shatunovskaya from members of the Alliluev family, who were seeking revenge for the deaths of Nadezhda, Pavel, Stanislav, and other relatives. This slanderous information was passed on to American spies by the leaders of JAC. And only God knew what they were planning on doing with the information. Apparently this personal note touched Stalin to the quick and played a decisive role in the speed with which events were to unfold.

It was speedy, yes, but not instant. In early January 1948, without waiting for Broverman to turn it into an acceptable transcript, the "Instance" was informed that "prisoner Goldshtein was forced to admit that back in 1946 his friend Grinberg, Zakhar Grigoryevich [on the staff of the presidium of JAC], told him that the Jewish Antifascist Committee was performing anti-Soviet, nationalistic work, and that all this work was headed by Mikhoels, who had made wide contacts with Jewish bourgeois nationalists in the USA and has the full support of American Zionists."

"Headed by Mikhoels . . ." He was to head that work for only a few more days.

8

THE MURDER OF
SOLOMON MIKHOELS

AMONG THE NUMEROUS public positions Solomon Mikhoels held was member of the Committee on the Stalin Prize for the Arts and Literature under the Council of Ministers of the USSR and head of its theater section. The committee was chaired by a Stalin favorite, an uncomplaining executor of his orders, "the Party's loyal soldier," the writer Alexander Fadeyev, who had another equally important position as general secretary of the Writers' Union of the USSR. The committee examined the candidates proposed for the prize and selected and presented works for confirmation by Stalin himself. Stalin made these decisions unilaterally anyway, but the process was made to look democratic. The members of the committee's presidium (that is, the section heads—literature, theater, music, etc.) met with Stalin, who listened to their opinions and then pronounced his judgments. They were also verdicts.

Nevertheless, the function of the committee and its leaders remained a highly important one. After all, in the majority of cases, Stalin's decision was based on the committee's collegial position: the leader selected the lucky ones from the group preselected by the committee. Stalin had reason to suppose that the functionaries he picked from among the country's truly outstanding cultural figures (this applied less to literature) would bring to his attention the very best in art that fit the standards of socialist realism. The committee and its numerous experts, associates, consultants, and reviewers worked conscientiously, fully aware of their great responsibility and the trust bestowed upon them by their beloved Party and government.

Every work proposed for the prize was studied (viewed, heard) by the committee's staff, who often had to travel far outside Moscow, since one of the unspoken but firm rules was to stimulate the creative cadres in the national republics and to support the Russian provinces. After the candidacies were approved, a multi-stage selection process began, which culminated in the final round, which involved the committee leaders.

These details are important to bear in mind as we reconstruct the tragedy that occurred in January 1948. Among the works proposed for the Stalin Prize that year were two plays that had not been premiered in Moscow: one from Leningrad and one from Minsk. Fadeyev, remarking that the selection for the final round was a very responsible decision and that the "Central Committee and Comrade Stalin personally" paid great attention to it and had total confidence in Comrade Mikhoels, insisted that the chairman of the theater section see at least one of those two plays. Undoubtedly, Fadeyev was convinced that he was performing a socially significant act. And he must not have even imagined that he was playing into the hands of people who wanted Mikhoels out of Moscow. It would be difficult and risky to fulfill Stalin's orders in the capital. Mikhoels was always among family, friends, and colleagues in Moscow, and it would be almost impossible to organize an "accident" under those circumstances.

Mikhoels was planning to go to Leningrad. That was the suggestion of one of his closest friends, the artist Alexander Tyshler. But apparently the Leningrad variant did not suit Lubyanka. They brought in the critic Vladimir Golubov, who wrote under the pseudonym V. Potapov, to work on Mikhoels. He was executive secretary of the journal *Teatr* and the author of one of the most delighted reviews of Mikhoels's play *Freilekhs*, sparing no superlatives—"most brilliant," "sparkling," and "wise"—and singling out Mey's virtuoso choreography of the wedding dances. And it was Golubov who unexpectedly insisted that Mikhoels go to Minsk. For the time being, it was merely persuasion.

The committee decided on December 22, 1947, to see the play, but, contrary to the tradition of many years, there is no information in the decision about who was to go to Minsk. "Decision of the committee" is of course bureaucratese: the committee did not meet for this and there was no discussion of it. And the chairman himself did not get involved in such details. "Technical"—that is, organizational—questions were dealt with by the apparat. If an order about the trip to Minsk did not give the name of the person to go, that could mean only one thing: the question had not yet been decided. Therefore, the documents and personal accounts allow us to say that on December 22 Mikhoels's fate may not have been sealed, but Stalin was on the threshold of a final decision. Still to be determined was where and how the drama's last act would take place and who was to perform it. It is quite probable that the mechanism for the operation, as well as the cast list, was worked out in that holiday season.

Mikhoels and his wife spent New Year's Eve at a party in the home of Moises Grinberg, chief of the music department of the All-Union Radio Committee. There are reminiscences of that evening, but none contain even a hint that Mikhoels let drop so much as a word about his coming trip to Minsk. It wasn't a secret, so most likely he did not know about it yet. This is confirmed obliquely by the travel approval receipt, which has survived: the city (Minsk) to which the committee member would be traveling and the date of the resolution (the committee's order) for this business trip (December 22, 1947) are filled in by typewriter. But Mikhoels's name is handwritten and the date the trip is supposed to end (January 10) is changed by the same hand to January 20. This receipt was issued on January 2, 1948.

Thus, the chronology of events is the following: Stalin made his decision in late December; on January 2, Mikhoels was told that the lofty mission of "reviewing the Belorussian play" was entrusted to him; since he could not leave immediately, and since the agents who were to perform the deed needed a reserve of time for unforeseen circumstances, the length of his stay was extended.

The travel receipt was signed by the assistant to the committee's chairman, Igor Nezhny, who also worked as administrative director of the Moscow Art Theater. His two jobs were made easier by the fact that the theater and the Stalin Prize Committee were in the same building. When Stalin was a few hours away from death and lay paralyzed at his dacha in Kuntsevo, Igor Nezhny was arrested, along with many others on the long list prepared ahead of time for arrest on "Day X." That most of them were secret agents of Lubyanka is now known for a fact. But each case requires concrete, indisputable proof. Let us be patient, it will come.

Naturally, neither Fadeyev nor Nezhny could possibly have known any of the details of the planned operation. But when they got orders from the Central Committee to send a certain person to Minsk at a certain time, they obeyed without question—especially since it was so simple to give it all a totally proper and unsuspicious excuse, which had already been used by Fadeyev: the Belorussian play was considered so significant politically that an objective evaluation could come only from the head of the committee's theater section.

I said that Mikhoels could not leave immediately. That is true, in a way. Of course, he was saddled with many affairs that did not allow him to take off instantly, and he was also not well. He had injured his arm in a fall and had gotten a tetanus shot, which made him feverish and uncomfortable. But, as a man of rare self-discipline and possessing a sense of duty, he would have put off his work and overcome his illness if he had received a call saying, "You must go as soon as possible," not only from Fadeyev or Nezhny, but from a much lesser committee staff person.

But there was an unexpected wrinkle. The poet Peretz Markish and his wife, Esther, offered to accompany Mikhoels. Minsk was the home of their friend Colonel General Sergei Trofimenko,* who was then commander of the Belorussian Military Region. The Markishes had met the general's family in Tashkent, where they had been evacuated from Moscow during the war, and later Mikhoels met them too, and their friendship became quite solid. Taking advantage of Mikhoels's trip, the Markishes wanted to spend some time with him in the hospitable circle of the general's home.† But this escort did not fit in with the plans at all. Mikhoels's departure had to be held back. Esther Markish, the poet's widow, writes in her memoirs:

---

* Sergei Georgievich Trofimenko (1899–1953), Hero of the Soviet Union, commander of several armies during World War II. After January 1948 he was hastily recalled to the Higher Courses at the Military Academy of the General Staff, and after he completed them he did not return to Minsk. He was sent to the Caucasus to command the Northern Caucasus Military Region.
† Some high-ranking Soviet military leaders showed loyalty and courage in regard to their persecuted and slandered friends from the Jewish Antifascist Committee: besides Trofimenko, Marshal Ivan Peresypkin of the communications corps and Colonel General of Aviation (later Marshal of Aviation) Vladimir Sudets.

"Literally a few hours before we were to leave, Markish had to turn down the trip: he had to read the galleys of his book." There is little doubt that the proofreading which had to be done with lightning speed for some reason (for the visit with their friends in Minsk would hardly have lasted more than two or three days) was created on purpose. Or as they say in Soviet bureaucratic jargon, urgently organized. They were not planning to kill Markish then, and the presence of a careful and observant witness could have ruined the operation.*

The main "persuader," Vladimir Golubov, was given the assignment of accompanying Mikhoels on the trip. Formally, he was going so as to review the play for his journal. But that was not the reason for Golubov's presence. He was a secret informant of Lubyanka and, as such, could keep an eye on every step Mikhoels made and, where necessary, on orders from Moscow, influence those steps.

According to the recently published memoirs of the last living close colleague of Mikhoels, Professor Belenky, the director of the school at the Jewish Theater, Mikhoels had gone to hear the famous Belorussian singer Larisa Alexandrovskaya (Belenky gives her name incorrectly as Alexandrova). She was in Moscow at the time, missing Mikhoels, who consequently spent five days waiting for her in vain. Alas, the memoirist fell victim not so much to faulty memory as to intentionally false rumors.

Alexandrovskaya was not nominated for the Stalin Prize that year. She was a laureate back in 1941. Perhaps Mikhoels's departure from Minsk had been delayed by people who insisted that he meet with the "state singer" (she headed the Belorussian Theater Society and was a deputy of the Supreme Soviet of the USSR), who was supposed to return from Moscow at any minute. But the formal goal of the Minsk trip was to see a different performance.

The play they were sent to see was never named, even though it was no secret. Why did the press suppress the play's name and even resort

---

* We cannot rule out the possibility that Itzik Fefer may have objected to Markish's proposed trip. He knew that Markish could not stand him, and apparently was paying him back in kind. Fefer's role in "Operation Mikhoels" will be discussed below. Fefer, as a leader of the Jewish Antifascist Committee, could have easily arranged an urgent need for proofreading Markish's book.

to falsification? All the newspapers mentioned the "plays that were candidates for the Stalin Prize." Actually, the important guests were going to see only one play—a contemporary saga called *Konstantin Zaslonov* at the Yanka Kupala Drama Theater of Minsk.

The question remains: who needed that cloak-and-dagger secrecy, and why? For all the absurdity of the situation, it is not so absurd a question. Of course, as chairman of the theater section, Mikhoels could have judged a play in any genre. But why did the committee and *Teatr*, a professional journal, send a specialist on choreography as the expert and reviewer of this play? Golubov had written a monograph on the great ballerina Galina Ulanova, ballet librettos, and many articles on the art of ballet. The committee and the journal had dozens of highly qualified specialists who would have made much better judges for a play contending for the Stalin Prize. If the play had been named, the incongruity would have struck people in the theater world immediately. But their sorrow and the blow they all felt pushed aside seemingly inappropriate details. Who could have cared what play Mikhoels and Golubov had seen in Minsk? And later, everyone forgot about it.

All of Mikhoels's close friends recall that he left with great reluctance and very strong forebodings. The train departed in the evening, and Mikhoels spent almost the entire day at the theater. The trip was to be very brief, yet he tried to finish up all the small, routine chores as if he would be gone a long time. The greatest impression (albeit in hindsight) was created by his unexpected farewell visit to the physicist Peter Kapitsa (later a Nobel laureate). They were in fact friends, but weeks and months might go by without their seeing each other, and there is no rational explanation as to why Mikhoels made a point of dropping in on Kapitsa two or three hours before the train just to say good-bye for a few days.

This mysterious episode is all the more astonishing in view of the information I received a few years ago. Now still hard at work in the Procurator's Office of Russia (until 1991 the Procurator's Office of the USSR), senior investigator for special affairs Sergei Gromov told me that in the KGB system, within the department for the liquidation of "traitors" and defectors, there was a particularly secret group, led by a married couple, which directly worked out the mechanism for murders and executed the plans. All the departments of Lubyanka had to submit to it without question, without demanding any explanations. This group, which carried out Operation Mikhoels, prepared a plan five years later, in early 1953, to kill Academician Kapitsa. It was only Stalin's death and the subsequent change in the political situation, when Kapitsa's sworn enemy Lavrenti Beria had other problems to deal with, that kept the plan from being implemented. They could not forgive Kapitsa (1894–1984) and his refusal to take part in the creation of the atomic bomb (Beria was in charge of nuclear science and technology at the time). Later another physicist, Abram Ioffe (1880–1960), also threatened to stop working on military projects if scientists were forced to speak out against their Jewish colleagues.

Originally intending to go to the train station straight from the theater, Mikhoels changed his mind at the last minute and went home to say good-bye to his wife. His contemporaries recall that Mikhoels's face that day was "Hippocrates-like," that is, bearing the mark of death. Of course, this could be an aberration of the memory, a temporary confusion. However, there is evidence in favor of the reality of those impressions, and not later ones, the most important of which is that Mikhoels had reason for his gloomy foreboding. His relatives recall that a few weeks before the tragedy some people warned him that death was near. The well-known actress of stage and film Faina Ranevskaya, not at all one to fantasize or falsify, recounted during the Khrushchev thaw that shortly before the trip to Minsk, Mikhoels told her that "he had received an anonymous letter with a death threat." I think that the calls and the letters were not threats but warnings of danger. The people getting ready to kill him had no reason to "scare off" their victim—on the contrary, their goal was to keep him lulled into a false sense of security. Nevertheless, people who adored this pure and noble man and his enormous talent were legion, and in the most varied circles, and they could have tried to warn him of the danger awaiting him (even by means of death threats).

It was January 7—five days before the murder. Three people besides his daughters and wife came to see Mikhoels off at the Belorussian Station: his best friend and colleague, the actor Veniamin Zuskin; the writer Vassily Grossman; and the poet Semyon Lipkin. But without a doubt, there were many more to see him onto the train. They pretended to be passengers, conductors, porters, and vendors, making sure that the approved scenario went off without a hitch.

The train started, carrying Mikhoels toward death.

HE ARRIVED IN MINSK on the morning of January 8. Mikhoels and Golubov were greeted at the station by people from the republic-level Committee on the Arts and the Belorussian Theatrical Society. But there were others there to meet them—just as in Moscow, they were portraying railroad personnel, porters, policemen, and citizens who happened to be on the platform on personal business.

Unfortunately, no document to which I have access reflects every hour spent in Minsk, but undoubtedly the reports of the agents surrounding the great actor in a tight ring have events down to the minute. Those reports have probably been preserved and one day will be published. For now, all we know is that on January 11 Mikhoels called home in Moscow for the last time and mentioned something that his relatives did not pay much attention to at first. He said that he observed breakfasting at the hotel restaurant his deputy in the Jewish Antifascist Committee, the poet Itzik Fefer, whom he had seen three days earlier in Moscow, where he handed over the reins of authority to him for the duration of his trip. Fefer had never mentioned a trip to Minsk, and he had no reason to be there. The most astonishing part was that Mikhoels said Fefer sat buried in a newspaper and pretended not to see him.

We can only guess why Mikhoels did not approach him. The scenarists could not have excluded that possibility and they must have prepared some excuse for Fefer's presence. Maybe Mikhoels did come over and they did talk, however briefly, but Mikhoels did not tell his family about it over the telephone, leaving it for his return to Moscow. There is no one left who can tell us now, but the episode in itself is significant, and we will return to it.

The events of January 12 are variously reproduced in the memoirs of his friends. But these are second-hand recollections—retellings of other people's accounts, what we call "broken telephone." There is one version according to which Mikhoels spent the whole day at General Trofimenko's house and went to see the play that evening. According to another version, he never saw the general or anyone from his family during his stay in Minsk. In either case, that worthy man's name was implicated in this bloody story.

If we drop the later layers of retelling and the details that are not incontrovertibly proven, we can say that around ten o'clock on the evening of January 12, as soon as Mikhoels returned from the theater, he got a phone call (another version has the call coming around eight o'clock, because Mikhoels had not gone to the theater that evening), after which he quickly dressed and left in the car that came for him. For reasons that remain obscure, Mikhoels spoke not on the telephone in his hotel room but on that of the concierge, who remembered that Mikhoels called his interlocutor either Sergei (a first name) or Sergeyev (a surname). General Trofimenko's first name was Sergei.

Usually the concierge in a major hotel, especially one with foreign guests, works with the secret police. In this case, when such an important operation (on the highest orders) was under way, this key position could not have been filled with a "neutral" person. Therefore, we can assume that he was doing his job. Thus, the killers needed to have "eyewitness testimony" that someone named Sergei had called. There is no proof that Mikhoels spoke on the concierge's telephone. This could have been a rumor that was intentionally spread. Subsequently Trofimenko maintained that he had never called Mikhoels. And that was probably the case: after all, Mikhoels knew the general's voice and would not have been fooled by a faker (he had a subtle actor's ear). So the caller must have said he was calling for or from Sergei. And told him something that made the weary Mikhoels set off immediately. Golubov, whom Trofimenko did not know, went with him. It is obvious that Golubov was carrying out his assignment: he had to make sure Mikhoels got in the car. He probably said he did not want to leave Mikhoels alone—for moral support and to ensure his safety—and naturally Mikhoels could not refuse, and why would he want to?

A new discovery in the archives confirms that the episode with "Sergei" had a twofold role in the bloody scenario: it served as a way of luring Mikhoels into a trap and it also confused the situation, hiding clues.

Subsequently, when the pretense of a thorough investigation was being created, General Bodunov, deputy chief of the Main Directorate of the Militia of the MVD USSR, wrote to Deputy Minister General Ivan Serov (who would head the KGB a few years later) in a "top secret" report (No. 6(a)583, February 11, 1948): "Mikhoels and Golubov-Potapov told the people from the Minsk theaters that they would be busy that evening, since they were planning to visit some friend of Golubov-Potapov—an engineer named Sergeyev or Sergei. Mikhoels and Golubov-Potapov categorically refused the offer of an automobile. . . . As a result of agent-operative and investigative measures, the version that Mikhoels and Golubov-Potapov were headed to the house of Golubov-Potapov's friend, the engineer Sergeyev, was not confirmed. All information gathered allows us to assume that Mikhoels and Golubov-Potapov for some reasons intended to visit some other person and were carefully disguising that fact from their acquaintances by using the made-up name of the engineer Sergeyev."

The absurdity of the alibi the Lubyanka is creating for itself in a secret document is clear, but the version written in its offices and carefully worked out has its own logic. Now we can see (and we will see more later) how many people on different levels and in different positions were dragged into the operation.

AT SEVEN O'CLOCK IN the morning on a quiet street along a deserted lot, rather far from the hotel, passersby noticed two bodies sticking out from the snow. They were Solomon Mikhoels and Vladimir Golubov. All their clothing, documents, and possessions were on them. Their watches ticked peacefully on their wrists: Mikhoels's gold watch had not been stolen, but the crystal was missing. They looked for it, but it was not found. Not surprisingly: the crystal had fallen out in a very different location.

Svetlana Allilueva, Stalin's daughter, gives very important information that helps us date events more precisely. "At one of our by then rare meetings at my father's dacha," Allilueva writes in her book *Just One Year,* "I came into the room while he was on the telephone. I waited. Someone was reporting to him and he listened. Then, to sum up, he said, 'Well, a car accident.' I remember his intonation very well—it wasn't a question, it was a confirmation, a reply. He wasn't asking, he was proposing it, the car accident. When the conversation was over, he greeted me and in a short while said, 'Mikhoels was killed in a car accident.' . . . He was killed, but there was no car accident. The car accident was the official version suggested by my father when he heard the report that the deed was done. . . . It is not hard to guess why they were reporting it to him."

It is not hard to guess, but there is an important detail missing in this tragic story. At what time did this conversation take place?

Stalin was a night person; he went to bed late and rose late. No one dared to wake him in the morning: the one exception was at dawn on June 22, 1941, when he was roused with the news of the German invasion. Yet by ten o'clock on January 13 the Jewish Theater in Moscow had already heard from Minsk that Mikhoels had died in a car crash. That morning my mother, a defense attorney, went to court for a criminal case that started at ten in the Sovietsky District of Moscow. She was home by eleven (we lived three bus stops away from the courthouse). One of the assessors in the trial was a man who worked at the Jewish Theater, and he was late. The worried judge called the theater a little after ten and she was told, "Don't wait, no one will be able to come. We had a terrible misfortune: Mikhoels died in a car accident." And Mother came home with that news.

There is no doubt: Stalin was informed of the execution of the special assignment on the night of January 12 (the KGB could have reported very late at night, but then Svetlana would not have been likely to overhear the conversation). And that means that the date of the actor's death must be corrected in all the encyclopedias and other reference books: he was killed on the 12th and not the 13th of January. There is an oblique but official confirmation for that: the date of death for Vladimir Golubov in the *Ballet Encyclopedic Dictionary* (Moscow, 1981, p. 153) is given as January 12. Yet they died together.

Anyone with even a remote connection to Moscow's Jewish circles was in on the secret: there had been no car accident, Mikhoels had been murdered. To keep people guessing, several rumors were spread. One was that Mikhoels had been attacked by muggers in the middle of the street, he fought them off, and he and Golubov were knocked down by a passing truck. There was a reason for this story: Mikhoels had been hit hard on the right temple, by a rock, the butt of a heavy revolver, or some other such object. In order to keep this piece of evidence hidden, as soon as Mikhoels's body arrived in Moscow (January 15), it was handed over to Professor Boris Zbarsky and remained in his custody for almost twenty-four hours. Zbarsky, who was a biochemist and not a pathologist, was head of a special laboratory that was charged with maintaining Lenin's mummy "at the proper level" in the mausoleum. No one had any intention of embalming Mikhoels, but Zbarsky was the best "makeup" man for the occasion. His laboratory was a subdepartment of the KGB, and that alone made the scientist a civilian employee of Lubyanka, and he knew how to keep his mouth shut. However, there was still the possibility of unwanted rumors flying around, and so desirable rumors were started by the KGB.*

IN THE BUSTLE OF the funeral, which required covering up tracks, the KGB made a big mistake. While Zbarsky was "working" (I cannot resist the quotation marks, even though, strictly speaking, the professor was indeed working), the artist Alexander Tyshler was allowed to see the body. He wanted to make a few sketches of Mikhoels on his deathbed. He is probably the only man aside from the "experts" to observe the naked body. Tyshler stated that "the body was clean, undamaged." But he made this statement not in 1948 but many years later, when not even the most naïve people believed the car accident story any longer.

On January 16, the funeral of Solomon Mikhoels was held, attracting huge crowds. The coffin lay on the stage of the Jewish Theater, and thousands of people passed to pay their respects. Among the mourners who came (to the house!) to express condolences to the family was the niece of Lazar Kaganovich, the daughter of Lazar's brother, Mikhail, who had shot himself in 1941 to avoid arrest: Yulia Mikhailovna Kaganovich did not hide that she was there not only on her own behalf but on that of the still all-powerful Lazar Moiseyevich. "She led us to the bathroom," recalled Natalia Vovsi-Mikhoels, "the only room where we could have privacy, and said quietly, 'Uncle sends his re-

---

* Four years later the wave of arrests would reach Zbarsky.

gards . . . and he told me to tell you to never ask anyone about anything.' In fact, it was not so much a warning as an order."

One speaker after another, all prominent cultural figures, addressed the funeral crowd. Alexander Fadeyev also spoke. He called Mikhoels an artist "crowned by the greatest glory," a man of extraordinary spiritual purity who would be remembered for centuries to come. Did he know any of the truth about Mikhoels's death? Did he guess? Did he realize that unwittingly he had played a part in the tragedy, urging Mikhoels toward his death in Minsk? Yet if Mikhoels hadn't gone to Minsk, they would have found another city and another excuse, since Stalin had given the order. And yet, and yet . . .

Recently a transcript of the speeches given at the funeral was discovered. "Transcript of a funeral" is not a natural combination, but it does exist. Of course, there were no stenographers in the crowded hall. But every word that went into the microphones was taped and then the transcript was sent to people on a special list.* Thanks to that, we now have a valuable document. And what is its value besides historical?

Among the orators was Itzik Fefer, speaking on behalf of the Jewish Antifascist Committee. It is incredible that at the time none of the grief-stricken people there paid attention to a very odd passage in his oration, which apparently could not have meant anything to people who were not informed. Without any connection to the context of his speech, Fefer felt it necessary to give this information: "I remember his last days. . . . I was in Minsk when the accident happened. We parted almost on the eve, at six that evening." And—even more astonishingly—there is a cut in the transcript: the page is neatly cut by scissors and the end of the speech is glued onto the passage cited above.†

It is made to look as if right after "six that evening" Fefer said "Mikhoels is the symbol of his people." The unknown editor did this

---

* This procedure was not exclusive to Mikhoels's funeral, but was used for all official funeral services, right up to the most recent times. The late director of the Central House of Literature in Moscow, Boris Filippov, told me that every civil memorial service held at the Writers' Union, just like the services in the other guild houses, was recorded on tape. Once the microphone was out of order, and the director decided to go ahead with the service, since the acoustics in the Maly Hall were excellent. But the radio electrician would not allow him to do so. The director knew what functions the "radio electrician" fulfilled. The funeral started ninety minutes late—they waited for the microphone to be repaired.

† This is the only cut in the entire transcript. There are no other omissions, touchups, or corrections.

in two copies (the second and third), which are kept in the All-Russian Theater Society (VTO) and the Central State Archives of Literature and Arts (TsGALI). But the original copy is in the KGB secret files, and someday the full text of this unparalleled funeral oration will be found.

Unparalleled because it belongs to a different genre. It is the official version of Mikhoels's accidental death (". . . when the accident happened") and its intention is to present a sort of psychological alibi for Fefer (or rather, for the people whose will he obeyed): to explain why he was in Minsk and what he did there for several days. This shameless attempt to justify himself, so inappropriate in a farewell address, speaks for itself, and the fact that the speech, hastily written at Lubyanka, later had to be edited in the transcript is further evidence that the "justification" was clumsy and self-revealing.

But now, at least, we learn that Mikhoels was not mistaken and in fact did see Fefer hiding from him at breakfast in the hotel on January 11; that Mikhoels's daughter, Natalia Vovsi-Mikhoels, did not mix anything up when she reproduced her telephone conversation with her father; and that Mikhoels and Fefer had met face-to-face a few hours before the murder. It is obvious that this information in Fefer's speech corresponds to reality. They were seen or could have been seen together, and it was important that Fefer himself reveal that fact first to stop the possible rumors.

Where did they meet? What did they discuss? How did their meeting affect the course of the tragedy that took place several hours later? Clearly, the sentences cut from the transcript contained a lie that had to be removed, a lie that might be as valuable as the truth if we were able to read it now: it would make clear what cover story the KGB was trying to create and then quickly abandoned.

The killers had been in a hurry. Once Mikhoels had seen the play, he could leave: trains to Moscow departed from Minsk frequently. They must have had a backup plan (after all, Stalin wanted this), but it would have complicated things enormously. Even if Mikhoels were not to leave immediately, the killers would not have more than a day at their disposal—a day when things would have been more difficult, if only because Mikhoels was surrounded by colleagues and friends from morning until night. Fefer and Golubov, probably not knowing about each other's role, separately ensured the operation, prodding the victim toward his death.

We will never learn precisely what Mikhoels and Fefer talked about that evening. Even the report, which may still be in a secret file at the KGB, would hardly contain the whole truth. But there was a meeting and it was part of the overt plan. Fefer clearly had a reason for mentioning the time. The play started at seven. They had met an hour earlier, at the hotel. It seems to me that, logically, Fefer's job was to talk Mikhoels out of returning to Moscow right after that play and to stay in Minsk at least overnight. Why else should they have met, only raising suspicions in Mikhoels? But if the victim was doomed anyway, then why should the KGB worry about suspicions he might have had? With whom would Mikhoels have shared them? Golubov? His fate was to be the same as Mikhoels's.

"Fefer sat glumly in Father's armchair," as Natalia Vovsi-Mikhoels described his call on the bereaved family on January 19, "and did not look in our direction. We were expecting a detailed account of their last meeting in Minsk. But he said nothing. And the longer that depressing silence continued, the clearer it became that it would be useless to ask. . . . We never did get the courage to ask him why he had suddenly turned up in Minsk."

So suspicions had arisen right away, and as we know, were completely justified. Of course, even very observant people did not have a sense of the impact of the event, the scope of the tragedy to come, did not think that Mikhoels's murder was merely the first nightmarish act in a long drama that was being created in the mind of the Supreme Playwright. Professor Moisey Belenky (who was to spend five years in the camps), then director of the Jewish Theater school, said, "We did not think then of physical extermination. When we brought back Mikhoels's body from Minsk (I was one of the six who went there for it), Markish whispered to me, 'Hitler wants to destroy us physically, Stalin wants to do it spiritually.' Destroying spiritually meant shutting the theater, the school. But we never thought about physical extermination, despite the tragic experiences of our people."

In the meantime, the Lubyanka version was being developed and instilled in the minds of the people. It was "supported" by the autopsy. On January 13, Chief Coroner Prilutsky of the Belorussian

Ministry of Health and coroners Naumovich and Karelina signed a certificate stating that the deaths of Mikhoels and Golubov were "the result of being hit by a heavy truck," that "all the ribs of the deceased were broken, the tissues of the lungs were torn, Mikhoels had a broken back and Golubov-Potapov a broken pelvis." Their conclusion: "All these injuries occurred before death." Now, when we know that they were dead by the time they were thrown out onto the street, when we know the evidence of the artist Tyshler, who had seen Mikhoels's clean, undamaged body, the tendentious lies of the coroner's report are even more glaring. Was there in fact any autopsy at all? Had the coroners signed a certificate written by someone else? In any case, they participated—against their will, most likely—in a lie. The list of people involved in Operation Mikhoels and tied to the web of a criminal secret grows longer.

Nevertheless, at the end of the winter of 1948, that is, a month or two after Mikhoels's murder, rumors began to spread. The most scandalous: "to avenge the accident of their leader" (note the Lubyanka-ese), the actors of the Jewish Theater were digging a tunnel from Malaya Bronnaya Street (the location of the theater) to Red Square (about two kilometers on a straight line) so as to blow up the Kremlin. Another rumor from the same mill: Mikhoels had been planning to turn over Birobidzhan to Japan, and now the Jewish Antifascist Committee was going to complete his plan. No one cared whether the rumors had any grounding in reality at all. The center for creating and spreading rumors, active for decades in the KGB (and probably extant today in some reorganized form), acted in the spirit of Goebbels propaganda (whether consciously or not): the cruder and more absurd, the more likely it was to be believed.

Parallel to this—in Stalin's favorite style—measures were being developed to put an end to the nasty rumors about the alleged new campaign of state anti-Semitism. Two resolutions were promulgated in April: "On Stalin Prizes for outstanding works in literature and cinematography" and "On Stalin Prizes for outstanding works in the arts." Naturally, a prize was given without any commentary to the Minsk play about a Belorussian World War II partisan, *Konstantin Zaslonov*, a typical mediocre piece of socialist realism. Many hacks received prizes for their portraits: two of Lenin, four of Stalin, and of

Molotov, Voroshilov, Dzerzhinsky, and other "leaders of the revolution." But Comrade Stalin's wisdom lay in this: of the 190 laureates from "the multinational socialist homeland," over 40 were Jewish.

The list begins with Ilya Ehrenburg: he was given a Stalin Prize First Class for one of his most colorless and flat works, the war novel *Storm*. Curiously, Stalin rejected the committee's proposal to give Ehrenburg a Second Class prize and insisted on a First (many years later, in his posthumously published memoirs, Konstantin Simonov described the meeting with Stalin, at which he was present). Besides the prize to Ehrenburg, the highest prizes went not only to the talented writer Emmanuil Kazakevich, not only to the major filmmakers Grigori Kozintsev (Ehrenburg's brother-in-law) and Mikhail Romm, but to writers of below-average quality (for instance, the children's author Iosif Likstanov), even though Stalin had a wide range of choices and could have found people more worthy. But he wanted Jewish figures—the most dependable propaganda screen behind which he could prepare the most poisonous dishes.

The original story was being drummed into people's heads: Mikhoels was the victim of an accident and had been a great actor, a great director, and, most important, a great patriot. The Jewish Theater was named after him, and several large and grand memorial concerts were dedicated to him. The most impressive ones were at the theater—posters announcing them in five-inch-high letters were plastered all over the city. The importance of the role these evenings were to play becomes clear when we compare dates.

On May 14, 1948, the state of Israel was officially proclaimed. Betting on its leaders as a force that would oppose British interests and wanting to push Britain out of the region and take a strong position in the Near East, seemed reasonable to Moscow then. Therefore, a large-scale anti-Semitic campaign at that time would not have been appropriate, and the order to march was not given. But neither was retreat sounded.

The immediate recognition of Israel by the Soviet Union was accompanied by deliveries of arms to rebuff attacks from the Arab states, which spoke out against the newborn nation. Although the United States had apparently announced its recognition a few hours earlier, Soviet officials insisted that the USSR was the first to recognize Israel.

In politics and in diplomatic practice, being first has no significance. Dozens of states inevitably become second, third, and twenty-third, and this in no way diminishes their worth or makes their relations less secure with the country they recognize a day, a week, or even a month later. Then why did Stalin insist on having this "gold medal"? Even Andrei Vyshinsky, then Deputy Minister of Foreign Affairs, who was justly dubbed a prosecuting diplomat, speaking at a working conference on a new textbook on the theory of state and law, suddenly announced out of the blue: "We were the first, the first, to recognize the state of Israel." He knew that his audience—hundreds of lawyers—would spread the word around the country that he had said it and that he had spoken with rapture.

And it was on that wave of brief and unfounded euphoria that two evenings in memory of Solomon Mikhoels took place at the Jewish Theater. I was present at both. The first occurred just ten days after Israel's official birthday: on May 24, 1948. Major figures of Jewish and Russian culture took part. They all spoke of Mikhoels as a loyal and passionate Soviet patriot. That was the order given from above, and they all followed the pitch sounded by the tuning fork. Noteworthy was Ilya Ehrenburg's speech. He was a writer who was exceptionally sensitive to every turn, even the tiniest, in Stalinist and post-Stalinist policy: his words were often used by the authorities to state important positions to his fellow citizens and the world community.

And this time Ehrenburg said,

> Now, as we recall the work of the great Soviet tragedian Solomon Mikhoels, bombs and shells are exploding somewhere far away: it is the Jews of a young state defending their cities and villages from British mercenaries. Once again justice collides with greed. Human blood is shed over oil. I never believed in Zionism, but now it is not a question of ideas, we are talking about living people. . . . This topic naturally is of concern to everyone here. . . . What did Mikhoels talk about all his life? About the friendship between the Soviet people and the Jews of the world, real Jews, not turncoats who are loyal to the golden calf of America, not Jewish fascists, for there are such people, but Jewish workers.
>
> Let us speak of people of labor and valor.
>
> The response of Vyacheslav Mikhailovich Molotov to the request for

recognition of the new state of Israel filled the hearts of the defenders of Palestine with hope and joy. I am convinced that in the old quarter of Jerusalem, in the catacombs where they are fighting now, the image of Solomon Mikhailovich Mikhoels, a great Soviet citizen, a great artist, a great man, is inspiring people to greater exploits.

Let us skip the typical Soviet rhetoric and the inappropriate suggestion—at a memorial evening for a slain actor—to "speak of people of labor and valor," the only representative of whom he named was Vyacheslav Molotov. And even the persistent reminder of the heroic acts of the man who deigned to recognize Israel. The hidden agenda of Ehrenburg's speech, given to him from on high, is crystal-clear: Mikhoels was to be separated from "turncoats" and "Jewish fascists" and presented as a "real Jew" and "great Soviet citizen."

The text of the speech serves as documentary evidence of the version I heard in the 1980s from Vladimir Terebilov, who then was chairman of the Supreme Court of the USSR. In the forties and fifties Terebilov worked in management in the procurator's office and later in the central apparat. In the brief Khrushchev thaw, he had the opportunity to look into some secret files and hear the stories of his colleagues who were involved in one way or another in certain notorious cases.

According to Terebilov, the original plan had been to say that Mikhoels had been killed by Zionists because he refused to join their terrorist conspiracy and remained an honest Soviet patriot. He would have been canonized and his name as a "real Jew" would be used against "not real" ones—"fascists" and "turncoats." That would achieve two things. Stalin's "solution of the Jewish question" would preclude accusations of anti-Semitism, and the proof of that would be the shade of the murdered Mikhoels. Stalin had arranged not only his murder but a nasty mockery of his memory.

The smokescreen around the visit to the mythical "Sergeyev" would have served any version they would later use. If Mikhoels were a victim of the Zionists, then they were the ones who lured him to that nonexistent Sergeyev. If he himself were a Zionist, then he and Golubov were going to a secret meeting and wanted to get away from their Minsk colleagues.

Operation Mikhoels required following the usual ritual (investigation, autopsy, etc.). Lubyanka sent a group of operatives to Minsk under the direction of Inspector for Special Assignments Colonel Osipov. The group diligently searched for the truck that had hit Mikhoels and Golubov. Naturally, they did not find it, and left after asking Belorussian Minister of State Security Tsanava to continue looking for the fatal vehicle. He promised to do so, of course.

But "public opinion" wanted more concrete information, and Stalin was tending to the version that Mikhoels was a victim of the Zionists.

And it was to develop this version that Lev Sheinin, head of the criminal investigation department of the procurator's office of the USSR, was sent to Minsk two months after the murder. His name was well known in the Soviet Union, and he had the reputation of being a highly sophisticated detective from whom nothing could be hidden. He created that image himself, publishing his "Investigator's Notes" from time to time, in which he reported in a very casual and relaxed style on the discovery and capture of the perpetrators of some hideous crime. Since he was the hero of all his stories, he became famous as the Soviet Sherlock Holmes. Vyshinsky, who liked him very much, helped create that image by including him among those who "investigated" the cases of the main "counterrevolutionaries" (Zinoviev, Kamenev, et al.). As the author of many popular plays (cheap melodrama but often performed) and screenplays for crime films, he had many acquaintances in the arts, and that is why using Sheinin to "check the circumstances of the accident" gave the sudden investigation authenticity and reliability. Apparently around March 1948, Stalin, who frequently changed course boldly, dropping old schemes and creating new ones, came up with the idea of replacing the accident version with the version of the fiery patriot murdered by vile Zionists.

Of course, Sheinin, with his natural slyness, would have executed any assignment given him: no moral brakes were present. All he had to be told was what had happened and how it was supposed to look. But apparently no one informed him of what was needed, probably because there were no clear orders from Stalin. And that was because Stalin changed his mind several times a day. The situation kept changing: both in Palestine and in the Soviet Union, there were conspiracies afoot, terrorists and killers everywhere, and the paranoia of the people's Leader and Teacher was growing daily.

There are two contradictory theories about what Sheinin was doing in Minsk. The first belongs to the then-secretary of the Central Committee of the Belorussian Communist Party, Mikhail Iovchuk.*
Vladimir Pimenov, professor and literary critic, took down what Iovchuk said: "When Sheinin was here, I thought that he was in a hurry to close the case, to find any acceptable formula to explain how the truck hit them. In fact there was no investigation at all."

The second theory seems more likely—if for no other reason than that no one, least of all Sheinin, needed to go to Minsk to confirm that there had been an accident: that was the official story already, case closed. Vladimir Terebilov, who was well informed, told me that Sheinin easily established that there had been no car accident at all and might have been planning his next edition of "Investigator's Notes" with the story of a sensational crime. But the active detective was hastily recalled to Moscow and told to keep quiet: Stalin had changed course yet again. Sheinin's story will be recounted later.

IN THE SPRING OF 1992, I discovered an important document in the secret archives of the Central Committee of the CPSU, which needs to be quoted almost in full to make sense. It is a letter from Lavrenti Beria to Georgi Malenkov, dated April 2, 1953. Malenkov was then the number-one man in the country, as head of the Malenkov-Beria-Molotov troika that ran the nation after Stalin's death, and Beria, accordingly, was number two: for a brief time he was back in his old office in Lubyanka, combining the Ministry of State Security and the Ministry of Internal Affairs into a powerful state mechanism that tried to seize power over the country (and might have succeeded if Beria had not been dealt with).

Here is the letter:

> *To the Presidium of the CC CPSU*
> *Comrade Malenkov, G.M.*
> *. . . In the course of checking the materials on Mikhoels we found that in February 1948* [an obvious error, it should read January] *in the city*

---

* Mikhail Iovchuk (1908–1990)—Party "philosopher," corresponding member of the Academy of Sciences, member of the Central Committee USSR.

of Minsk, the former deputy of the MGB USSR Ogoltsov and former
minister of the GB of the Belorussian SSR Tsanava† on the orders of the
Minister of State Security Abakumov performed an illegal action for the
physical liquidation of Mikhoels.*

*In connection with this Abakumov was interrogated at the MVD
USSR and explanations were received from Ogoltsov and Tsanava.
Abakumov testified about the circumstances of this criminal action: "As
far as I recall, in 1948 the head of the Soviet government J. V. Stalin
gave me an urgent assignment—to quickly organize the liquidation of
Mikhoels by workers of the MGB USSR, assigning it to special people.
It was known then that Mikhoels and his friend, whose name I do not
recall, had arrived in Minsk. When this was reported to Stalin, he
immediately gave orders that the liquidation be done in Minsk. . . .*

*When Mikhoels was liquidated and this was reported to Stalin, he
appreciated it highly and gave orders to award the men medals, which
was done.*

*(MGB USSR agent Golubov, V.I., who accompanied Mikhoels, was
also liquidated.)*

*There were several alternatives for getting rid of Mikhoels: a) car
accident; b) being run over by a truck on an unpopulated street; c) since
neither was foolproof, the following decision was made: to use an agent
to invite Mikhoels at night to visit friends, send a car to the hotel to pick
him up, bring him to the country house of Tsanava L.F., where he would
be liquidated, and then bring the body to a quiet street in the city, put
it on the road leading to the hotel, and run it over with a truck. . . .
This is what was done. To keep it a secret, Golubov, who had gone on
the visit with Mikhoels, was also killed. . . . (They were run over by a
truck at the country house.)*

The MVD deems it necessary to:

*a) arrest and bring to justice Deputy Minister of State Security
Ogoltsov S.I. and former Minister of State Security of the Belorussian
SSR Tsanava L.F.*

---

* Sergei Ivanovich Ogoltsov began his career in the NKVD in Leningrad and in 1946 was
made first deputy of the Commissar of State Security and a lieutenant general. He was shot
after Stalin's death.
† Lavrenti Fomich Tsanava joined the Cheka-GPU in 1921. A close colleague of Beria, he rose
to power when Beria replaced Yezhov as Commissar of Internal Affairs of the USSR. Beria
made him Commissar (later Minister) of State Security of Belorussia, at which post he
remained until September 1952. A lieutenant general, he was shot in 1953.

b) rescind the Decree of the Presidium of the Supreme Soviet USSR awarding orders to the participants in the killing of Mikhoels and Golubov.

2/4/1953   *L. Beria*

Let's start with the date. By April 2 Beria had prepared for the second of his series of planned actions that were meant to bring him unlimited power, based on the denunciation of Stalinism and the shunting aside (or, more likely, getting rid) of the Stalinist leadership. The first action took place on March 27, the promulgation on his initiative of the Decree on Mass Amnesty of Criminals, which (according to his plan) would recruit millions of people to his side. The second was planned for early April: the rehabilitation and release of the "killer doctors," of which more later.

The Politburo was scheduled to meet on April 3, and it was supposed to pass the appropriate resolution. The meeting took place, the resolution passed, and that same evening the doctors were released. The letter to Malenkov was part of Beria's plan to discredit Stalin and especially the MGB when Beria was ousted and Abakumov, whom he hated, was in charge. That monster had already been in prison for almost two years, and now Beria intended to finish him off. Naturally, a pro like Beria had no trouble getting the statement he wanted from his prisoner. But a close analysis of Abakumov's "explanation" gives no cause to doubt its veracity.

Everything that was known then and which became known later is in fact in agreement with the testimony of the chief of the killers. Now, thanks to that laconic and dispassionate confession, we know that the car that allegedly came from General Trofimenko took Mikhoels and Golubov to Tsanava's house, where they were killed. The only dubious element was the story about the truck driving over the bodies. This information contradicts the statement by the artist Tyshler, who had seen Mikhoels's body unmarked. But this detail is not essential. It could be that no vehicle ever touched the bodies, but the intentional spreading of this version was due to the fact that it was proposed by Stalin himself and therefore brooked no discussion. Another contradiction with what we already knew is more important. According to Abakumov, the orders to kill Mikhoels came from Stalin when Mikhoels was already in Minsk. That is doubtful. All the painstakingly gathered details (how Mikhoels was forced to go to Minsk, how his trip was covered) suggest that the decision had been made before the New Year and that Minsk was selected as the most convenient place for the killing. Arguments in support of this theory are Golubov's persuasions, his accompanying Mikhoels to Minsk, and his tragic end as Beria relates it (Golubov was liquidated as an agent accompanying the actor).

Lavrenti Tsanava was given the Order of Lenin on January 27, 1948, "for exemplary execution of a special assignment from the government." On April 7, 1953, that decree was repealed without any explanation. Therefore, those must be the respective dates for the decoration of the other men and for the rescinding of the orders which they had earned. But the names of the killers of Solomon Mikhoels are still kept a deep secret.

9

HOLOCAUST:
THE FINAL PAGE

A CLOSE READING of the documents reveals that the murder of Mikhoels slowed down the scenario. Orders from above were awaited, but they did not come. The magnificent funeral for Mikhoels did not fit the scheme in which he was immediately to be declared an American spy and Zionist agent. The version in which Mikhoels was to play the role of a victim of Zionism rather than its agent is obliquely but convincingly supported by the materials to which we have access. The interrogations of previously arrested "conspirators" in February–March 1948 do not have a single mention of counterrevolutionary behavior by the murdered actor. His name simply vanishes from the transcripts in any context—positive, negative, or neutral. But it does appear in other official documents. His name was given to the State Jewish Theater and the Jewish Theater Studio, and two impressive memorial evenings were held in Moscow.

The extinction of JAC and of Jewish Soviet culture was postponed for a while, but that does not mean the actions planned by Lubyanka had stopped. On January 28, 1948, Grigory Sorkin, head of the photo department of the Soviet Information Bureau, was arrested. He was charged with espionage, and the first "source of espionage information" was given as JAC and his own institution, the Sovinformburo. The shells were landing very close to Lozovsky now. After all, he was the head of Sovinformburo.

This is what Sorkin said in May 1954, having served only six years of his twenty-year sentence. "From January 24 to February 22, 1948, while in Lefortovo Prison, I was subjected to daily beatings with a rubber club, and the blows . . . were struck all over my body, but mostly in the buttocks, as a result of which bloody wounds formed which took over four months to heal." Six years later medical experts found "star-shaped scars," the result of "blows by a blunt object." What did his torturers want from Sorkin? He himself was of very little interest to them. They wanted him to confirm that "Lozovsky, Markish, and other JAC activists had sold out to the Americans and Zionists." Mikhoels was already dead and cremated—his name was not mentioned. But when it would be necessary to publicly proclaim him a traitor and spy, they would have the evidence. He could easily be among the "other JAC activists."

As I have said, there were certain circumstances that kept Stalin from making a decision, thereby prolonging the death throes of JAC— and of more than just JAC. Its fate automatically involved the fate of thousands, perhaps hundreds of thousands, and more.

Stalin's large gesture—a hasty and well-publicized recognition of the state of Israel—had two goals. I have already spoken of his desire to fill the vacuum created in Palestine by the withdrawal of the British. Many of the government leaders of the new state had come from Russia, the Ukraine, and Belorussia, from regions that had a connection with the Soviet empire. Not sentiment and nostalgia but sober calculation (the USSR still had several million potential citizens of Israel) should have prompted a similar response from Israeli officials to Stalin's demonstrative gesture. But the Israelis were cautious. They were much closer to the White House than to the Kremlin, and America was not very happy with the prospect of Stalin's influence extending to the Near East. Britain was quickly adjusting to the new political reality. No one was in a hurry to jump into Stalin's arms.

The second goal of Stalin's recognition was to neutralize the rumors about his changing course in nationality policy. The rumors were supported by facts. It was getting more difficult for people with certain data in their papers to find work and housing and to enter college. Now those rumors and concerns would lose their foundation. He felt that he had a psychological and political alibi for future events (arrests, exiles, propaganda campaigns).

On September 3, 1948, Israel's ambassador Golda Meir (the Soviet press reported the arrival of Golda Meyerson) arrived in Moscow with the first diplomatic mission. She soon visited a Moscow synagogue because it was the Jewish New Year. There were many people in attendance, and the crowd blocked the small street, where the synagogue stands to this day. There was a very warm reception for the Israeli ambassador. Later, as the story went through second-, third-, and fifth-hand retelling, the New Year's celebration in a quiet Moscow street became "a gigantic parade down Gorky Street, traffic stopped in midtown for several hours in honor of Golda Meir" (this was in a letter from Muscovite I. P. Poznyakova, in response to one of my newspaper articles).

Downtown had not been blocked off and there was nothing particular about the ceremony at all. So many people came to the Moscow synagogue for Passover that starting in the spring of 1945 traffic was stopped not in the "center" of Moscow but on the street where the synagogue was located. And at this time, on the recommendation of the World Council of Rabbis meeting in Jerusalem, Stalin permitted Moscow Jews to organize a memorial service for the six million Jewish victims of the Nazis. The tenor Mikhail Alexandrovich, now living in the West, who was a cantor in his youth and later an Honored Artist of the RSFSR and recipient of the Stalin Prize, was invited to chant the "El Molei Rakhamim" and other prayers. Major government figures, marshals and generals, and celebrated artists attended—over twenty thousand people, though the Moscow synagogue can accommodate a little over fifteen hundred. That evening they raised over half a million rubles for the postwar restoration of the country. The solemn Kaddish was repeated in 1946. In 1947 it was banned.

However, there was no ban on celebrating the major holidays, Passover and Yom Kippur. The arrival of the first Israeli ambassador permitted Abakumov, head of the MGB, to urge Stalin to make the decision the Lubyanka needed. After all, the "conspirators" were being held in the Inner Prison of the Lubyanka and Lefortovo, the cases were prepared; Stalin's indecision was tying the hands of the interrogators.

Stalin made a decision. The switch in the policy toward Israel was reflected in the publication of Ilya Ehrenburg's article "Response to a Letter," in *Pravda* on September 21, 1948. It was written as a reply to a letter from a certain Alexander R., "a German Jew from Munich."

There isn't the slightest doubt that the letter was a fabrication. Nor is there any doubt that Ehrenburg was executing a commission directly from Stalin. There had been a shift in policy on Israel and the world must be made aware of it.

"What is the attitude of the Soviet Union to the state of Israel?" asked the "author" of the letter. "Can we find in it the solution to the so-called Jewish question?" The hopelessly Soviet language (the "so-called" alone speaks volumes!) made the artifice of the publication all too obvious. Perhaps Ehrenburg was trying to tell the West that he was only doing his duty?

"The Soviet government was the first to recognize the new state," Ehrenburg reminds the reader. "It energetically protested against the aggressors, and when Israel's army was defending its lands from the Arab legions commanded by British officers, the sympathy of the Soviet people was on the side of the victims, not the side of the offenders." Stalin's voice is apparent in other passages as well, where the famed writer persistently writes of "attacks by British hirelings," "invasions of Anglo-Arab troops," and "Anglo-American capital."

But the aim of the publication was to answer the letter's second question. "The resolution of the 'Jewish question' depends on the victory of socialism over capitalism. All free Jews consider the Soviet land their homeland and they are proud that they are citizens of the country where there is no more exploitation of man by man. Citizens of a socialist society regard people in any bourgeois country, including the people of the state of Israel, as travelers who have not yet found their way out of the deep forest. Citizens of a socialist society could never be attracted to the fate of people carrying the yoke of capitalist exploitation."

The extraordinary clumsiness and primitive propaganda clichés have nothing in common with Ehrenburg's brilliant style. But Stalin needed his name on that article. His grandiose and nightmarish plans were forming and he needed Ehrenburg to remind the reader that it was Stalin who had said back in 1931 that "Anti-Semitism as an extreme form of racial chauvinism is the most dangerous vestige of cannibalism."

The article appeared exactly three weeks after Meir arrived in Moscow. The euphoria her visit had created in some circles had to be quashed. But the arrival per se could not have served as the reason for the sharp turn in policy, of course. Almost all memoirists of that period and, alas, even historians, attribute almost fateful significance to the meeting between Meir and Polina Zhemchuzhina, wife of Molotov. The encounter took place at a reception Molotov, as Minister of Foreign Affairs, had given for the diplomatic corps on the thirty-first anniversary of the October Revolution.

Zhemchuzhina was not merely Molotov's wife, but a person well-known in Party and government circles. She was not only the wife of the second-most important man in the government, but also a person with her own credentials. She had been People's Commissar of the Fish Industry, head of the state perfume trust (the TEZHE, famous in the thirties), and a member of the Party's Central Committee. But, most important, she had a been a close (and perhaps the only) friend of Nadezhda Allilueva, the last one to have seen her alive, and the person with whom Stalin's wife had shared her feelings literally minutes before her tragic end. This alone made her the target of Stalin's revenge. Zhemchuzhina was often "criticized" (that is, badgered) and dismissed from her posts, and in February 1941, at the Eighteenth Party Conference, was removed from the Central Committee for "failures in work." At that same conference Stalin fired Maxim Litvinov from the Central Committee and berated Mikhail Kaganovich so strongly that the latter put a bullet in his head a few weeks later.

Molotov manfully abstained from voting on the expulsion of his wife from the Central Committee, but two years earlier he had announced that "because of the loss of vigilance of Comrade Zhemchuzhina German spies made their way into the apparat she directed." That time—for the German spies—she got off with a stern reprimand. This time, in 1941, at the height of the passionate love between Moscow and Berlin, the spies could only be American or British. But as long as Molotov remained "the most faithful and closest comrade-in-arms of the great Stalin," her life was spared.

The real name of the Jewish girl who was born "beyond the Pale" and lived there until she was twenty-four was Perl Semyonovna Karpovskaya. "Pearl" in Russian is *zhemchuzhina* and that became her Party pseudonym and later her official surname. In 1918 she joined the Party (and used the pseudonym while carrying out Party assignments in the rear of White General Denikin's lines) and three years later came to Moscow from the Ukrainian city of Zaporozhe as a delegate to the International Women's Conference. She never went back, and moved to the Kremlin to live with Vyacheslav Molotov, who had fallen in love with her at first sight. That love, which continued throughout his life, did not keep him from betraying his wife "in the interests of the Party." Toward the end of his life, he confessed to Felix Chuev, "I had great luck in having her for my wife. She was beautiful and smart, and, most important—a real Bolshevik, a real Soviet person." So this is the most important thing in love. And it is clear that he believes it. "She suffered in the hard times," Molotov continued, "but she understood everything and not only did not blame Stalin, but also would not listen to anyone else criticize him."

In late 1991, among the other paper for recycling that flooded the "free" Soviet book market during perestroika, there appeared a book by Stuart Kahan, who presents himself as an American journalist and a nephew of Lazar Kaganovich. The book is called *The Wolf of the Kremlin*. A knowledgeable reader finds so many facts that have no relationship to reality on every page that great doubts arise about the rest. For instance, contrary to Kahan's statements, Polina Zhemchuzhina was not "a rather close friend" of Golda Meir, who describes their only meeting in Moscow in great detail in her memoirs.

In Meir's *Autobiography*, written many years later, she recounts how Zhemchuzhina came up to her at the reception and said that she was very glad to meet her. Zhemchuzhina did not fail to add that she spoke Yiddish,* expressed an interest in meeting the ambassador's daughters, and asked about kibbutzim in Israel. "We spoke for a rather long time," wrote Meir. "In parting, Polina Zhemchuzhina said, 'If things go well for you, then things will be good for Jews all over the world.' "

Did Polina ask permission of the Minister of Foreign Affairs for this conversation? Did she at least inform her husband after the fact? We don't know. What we do know is that every word of that conversation was immediately in the hands of the "organs." "After our conversation," Meir concluded, "Polina Molotova was arrested." After—yes.

---

* With foreign diplomats Zhemchuzhina attempted a strange mix of Yiddish and German, which she delicately called "the Austrian language."

But only because of that? It's possible that this was the last straw for Stalin. Upon reading the report, Stalin told his favorite, who was no longer that, "It is time for you to divorce your wife." Molotov immediately told his wife, "Polina, we have to get a divorce." As Chuev reports, Polina reacted in the style of Party etiquette, "If this is what the Party needs, we will divorce." She packed her things and moved in with her sister. There were no problems getting the divorce. This was late 1948. In February 1949, Zhemchuzhina was arrested.

The arrest was preceded by the humiliating procedure of "discussion of the personal case" at a meeting of the Politburo with the participation of "Party activists." Among the invited guests was Alexander Fadeyev, head of the Writers' Union. The writer Mark Kolosov quotes Fadeyev's first wife, Valeria Gerasimova, in his memoirs: "Zhemchuzhina was accused politically—hostile subversive work. And terrible filth was added to that. The scheme was that she was allegedly living with her secretary (a young man) who was an agent for a capitalist government, America, I think. Using her closeness to Molotov, Zhemchuzhina obtained and passed on state secrets to the enemies of our country."

This requires some explanation. Zhemchuzhina's secretary when she was running the textile industry in the Ministry of Light Industry USSR was not a man but a woman (Melnik-Sokolinskaya), who was arrested with her boss. Both categorically refused to admit their guilt in espionage, even though they could not deny the obvious fact that secret documents were missing. There is no doubt that the documents had been stolen by MGB agents. However, Stalin needed Zhemchuzhina to be accused not of losing vigilance but of selling out to the Zionists. This would be a blow not only against her but against "his closest comrade-in-arms." In order to break her, and clearly not without Stalin's approval, the MGB beat an admission out of two arrested ministry workers that they had participated in "group sex" with the elderly Bolshevik woman. Neither Party discipline nor deep humiliation paralyzed Zhemchuzhina or kept her from resisting the charges. So it is unlikely that adultery had been discussed during the examination of her personal case, which occurred before the arrest and investigation. The group-sex episode had not yet been fabricated.

Politburo member Molotov participated in the discussion of his wife's personal case, listened to all this insulting nonsense, and (since the Party required it) voted along with everyone else for her expulsion from the ranks. But eight years earlier, when Polina Zhemchuzhina was being expelled from the Central Committee, he had dared to abstain from the vote.

Now that it is possible to read the four-volume file of the Zhemchuzhina case, we can see that the action not only was directed against Molotov, or the JAC, but also was part of the general scenario of organized genocide of the Jewish people. Contrary to what Roy Medvedev writes in his book *All Stalin's Men*, Zhemchuzhina was never "one of the leaders of the Jewish Antifascist Committee," although they persisted in trying to pin that on her. She was reminded of the fact that in the mid-thirties she had traveled on business to the United States and that Roosevelt had received her. That formal meeting is among the charges and is presented like a dangerous criminal act. Even more pernicious is her "contact with her millionaire brother living in the USA." No one ever counted his millions but she did have an American brother. In the file he is called "Karp," but it is not clear if that was a family joke or if he had shortened his name, Karpovsky, when he emigrated.

The file has a copy of only one letter from Polina Zhemchuzhina to her American brother, dated October 5, 1946. Its counterrevolutionary content can be seen from such lines as: "We live very well. Restoration work is well under way in the country, there is extensive work on healing the wounds made by the fascist aggressors. The people are laboring selflessly and successfully fulfilling the new five-year plan." The dreary style of a small-town Party propagandist is not a criminal offense. And how did the letter ever get into the hands of the glorious Chekists?

Another, equally criminal letter was found during a search of Zhemchuzhina's files and added to her case as alleged evidence of her ties with JAC, or more precisely, her ties with Mikhoels personally. In the letter, dated April 18, 1945, Mikhoels asked for her help in getting the critic and essayist Abram Gurvich, stricken with partial paralysis, into the Kremlin Hospital, where the quality of care was high. This is obviously criminal. By involving Zhemchuzhina in saving the life of a Jewish critic, he was clearly counting on her efforts in saving the participants of a Zionist conspiracy.

Zhemchuzhina was charged with several nightmarish crimes. For instance, that she was present at a memorial service at the synagogue on March 14, 1945. Apparently, this was the service described earlier. The investigation materials mention that among the people at the synagogue that day were "academicians and generals" (unnamed) and the actors Mark Reizen, Solomon Khromchenko, and Leonid Utesov (Mikhail Alexandrovich mentions them in his memoirs too). Zhemchuzhina was among the guests of honor (and even took a place below and not in the balcony with the women). Her presence was never in doubt and was corroborated by many objective witnesses. But during the investigation she categorically denied even this obvious fact, without any explanation.

She was accused of "enjoying the nationalistic play *Freilekhs*, produced by the Jewish bourgeois nationalist Mikhoels at the Jewish Theater"—the very same play that had been awarded the Stalin Prize. She was also accused of coming to the funeral to bid farewell to Mikhoels and to express her condolences to the orphaned theater. And finally, it was a crime that Mikhoels allegedly (and probably actually) said to Fefer about her, "She is a good Jewish daughter." Fefer, it goes without saying, was the main witness against Polina Zhemchuzhina. But there were other accusers as well, including her closest relatives. And she never held it against them.

Zhemchuzhina was moved around several prisons—the Internal Lubyanka, Butyrka, and Lefortovo. She was at last placed in the Sukhanovo near Moscow (Beria's favorite), but in an investigator's office, which was more comfortable than the crowded, stinking prison cells. "Even we warders were not allowed to look through her peephole," said MGB Lieutenant P. V. Maltsev, who worked as a warder at the Sukhanovo Prison from 1939 until it was shut down in 1953. The situation of the disgraced Second Lady of the land was remarkably different from that of the others who shared her fate.

We will return to her "trial," but here I would like to mention that she did not hold her arrest against anyone, and she continued to idolize Stalin even after her ordeal. This is covered in detail in Felix Chuev's book, *One Hundred Forty Conversations with Molotov*, which I have quoted frequently. Ivan Standyuk, another writer with right-wing tendencies, handles this theme in his article, "Confessions of a Stalinist." "Every time we sat down at the dinner table, Molotov found the right moment to raise a toast to 'the great continuer of Lenin's cause.' We all would rise, and she would, too, Zhemchuzhina, touch glasses with us and then add a few words praising Stalin."

I have the unpublished manuscript written by the wife of a former Soviet diplomat. Galina Erofeyeva (mother of the Russian writer Viktor Erofeyev) met with Zhemchuzhina in the forties, the fifties, and the sixties. Erofeyeva writes that by the sixties "when mentioning Stalin, Zhemchuzhina spoke his name with reverence, 'Josif!' and called him 'a great man.' " Once, when the conversation turned to the tragic fate of a defector Soviet diplomat, Fedor Raskovnikov, who had written a famous open letter to Stalin, Erofeyeva heard something that "stunned me to the bottom of my soul. Polina . . . was standing against the balcony column, her arms behind her back. She tossed back her head and said to me, 'It's better to die in your socialist homeland than live in a capitalist country.' "

Zhemchuzhina was an iron Stalinist, but her fanaticism did not keep her from being a "good Jewish daughter."

Zhemchuzhina died on May 1, 1970, on the great proletarian holiday. She was buried in the "government" Novodevichy Cemetery to the music of the Soviet anthem, played by a military band. As the coffin was lowered into the grave, Molotov asked Bulganin, who was standing next to him, "Will they play that anthem at my funeral?" Bulganin nodded. "Certainly." But I do not think they did.

THE LUBYANKA HAD DEVELOPED a scenario that was primarily oriented to Stalin's growing paranoia. In 1947 Stalin had a mini-stroke, followed by several others over the next two years, which affected his speech and caused partial paralysis of his right hand. He often had powerful headaches, dizziness, and nausea caused by the spasms in his brain. This heightened his suspiciousness. He took on faith any information of a conspiracy against him, especially involving members of his entourage, because it merely confirmed his own convictions.

There was another point that ensured Stalin's support for this scenario. It touched on his sore spot—his wife's tragic death and his
relations with the Alliluev family and their friends. It was also incredibly simple, extremely accessible, and, most important, had a
certain logic, if you can call the ability to bring together "facts"
invented by a sick imagination logic. The success of the scenario lay in
its pathetic primitiveness. It was built on one main theme. In order to
get at the secrets of Comrade Stalin's personal life (what for?), they
used international Zionism and the Jewish wives of major Soviet figures or those Jews who had managed to hold on to their important
posts.

This seemed such a likely hypothesis that it was quickly accepted.
Bronislava Solomonovna Poskrebysheva, the wife of one of the people
closest to Stalin, his private secretary, Alexander Poskrebyshev, was
arrested. So was Esfir Khruleva (née Gorelik) the wife of Army General
Andrei Khrulev, who had commanded the rear in the war and played
a significant role in Russia's victory. They arrested Air Force Major
General Georgi Uger, deputy chairman of the Committee on Radar
Technology, headed by Malenkov. They took Revekka Levina, corre-
sponding member of the Academy of Sciences, a famous economist.
The list goes on.

Each one of them could have been charged with any sort of treachery
(giving the enemy military secrets or secrets of the Soviet economy),
especially the last two. But they were all accused of the same thing—
informing the Zionists, and through them the American intelligence
services, about the personal life of the unnamed head of the Soviet
government. It turned out that they all, if not directly then through
someone else, "had access" to members of the Alliluev family—General Uger, through circumstances that would take us too far afield,
lived in the same apartment as Yevgenia Allilueva; Isaak Goldshtein,
who had known Yevgenia Allilueva in Berlin in the twenties, worked
for Levina at the Institute of Economics; Khruleva met her when they
were evacuated during the war. And so on. They were all tied to the
same chain. And from Allilueva through Lidia Shatunovskaya it led to
Mikhoels. And from him to the entire JAC.

Only one "unworthy" wife (perhaps she was not the only one; after
all, there were no lists of them) was fortunate enough to escape the fate

that befell the others, even though she had "ties to world Zionism" through the members of JAC—Roza Peresypkina, wife of Marshal Ivan Peresypkin. It was at their country house on Nikolina Gora, among famous generals, that Peretz and Esther Markish spent New Year's Eve 1949.

What had begun as a Lubyanka campaign against a narrow circle of people who were delivering information on Stalin's personal life to America for some bizarre Zionist reason, followed its inexorable inner logic and sucked new people and new plots into its orbit. The time bombs placed at varying periods started to explode.

On December 25, 1945, Matvei Shkiryatov, who held an apparently modest post as deputy chairman of the Committee of Party Control but actually had wide inquisitorial powers, wrote to Malenkov:

> . . . at the present time JAC has no definite program. While supervision over its work was bad before, now no one is in charge of the Committee at all. The materials in Yiddish being sent abroad are not subject to thorough political editing. . . .
>
> The desire of the JAC to turn this organization into some Commissariat on Jewish Affairs is politically harmful and is a distortion of the goals that were defined at the creation of JAC. . . .
>
> Our profound conviction is that JAC cannot be left in the state in which it is now, and there is an urgent need to examine the question of its future work.
>
> If its future existence is going to be deemed necessary, then the circle of its activity must be determined, its leadership strengthened, with the selection of firm political leaders, or else the organization must be disbanded as having exhausted the tasks placed upon it in the years of the war.

We do not know whether Malenkov reported this suggestion of Shkiryatov's to Stalin, but it could not have been acted on either fully or partially without the leader's approval. There were no repercussions from this *cri de coeur*; even Mikhoels remained in his job—no "firm political leaders" were found to replace him. But the proposal in this memo remained on the agenda. And in less than a year's time, they returned to it.

On October 12, 1946, the recently appointed Minister of State Security, Viktor Abakumov (replacing Vsevolod Merkulov), signed a long memorandum addressed to the Central Committee and the Council of Ministers, that is, to Stalin, who was head of both. The memorandum was called "On Nationalistic Manifestations of Some Workers of the Jewish Antifascist Committee." In point of fact, it was not about "some workers" (Mikhoels, Markish, Kvitko, Shimeliovich, et al.), but about the committee as a whole. It was accused of forgetting "the class approach, which has been replaced by an approach on national principles"; and of "establishing foreign contacts on the same national principles." Also, in foreign editions about the life of Soviet Jews, it "exaggerated their contribution to the achievements of the Soviet Union in science, technology and culture." And finally, a special section of the memo, written in a particularly harsh, even hostile, tone, noted that the committee "has taken on the function of the chief representative on the affairs of the Jewish population and intermediary between that population and the Party-Soviet organs." The summary conclusion of the memo was that "the further activity of this committee is politically harmful and intolerable." In a clearly agreed-upon move, the minister was supported by one of the new members of the hierarchy of Party ideology, Mikhail Suslov. In his appeal to Stalin on November 26, 1946, he also called for the liquidation of the committee.

These memoranda are astonishing not in their conclusions (which are a priori and prompted by Stalin's change in policy) but in their arguments. It is truly difficult to invent a more ridiculous approach. What other basis for seeking foreign contacts could the committee use other than "national principles," on which it was created in the first place? The Antifascist Youth Committee sought contacts on age principles, the women's committee, on gender principles, and scientists, on professional principles, and the Antifascist Slavic Committee naturally sought unity with Slavs (the "national principles") and not with the Japanese or Brazilians. But who cared about elementary logic? The very presence of argumentation, however absurd, was merely a bow in the direction of traditional protocol, always observed in Party etiquette.

But Stalin was not prepared to shut down the committee in late

1946. The foreign policy situation was not right for it, the way Stalin saw it, nor had the proper psychological preparation inside the country been done. That is why—and I stress this again—we must not mix up the dates in analyzing events involving the committee; 1946 was not 1948 or even 1947—the situation changed with lightning speed.

Stalin refrained from disbanding JAC then, but silently took notice of the memoranda. This was a signal not only for the organization of numerous checks of the committee's activities, which created a pre-storm atmosphere, but also for collecting voluminous amounts of compromising material against it. Even if Mikhoels and his friends did not know (and they had to know) the efforts and speed with which Lubyanka was creating dossiers against every JAC member, at least the story of the stifling and then total ban of *The Black Book* should have served as a warning to them. The confessions beaten mercilessly out of Goldshtein and Grinberg were angled to fit the leader's conviction that there was a global Jewish conspiracy against him and were written with their main (if not only) reader in mind—Josif Stalin.

A curious fact that is interesting in its dreary and typical cynicism should be noted. Two days before the killing of Mikhoels, in which Fefer played a key role for the Lubyanka, Fefer himself figures in yet another memorandum from Abakumov, addressed to the Central Committee. He is named as one of the spies, wreckers, and terrorists "exposed" in their "clean-breasted confessional statements" by Goldshtein and Grinberg. Abakumov sent another memo to Stalin, Molotov, and Malenkov on March 1, 1948, which had "new data" on the JAC conspirators, and called the committee itself "a hotbed of Zionism." But it was still too soon. Abakumov's ministry was doing its usual business—arresting, torturing, and acquiring necessary statements. Stalin was taking a broader view. It was less than three months to the establishment of Israel, and the game around that event would force him to slow down any actions that would deprive him of room to maneuver.

But his hopes of gaining political space in the Near East through Soviet Jews in Israeli command positions burst quickly. Britain did lose its former positions in the region, but the vacuum was not to be filled by the Soviet Union. Israel was clearly drawn to the United States. In the cold war, American Jewish organizations, including many that had been pro-Soviet (in the very recent past), did not want to support the Kremlin. Stalin was frightened by the flood of letters that the Lubyanka comrades reported to him (probably with some exaggeration). Heroes of the war, awarded so many medals and ribbons, were pleading to be sent to Palestine to repel "Arab aggressors and British fascists." He was particularly incensed by the information from Abakumov and Suslov that some Jews were already collecting money to build a Jewish Soviet squadron, the Josif Stalin, for Israel. As we know, Soviet military specialists under false names and under top security were sent to the Near East to fight on the side of Israel, but that was the exclusive prerogative of the Kremlin, one of its most secret activities, and no one could be allowed to take over that function and do it covertly. Stalin saw in it a psychological readiness on the part of the volunteers to be under the jurisdiction of two states—the homeland of all the workers and the homeland of all the Jews—something that was categorically impossible in his mind, especially since they could set off a chain reaction. The mass expressions of sympathy for Israel addressed to Golda Meir in Moscow substantiated the reality of that threat.

And the words "contact with foreign organizations and citizens" angered Stalin. Such contact—a hint at freedom, albeit inner, spiritual freedom—meant an independence from the "organs," which controlled all acquaintances and ties. Stalin and the Lubyanka preferred an absence of contacts to controlled contacts. The great fighters for the happiness of humanity were constantly imagining the use of enciphered texts, secret codes, and passwords. For instance, George Kennan, then attaché of the United States (and future ambassador) gave Mikhoels a letter of thanks for the committee's condolences on the death of President Roosevelt. The White House letter made the rounds. It was sent for special study to the Lubyanka. The copy in the archives is marked, "Correct. Senior Operative 3 dir. 3 Main dir. MGB Major Titov."

Throughout 1948 the MGB flooded Stalin with reports and memos on the sinister activities of JAC, adding ever new "facts" to the already bulging files. Abakumov sent a particularly vicious report of March 26, 1948, to Stalin, Molotov, and Central Committee Secretaries Zhdanov (who would die under suspicious circumstances five months later) and Kuznetsov (who would be arrested within eighteen months and executed in the "Leningrad case"). The memo was called "On the Espionage and Nationalistic Activity of the Jewish Antifascist Committee." This was the first time the word "espionage" was used in regard to JAC. Abakumov maintained that Mikhoels was known "long before the war as an active nationalist, he was a kind of banner for nationalistic Jewish circles." Therefore he was informing Stalin that he had given a standing ovation, awards, and medals, and the prize in his own name to a nationalist and spy, who was known in that capacity for a long time to the "organs," and therefore to Stalin. The organs would not have hidden such important information from the leader.

It would be a great mistake to see this flood of memoranda as independent activity on the part of the Lubyanka. Stalin never gave such orders directly, crudely, or openly. But Abakumov's people had no doubt that they were fulfilling Stalin's instructions. His heightened interest in the entertaining reading provided by the memos was Stalin's support for their work. If he had frowned or moved a finger, their activity would have ceased instantly.

In late 1947, stunned by the ban on *The Black Book* and realizing what it meant, Mikhoels obtained a meeting with Kaganovich and Molotov (perhaps using Zhemchuzhina as an intermediary). This must be the meeting that Esther Markish thought was to discuss the fate of the Crimea, when in fact that plan had long been discarded. Mikhoels, Peretz Markish, and the others at the meeting tried to save *The Black Book*, but even more so the committee, and, even more important, all Soviet Jews from genocide. The meeting ended in nothing, but at least it took place. Now, at the end of 1948, any such meeting was unthinkable. Mikhoels could not be replaced. No one tried to undertake anything—they just abandoned themselves to their fate. No one can be blamed for that in hindsight. There was nothing to be done.

The long meditation of the Kremlin's leader culminated in a decision. In the minutes of meeting No. 66 of the Politburo of the Central Committee, November 20, 1948, No. 81 on the agenda (which means eighty items were discussed before this) says:

On the Jewish Antifascist Committee. Confirm the following resolution of the Bureau of the Council of Ministers of the USSR: "The Bureau of the

Council of Ministers of the USSR instructs the MGB USSR to disband the Jewish Antifascist Committee immediately, because, as the facts show, this Committee is the center of anti-Soviet propaganda and regularly provides anti-Soviet information to organs of foreign intelligence.

"In conjunction with this the publishing organs of the Committee are to be shut down and the Committee's files confiscated. For the time being, no one is to be arrested."

This text probably needs no commentary, but I will make a few brief remarks. The toying with formalities (the Politburo confirms the decision of some bureau of the Council of Ministers, which has never been found in the archives) should not be surprising, since the same man was head of both the Politburo and the Council of Ministers. The Politburo deciding on who is to be arrested when—without camouflage—is also nothing new. But the instructions to disband JAC given to the Ministry of State Security are curious. This must be the first document unearthed to date that authenticates the fact that JAC even formally was a structural subdivision of the Lubyanka. Before this we had assumed that the NKVD-NKGB-MGB had de facto but not de jure control over the ill-starred committee. Now everything falls into place.

There is a version (which comes from literary scholar and economist Efim Dolitsky, who spent seven years in the GULAG on charges of Zionism) that a few days before the final decision on liquidating the committee was made, Suslov called in its members and, after a few formal words of sympathy for the sacrifices endured by Jews during the war and the need to restore Jewish national culture, suggested that the committee initiate "the unification of representatives of that nation, scattered in various regions," in some empty area in order to create a "compact national majority." The Crimea was out of the question by then, so he could only have been speaking of the Far (very, very far) East. According to this story, Ilya Ehrenburg did not participate in this meeting and Solomon Lozovsky and Peretz Markish spoke up against it sharply. "I do not feel it possible," Lozovsky is supposed to have said, "to act in the role of preacher [of this idea], who can expect nothing but scorn."

Even more categorical was Peretz Markish's alleged response to Suslov's idea: "What am I supposed to say to my people? I am supposed to say '*lekh lekho*,' the archaic way to say 'Get lost'? Where, why, for what reason? Where to? Maybe I'm just supposed to give them the name of their station of destination? But when did I become a railroad stationmaster . . . who announces where the train is going? Why? What else can I say except to announce that these were my orders? I doubt this is what my people expect of me, but there is nothing else I could say. Will anyone find it convincing if I say I am going with them?? . . . I cannot strike my people in the back."

This version, and the even more unlikely text of the speeches supposedly spoken by the suicidal heroes, has no documentary substantiation nor any corroboration of anyone who heard anything from the people at this meeting. Yet the historian A. Vaisberg, who found the memoirs of Efim Dolitsky after his death in 1984, does not exclude the possibility that the meeting did take place and that Suslov, on Stalin's direct orders, was seeking to formulate the first, rough-draft version of plans to deport Soviet Jews to the Far East—a deportation that would have been effected by the Jews themselves, in the persons of their leaders, and in the name of their own good, to save the nation and develop its culture. If this meeting in fact occurred, then it's possible that by agreeing, the committee members could have saved their lives and changed the course of the scenario. But they did not agree.

Perhaps Lozovsky and Markish did not make such brave speeches. But Stalin could have sounded out the situation through Suslov before making up his mind. This passage from Markish's putative speech obliquely supports that—a strange reaction to the "well-meaning" project proposed by Suslov. "Now, before the wounds of the war are healed, the conditions in which the majority of the Jewish populace of the country finds itself, apparently, demands the preservation of the Jewish Antifascist Committee. . . . If all this did not exist, then the necessity for preserving the Jewish Antifascist Committee would be gone. It exists, even though the range of concerns with which the Committee deals has changed significantly." If they are talking about the creation of the Jewish Soviet Republic, albeit in the Far East, then why should Markish suddenly hurl himself on a spear in an attempt to save the committee? Perhaps the question under discussion really was the fate of JAC? Or did Markish simply understand the real reason for Suslov's treacly suggestion?

In any case, on November 20, 1948, the committee ceased to exist. "For the time being no one is to be arrested," Stalin instructed. But JAC member David Goldshtein had been arrested back in September. Stalin's moratorium was short-lived, ending in December. Mass arrests began. The first to be taken was Fefer—on December 24. A day or two earlier, he had come to the Jewish Theater with the Minister of State Security. They locked themselves in Mikhoels's office and went through the desks and files. Fefer translated the documents in Yiddish for the minister. After he had completed his work, Fefer was moved into the Internal Prison at Lubyanka.

The following evening was Veniamin Zuskin's turn. Taking over as administrator of the theater after Mikhoels's death, Zuskin suffered terrible stress. In the summer of 1948 the theater went on its first tour after the death of its founder and the last in its history, to Leningrad. They brought the incomparably cheerful *Freilekhs*, the tragic *Ghetto Uprising* by Peretz Markish, the everlasting *Wandering Stars* by Sholem Aleichem, and five other plays that were great hits. But Mikhoels's heir, the troupe's best actor, categorically refused to go to Leningrad. No one understood why—Zuskin was not capricious and had great discipline as an actor. Moisey Belenky, the director of the theater's school and now a professor of philosophy (who spent six years in the camps), recalls, "Before the theater left for its last tour, Zuskin invited me to his house several times, and tried to tell me something profoundly secret. But he couldn't say it, even though we were alone in his house on Tverskoi Boulevard. He was afraid. And he had good reason—he was under surveillance, and I had my own 'tail,' too. But we were not thinking about physical extermination then."

A few days after the theater left, Zuskin's close friend Dr. Boris Shimeliovich signed him into the Botkin Hospital, where he was chief surgeon. Zuskin was on a regimen of sleeping pills to reduce his stress. He was arrested at the hospital—sleepy, but conscious of what was happening to him. They wrapped him in a sheet and blanket and carried him out. Zuskin woke up in a prison cell.

In January there was an avalanche of arrests—several people daily, not only in Moscow, but in Kiev, Odessa, and Minsk. According to writer Alexander Borshchagovsky, 144 Jewish writers were arrested. One candidate for arrest, the Russian poet Mikhail Golodny (Epshtein), whose songs about the Red Army commander Shchors and the sailor Zheleznyak were enormously popular then, suffered the fate of Mikhoels. He was the victim of a hit-and-run in broad daylight in Moscow. He was buried on January 23. Kvitko, Bergelson, and Belenky came to pay their respects. They were arrested that night.

A few people were still free. On the anniversary of Mikhoels's death, Georgi Malenkov called in Lozovsky and in the presence of the chief Party executor, Matvei Shkiryatov, tried to get him to confess to criminal activities. Lozovsky denied the accusation, and then Malenkov and Shkiryatov composed a note to Stalin, "to remove S. A. Lozovsky from the Central Committee for politically unreliable ties and behavior unworthy of a member of the Central Committee." Stalin ordered his comrades-in-arms to be polled as to whether they agreed to Lozovsky's removal from the Central Committee and his expulsion from the Party (right away—why wait?). No one disagreed, and on January 18 the resolution was passed.

It is amazing that this experienced apparatchik, who had dwelt so long on the Party Olympus and knew the Kremlin's secrets so well, could be so naïve. Perhaps he considered his escape from the Great Terror a sign that his luck would hold forever. Almost all the members of his committee had been picked up, he had just been expelled from the Party, and all he could think about was his transportation problem. He appealed personally to Deputy Foreign Minister Vyshinsky on his stationery as deputy of the Supreme Soviet: "I find myself at a loss from the point of view of transportation—I will no longer have a Central Committee car. Could the Ministry of Foreign Affairs help me out in this, for my more than seven years of work, at least for the duration of 1949 or until I am offered other work?"

Lozovsky was quickly given another form of transportation and other work. They came for him on January 16. The next day, Peretz Markish was arrested. Mikhoels's name appeared in all the transcripts: "enemy of the people," "American spy," "Zionist agent."

A Politburo commission created by Mikhail Gorbachev and chaired by Alexander Yakovlev came to the conclusion in late 1988 that "the direct responsibility for the illegal repression of people arrested in the Jewish Antifascist Committee case was borne by G. M.

Malenkov, who was directly involved in the investigation and trial." In actual fact, Malenkov was appointed by Stalin to run the operation. He was zealous, cruel, and vile, but no more than the executor of a higher will. No one would have dared start an independent action of this sort—of such scope, with such people and such obvious international repercussions—under Stalin. Stalin himself preferred not to leave written evidence, and it is therefore unlikely that we will ever find his instructions to Malenkov.

By the same token, it was Stalin's order to disband the Jewish sections of the Writers' Union and to shut down all the Yiddish press, even though formally the initiative belonged to Alexander Fadeyev, general secretary of the Writers' Union of the USSR. This faithful servant of Stalin's sincerely subordinated his talent to unquestioning servility to the despot and killer, and brought a "proposal" to the Politburo for eliminating Jewish literature in the Soviet Union since it had turned into a hotbed of Zionism. And in protocol No. 67 of the Politburo meeting of February 8, 1949, there is this, "109. On disbanding associations of Jewish writers and closing almanacs in Yiddish. (J. Stalin) Resolved: accept the proposal of the board of the Writers' Union USSR (Comrade Fadeyev, A.A.)."

The fact that by this time a decision had been made at the top not only dealing with the fate of the committee or some trial or other, however large in scope, but also developing a plan for the Stalin solution to the Jewish question (a variation on the Hitler plan) is confirmed by the start of a violent propaganda campaign against "rootless cosmopolitanism," which attended the mass arrests. It was launched in *Pravda* with an editorial titled "On an Anti-Party Group of Theater Critics." It was published on February 2, 1949, just after the arrests of almost all the Jewish writers.

Why did Stalin decide to start with theater critics? The usual response along the lines of "And why toward the end of his life did he suddenly become a theoretical linguist?" merely shows that there is no explanation. But by sheer accident (I was looking for one document and came across another) I found in the archives of the Central Committee a denunciation that served as the detonator of a prepared explosion. The soil was tilled, but there was no seed. And then it appeared.

. . .

ON DECEMBER 10, 1948—three weeks after JAC was closed—a letter came to Stalin from a barely literate journalist who worked in the arts section of *Izvestia*. The author, Anna Begicheva, fifty years old, who says of herself that she is always fired "because of her squabbling and hard-to-live-with character," began her denunciation on a hysterical shriek: "Comrade Stalin! There are enemies at work in the arts. I am willing to answer with my life for these words." The enemies—"European-American agents"—were theater critics named by the snitch—"rivals" of that typical Soviet ignoramus with two college degrees. And they were all persons of a "certain" (or as they used to say then, "corresponding") nationality.

It was a fortunate prompting. This gave form to what was in the air. The letter is marked up. The recipient read it with a pencil in hand. And the reaction was swift. On January 24, 1949, the Central Committee passed a resolution to start a campaign against "rootless cosmopolitanism," and that formulation appears for the first time in Begicheva's denunciation. And all the names of the "cosmopolites" that she gave moved into newspaper articles inspired from above. If a critic wrote under a pseudonym, his real name was given in parentheses, so that no one could have any lingering doubt what the article was talking about. The first group of the plague-infested were the best theater critics of the times—Abram Gurvich, Iosif Yuzovsky, Alexander Borshchagovsky, Iogann Altman, Yakov Varshavsky, Efim Kholodov (Meerovich), and young Daniil Danin (Plotke) and Boris Runin (Rubinshtein). And as usual—previously, then, and later—to be able to deny indignantly any accusation of anti-Semitism, they included a Russian (Leonid Malugin) and an Armenian (Georgy Boyadzhiev).

This was a carefully thought-out and well-organized psychological treatment of the populace before the coming cataclysm planned by the crazed dictator. There isn't the slightest doubt that this was his work, and now there is direct proof. In the former Central Party Archives I found a personal report to Stalin from the ideology secretary of the Central Committee, Dmitrii Shepilov, dated February 4, 1949, "on the reaction of the Soviet public" to the newspaper campaign against the "rootless cosmopolites." Shepilov writes openly (nothing to hide from the leader) and assures him, "We will execute all your orders like Bolsheviks, Comrade Stalin." The orders were readily implemented by mediocrities and scribblers who rejoiced in the opportunity to get rid of their "persecutors" and were intoxicated by the vistas that were opening before them. One of them—the wretched prose writer Arkady Perventsev—shouted at the brilliant critic Iosif Yuzovsky when the latter tried to remind him of some of his articles praising Soviet literature, "Don't blaspheme, pygmy!"

Another—one of the most despicable literary executioners—Anatoly Sofronov, demanded that the rout of the "anti-patriots" be brought to its conclusion, "rooting out their final remains." He always had a moral alibi at the ready to preclude accusations of anti-Semitism—Sigizmund Kats, the composer, who wrote songs to his lyrics and was his "domestic Jew." "My dear friend Ziga," Sofronov would say, after destroying yet another "cosmopolite."

The list of people who were known in those years for destroying "cosmopolites" is full of people like Nikolai Gribachev, who nevertheless managed to do well and was puffed up with more awards and medals under Nikita Khrushchev, who overthrew Stalin's reputation, and "stagnation" Brezhnev, and perestroika Gorbachev. Mikhail Bubennov, a drunkard and pathological anti-Semite, distinguished himself even in that company. He took the pure Odessa accent of Russian writer Valentin Katayev for a Jewish one and he believed the rumors that Katayev and his brother, Yevgeny Petrov, another popular writer who died in the war, were both Jews hiding under pseudonyms. So Bubennov attacked Katayev's novel *For the Power of the Soviets* in an openly anti-Semitic way. The novel is a shameless piece of toadying but has nothing of Bubennov's *bête noire* about it.

Even before that, Bubennov wrote an article in *Komsomolskaya Pravda* entitled "Are Literary Pseudonyms Needed Now?" Calling for an end to the practice, he maintained that they were used to hide "people with antisocial views on literature who do not want people to know their real names. It is no secret that cosmopolites in literature are very eager to use pseudonyms."

The editor-in-chief of *Literaturnaya Gazeta*, Konstantin Simonov, dared to disagree sharply with Bubennov, calling his article "discourteous and brazen," "incorrect in essence and garish in form." The heavy artillery was then brought in. A new article against pseudonyms was written by Mikhail Sholokhov, a future Nobel laureate in literature. "Whom is Simonov defending?" the living legend demanded intimidatingly. "What is he defending? You can't tell right off the bat." In a new reply, Simonov said he "was prepared to learn much from many, including such a master of literature as Sholokhov. One thing I would not like to learn from Sholokhov—that crudeness, those strange attempts to stun another writer with which he writes on a private matter after five years of total silence when the most significant problems of literature were being discussed." Of course, Simonov was prevaricating. He knew the reason for this article. And he was so brave because he knew more than his opponents. Even more than Sholokhov.

Because once Stalin had unleashed a wild anti-Semitic campaign, he washed his hands of the whole thing and let it be known that he had nothing to do with it, that he was still the great internationalist he had always been. It is no accident that in the latest volume of his collected works (which turned out to be the last), Stalin permitted the publication for the first time of his answer to an American named Barnes, dated March 20, 1933, with the lines, "the USSR is one of the few states in the world where a display of national hatred is persecuted by law. There has never been nor can there be a case of someone in the USSR becoming an object of persecution because of his national origins." Signing "at your service," Stalin knew that his every line was read through a microscope and that this publication at the height of the anti-Semitic persecutions would create the necessary effect. It would mean that the persecutions were not Stalin's work. Rather, they were the hostile policy of local anti-Soviet types. And it was time to sound the alarm and alert Comrade Stalin to the actions of renegades from Marxism-Leninism. The specialists at the Lubyanka intercepted the alarms and took their own action.

The director of the campaign against rootless cosmopolites was the deputy head of the propaganda department of the Central Committee, Professor Fedor Golovenchenko, a primitive and petty man, totally uneducated, even though he was considered a Dostoevsky expert. As Mikhail Voslensky tells it, the professor once said at a Party meeting,

"Now we use the word 'cosmopolitanism.' And what is it when it occurs at home? How do we say it in simple worker's language? It means that all these Moishes and Abrahams want to take our jobs." Very pleased by this convincing and clear explanation, Stalin punished the commentator by throwing him out of the Central Committee and sending him back to his scholarly research.

But this did not seem to be enough for Stalin. He had to speak out directly on this acute issue which was agitating the whole world as it watched Moscow in horror. If Stalin were to make such a statement in the press, the local authorities would take it as a condemnation of anti-Semitism. But that was something Stalin did not want at all. Everyone had to know that he had nothing to do with the pogroms, but in a way that would not leave anything in print to be referred to later.

And for that he used a discussion of candidates for the Stalin Prize in the Kremlin, in a rather small circle, but perfectly adequate for the word to get out. Among the competitors was the Russian writer Orest Maltsev, who came from a peasant family in the Kursk region and whose real surname, Rovinsky, sounded very Jewish, which was what had prompted the crafty and servile Orest to select a pseudonym. The candidate list showed the author's real and literary names. And that gave Stalin a fortunate excuse to speak out on the major topic (I am using Konstantin Simonov's notes).

"Why Maltsev and then Rovinsky in parentheses? What is the matter? How long will this continue? Last year we talked about this and forbade nominations giving two surnames for the prize. Why is this being done? Why is a double surname written? . . . A man has the right to write under any pseudonym he picks for himself. But apparently, it makes someone happy to stress that this man has two names, to stress that he is a Jew. Why stress that? Why do that? Why create anti-Semitism? Who needs this?"

Who needs this? Put that way, there was only one answer. Anyone at all, but not Stalin. "That evening he played for us, the intelligentsia, whose conversations, doubts, and concerns he knew from his own sources," wrote Simonov, "a play on the theme—stop thief! and let us know that what we did not like was emanating from someone else, but certainly not from him."

There was a story told in those years about a journalist who, either seriously or jokingly, suggested that at every mention of Soviet leaders their real names be given in parentheses—Lenin (Ulyanov), Stalin (Dzhugashvili), Molotov (Skryabin), Kirov (Kostrikov). And he paid for his daring by expulsion from the Party and loss of his job. Whether this actually happened or was just one of the bitter jokes of the period, Stalin must have remembered his own pseudonym. While he was willing to be perceived by the millions of his countrymen and "workers of the world" as a tyrant, despot, and absolute ruler, he did not want to be a laughingstock. So he put a halt to the campaign against pseudonyms, once it had already done its work.

The rumors that "Stalin knows nothing about it" seemed to be spread capably, but there were no changes in the "personnel policy," the policy, that is, of firing Jews from every place possible. The heads of scientific and research institutes and the deans of departments received instructions from their supervisors in no uncertain terms—get rid of Jews who are on the job and do not hire any new ones. These instructions went to administrators who were Jewish. First they fired their Jewish subordinates, and then they were removed by their bosses.

I remember a curious episode that my mother told me around that time. A Moscow lawyer originally from Belorussia, Nikolai Borovik, whom everyone considered Jewish (which he was), had the foresight to appeal to the courts on the eve of his probable dismissal "to establish the fact." He gathered some documents and brought in witnesses from his hometown and asked the court to recognize him as a Belorussian by nationality. His plan was that an official court determination of his nationality should be a reliable shield against all possibilities.

The court heard the case with zeal, and Borovik thought there could be no doubt of its decision because all the "evidence" pointed to only one conclusion—Belorussian, and nothing but. The court's decision stunned him. It said that the court by law can establish only those facts that have juridical significance. Since in our great Soviet country, living happily under the sun of the Stalin constitution, all citizens were equal, regardless of nationality, since no benefits or disadvantages depended on nationality, and therefore the question of nationality had no juridical significance, the fact thus could not be established in the courts. The blatant demagogy of the decision combined with its formally flawless legal casuistry amused us, and we laughed at the judge's clever circumvention of the problem. (It would have cost him his hide three times over if he had found for the claimant.) Now I realize that there was nothing to laugh at. This Borovik was merely trying to save his life. Of course, denying one's roots, one's blood, was not the most worthy way. But who could throw the first stone?

After all, in trying to save himself, he was not endangering anyone else, he was not like the Judenrat who helped kill their own people in Hitler's concentration camps to stay alive. Many Soviet Jews acted differently. As his contemporaries tell it, the filmmaker Mark Donskoi shouted out at a public execution that another, no less celebrated filmmaker, the "cosmopolite Trauberg, is totally in sync with the fascist reactionary theoreticians of the West." The absolutely illiterate staff member of *Pravda* Alexander Magid, whom everyone avoided like the plague, wrote a denunciation addressed to Stalin (it was recently found in a Party archive) exposing "the journalists Gershberg, Brontman, Goldenberg, Ryklin, Izakov, and other Zionists who have crept into the central press organ of our beloved Party," and bragged that when people complained about the persecution of Jews he replied, "They are firing not Jews but scoundrels. They are arresting not Jews but spies." There is no information that Stalin himself read the denunciation, but it was seen by Malenkov and Suslov, Shkiryatov and Poskrebyshev. "Measures were taken." The accuser lived until 1987, happily exposing Zionists—and departed this world as a man who could not write a decent sentence, yet belonged to two professional unions, for writers and for journalists.

Stalin was against the Jews, but not ones like him.

STALIN'S HUGE BROOM WHICH was purging Zionists and American agents from all the cozy spots they had found for themselves had to take on the ministry that was using that broom against the people. It had happened before in the thirties, the model was developed, and there was nothing fundamentally new about it. Back in the thirties, during the Great Terror, which the country refers to by its code name, "Nineteen Thirty-seven," the search was for Trotskyites and counterrevolutionaries. Naturally there was an abundance of them in the Lubyanka, where thousands of executioners were purged, people who had worked faithfully and ruthlessly at weeding the Soviet garden until the very moment of their own arrests. Now Zionists and conspirators were the enemy—surely they would be found at the Lubyanka too?

The search had even greater potential because the ministry of Yagoda-Yezhov-Beria and their successors did not suffer from a lack of "persons of Jewish nationality." Nor had the campaign that began in the late thirties to fire Jews affected the Lubyanka. "Work ability" was more important than biographical data there, if by that we mean question five (all Soviet citizens had to fill in applications for work or study, and question five was "nationality"). Apparently Stalin did not care who was executing his most important and most responsible assignments as long as they were done well and on time. Perhaps now, in late 1948, he felt that the most fateful deeds were done—Trotsky was killed, the Lenin guard was destroyed, the war won, the "traitor nations" exiled, and General Vlasov, who had dared to raise the Russian Liberation Army against Stalin, was captured and hanged. What more was there to do? The rest could be accomplished by the new young people of good proletarian stock. The old workers could retire—along with the other Zionists.

We do not know just how Stalin phrased it, but the new task was clear—free the Lubyanka from the old cadres who had sold out to Zionists and imperialists. Some contemporary authors, who are not too well versed in the spiderlike, internecine struggles in the Kremlin of that period, tend to blame Beria, who was settling scores with his closest colleagues. But that is not so. On the contrary, the new wave of purges in the Lubyanka apparat struck Beria—obliquely, but still painfully. The victims were his best cadres, for whom he bore Party responsibility. Beria at that time was away from the Lubyanka, having been moved to atomic energy. His discreditation was part of Stalin's plan to put almost his entire entourage in the dock. Even after he took away Beria's Lubyanka troops and the whole apparatus of repression, Stalin still feared the vicious man in the pince-nez.

The two goals—reshuffling personnel for "national equilibrium" and purging Beria's former colleagues—were complementary. They could be done in one blow. It began with the firings.

In 1988, with the help of readers who responded to one of my newspaper articles, I found a veteran of the Lubyanka investigations hiding out in the city of Kaluga, not far from Moscow. Yakov Raitses, a fabricater and sadist, took part in the secret killings of major Soviet military leaders in October 1941 on Beria's orders.* He was also involved in the "young terrorist" case, whose victims included the budding screenwriters Yuli Dunsky and Valery Frid. My five-hour conversation with this monster deserves a separate publication. Here I present only the part that deals with our topic.

According to Raitses, he was called in by "the bosses" in 1948 and told "to get out of there" as fast as he could. "There is nothing for Jews in the organs anymore," a general told him. Raitses stubbornly refused to name him because he worried about revealing state secrets, as he put it. "But since you have worked well and we have no complaints against you, we will not toss you out on the street but quietly transfer you to police work in some provincial place like Kaluga. Keep on working and keep your mouth shut." Raitses says that several dozen workers were fired this way, but many remained and he envied them, cursing the general who had tricked him, since quite a few Jews for whom there "allegedly was nothing at Lubyanka" were still flourishing there. But in two or three years he saw just how lucky he had been and the "flourishing" ones had merely been given an extension for which they paid dearly.

Another Lubyanka monster, Boris Rodos, much more vicious than Raitses, had some luck too. This sadist, who did not get through four grades of school, became a colonel and even a "professor" at the Academy of Internal Affairs, where he taught a bizarre subject—the methods of working over prisoners inside their cells. The blood of Babel, Meyerhold, innocent academicians, generals, actors, and doctors is on his hands. He was also told to get out of there as fast as possible before "they start catching Jews like rabid dogs," as Bakumov put it. Rodos didn't bother to wait for a new job and just left. After Stalin's death and Beria's arrest the government sought him out to bring him to justice. He was found in a high post, head of anti-aircraft

---

* More on this in my book *Stalin's Prosecutor: The Life of Andrei Vyshinsky*, Grove Weidenfeld, New York, 1991, pp. 221–27.

defense for the department store in Simferopol. He had the honor of being personally heard at the Politburo, and Khrushchev, who described it in his secret speech at the Twentieth Party Congress, said Rodos was a man "with the brains of a chicken." Rodos was executed in April 1956.

The arrests in upper echelons of the Lubyanka began in 1951. The signal for the arrests was the fall of Minister Viktor Abakumov himself, arrested on July 12. The next day he was followed by one of the most vicious KGB executioners, Lev Shvartsman, deputy chief of the investigation department for most important affairs. This monster was involved in the falsification of many cases. He personally tortured Mikhail Koltsov, diplomats, major scientists, and cultural figures.

Stalin was given a report on the discovery of a major Zionist plot in the bowels of the MGB. His reaction was easy to predict—it untied the hands of the authors of the provocation but also served as instructions for the new minister, Semyon Ignatiev. Now he knew what to do and to whom. Among those arrested after that signal were MGB generals Leonid Raikhman and Naum Eitingon, the "genius of wet crimes," whose work record culminates in the murder of Trotsky, for which the head of the terrorist group received the Order of Lenin (and then the military order of Suvorov First Class).

From the long list of the Lubyanka's Zionists we will examine only the already familiar Lev Sheinin. Even though he was not in the secret police but in the procurator's office, he was considered a Lubyanka Zionist conspirator and listed as the link between the "Mikhoels-Shimeliovich band" and the "Shvartsman-Eitingon band." Apparently while investigating the "accident of the Jewish bourgeois nationalist Mikhoels," he actually was trying to confuse the investigation, on orders from the bourgeois nationalists and agents for American intelligence services, in order "to discredit the organs of state security."

Of course, Sheinin was doomed because he was mired too deep in the blood and slime of the Lubyanka. Here is an excerpt from Lev Shvartsman's own explanation offered to the investigation of 1954–1955, when the timid exposure of Stalinism's crimes began. For all its vagueness (the assumption was that Shvartsman's former colleagues, to whom this explanation was addressed, did not need any deciphering), his confession re-creates the atmosphere of those years and shows how inexorably the ring tightened around yesterday's omnipotent favorite of Beria and Vyshinsky.

> *We kept Sheinin out of active agent investigations, otherwise he would have certainly been burned because of his uncontrollable tongue and careless ties. A long chain of connections would have followed him, including ties in the organs. If Sheinin had been arrested, it would have meant great trouble for me. In conversations with him we often complained about the situation of Jews and the attitudes toward them. When the question of his arrest came up, I was upset and tried to prevent it.*

Shvartsman gave his "explanations" in the hiatuses between attempts to simulate madness. One day he would refuse the prison food, claiming that "the soup was made out of Aunt Tsilia," and then, hungry the next day, he would wolf it down and denounce his closest friends. His explanation seems to relate to events in late 1948 or early 1949. So the possibility of Sheinin's arrest had arisen even then, and Shvartsman, still riding high, tried to prevent it, worried not about Sheinin, but his own neck.

But what "careless ties" could the Soviet Sherlock Holmes have had? He was so successful in uncovering all kinds of conspiracies and had almost found Mikhoels's killers. It had to be connections with Jewish cultural figures who were suddenly turned into agents of international Zionism, and relationships with important figures in the "organs" who had been close to the top, had given Comrade Sheinin special assignments, and had then fallen into disfavor and became "contagious," infecting Sheinin too. It began with losing his job.

For two years the "number-one investigator of the land" was out of work. He was promised a post as director of a scientific research institute, but it fell through. They even barred his way to becoming an advocate. And yet the unemployed jurist managed to get the Stalin Prize in 1950 for the toadying and lying film *Meeting on the Elbe*. Stalin was still using his personal prize as a sidetracking maneuver.

And all the while Sheinin's dossier grew with new papers marked "Top Secret." Mikhail Maklyarsky, an arrested colleague (a Chekist and screenwriter), agreed to corroborate that Sheinin had allegedly confessed to him that he had sold himself to foreign intelligence services in Nuremberg (where he was assistant to the chief Soviet prosecutor at the war-crimes trials). On instructions, the obedient Maklyarsky, who remained a faithful Chekist even in the cells, stated that Sheinin "talked with a representative of the Jewish Telegraph Agency about organizing an independent Jewish state in Palestine and expressed the desire that many Jews living in the USSR would be able to move there." At that moment, such an accusation was deadly.

Sheinin was taken from a train as it approached Moscow and arrested on October 20, 1951. He was returning from a vacation on the Black Sea. The formal basis for the arrest was, according to the case file,

> *statements by detainees Fefer I.S., Shimeliovich B.A., Markish P.D., Zuskin V.L. . . . about his nationalistic activity and criminal ties with Jewish nationalists; and also the statements of detainee Shvartsman. . . . Sheinin had close ties with Mikhoels, according to whom he was known to them as a Jewish nationalist.*
>
> *Shimeliovich called Sheinin an active Jewish nationalist and stated that Sheinin had expressed his dissatisfaction with the conditions of life in the USSR, had treacherous feelings, dragged nationalistic views into his literary works, and maintained close ties with Mikhoels and was familiar with the hostile work done under cover of the Jewish Antifascist Committee.*

We should by now have grown accustomed to the falsifications of the Lubyanka crew, but the levels they reached in the late forties and early fifties are amazing. They no longer even tried to give a semblance of truth to the charges or to present facts, however tendentiously selected and demogogically interpreted. Sheinin was not acquainted with Fefer, Markish, or Zuskin, and he knew Dr. Shimeliovich only as a patient who would have saved his "treacherous feelings" for a psychiatrist, which Shimeliovich was not. He could not have had "close ties with Mikhoels" because they belonged to different cultures, interests, and circles. Sheinin's literary works can be criticized for many things, but they certainly had no "nationalistic views." As for the "conditions of life in the USSR," which everyone knows, why would Lev Sheinin be in the least dissatisfied with them? He was among the pampered and flourishing.

But all these statements nevertheless could not have served as a basis or even an excuse for Sheinin's arrest because the decision for it was made prior to these statements, which were falsified to suit the case against him. Paradoxically, it was Abakumov who had Sheinin fired from the procurator's office and left unemployed for two years, yet Sheinin was arrested for complicity with Abakumov in his alleged villainy. (There is no doubt that Abakumov was a villain, but he was not guilty of the villainy of which he was accused. Similarly, Genrikh Yagoda was an executioner, but not a British spy.)

It is obvious that the goal was to get rid of this man who knew too much, privy in the most direct way to the Lubyanka's deeds. The executions continued, but were done by other hands. The former killers had to go. And they were removed, added to the conspiracies the ministry was investigating. If the Jewish card had not been in play, Sheinin would have been accused of something else. But the Jewish card was handy. He was guilty of the same thing as the rabbit in the story—the predator was hungry.

The KGB finally came up with a role for Sheinin. He was supposed to have headed a group of writer-spies who sold their homeland exclusively out of nationalistic considerations. As opposed to those arrested in the JAC case, the writers who wielded their pens under Sheinin wrote in Russian and their works were considered Russian literature. But nevertheless they "bore nationalistic notions" simply because they were Jewish. As usual, Ilya Ehrenburg, whom Sheinin did actually know well, was at the center of the investigation. Sheinin's statements say that Ehrenburg "complained about the wary attitude toward Jews in some local areas and about excesses in these questions." It's quite likely that Ehrenburg did say something to that effect, but the people putting together a major trial out of this paperwork attributed these statements to "assignments from foreign intelligence" and "intrigues of international Zionism."

It is interesting to see the role Sheinin gives to himself in these conversations. "I unfailingly told Ehrenburg that it's their own fault for many Jews and that the Central Committee would punish the people acting excessively and would restore order." Later he added to this self-defense, "The investigators focused on these statements and told me that either I signed the formulations of the investigators or I would be beaten. I signed this boilerplate, knowing that the facts given as their basis would not show cause for a crime and that this would be discovered by the first objective eye."

Sheinin was also supposed to admit that he was a nationalist and anti-Soviet person, involved in a conspiracy with nationalists and anti-Soviets like Vassily Grossman. On October 31, 1951, Sheinin signed this "confession." "We dramatists formed groups on a nationalist principle and supported one another mutually . . . working to forestall the future rise of Soviet literature and art by praising each other's flawed works." The formulas were the same ones that appeared daily in the newspapers then—the battle against "rootless cosmopolites" in literature, theater, and film was in full swing.

The KGB put together a team of Jewish spies, destroyers of Soviet literature, for the defendants' table. Besides Sheinin, there were Ilya Ehrenburg and Vassily Grossman and other writers, primarily playwrights—the talented Alexander Kron, the mediocre Tur brothers (Leonid Tubelsky and Petr Ryzhey) and many more. Two are alive and well today. Iosif Prut is in his nineties and Alexander Shtein is over eighty. The Sheinin file shows that parallel to the Jewish Antifascist Committee case they were preparing for yet another trial—of nationalist writers. It is hard to compare them in terms of publicity and sensationalism, but the second trial could have made just as much of a splash. All the planned defendants were well known then.

As I LEAFED THROUGH the files, I tried to discover some standard, some logic for the division of people, charged with the very same crimes, into two groups. Some were prepared for big trials and their "investigations" were dragged out for three years; others were sent directly to the Military Collegium or the Special Commission (the "Troika") for immediate sentencing or execution.

Lozovsky, Markish, Fefer, and others were still under investigation, awaiting trial and sentencing, while dozens were sent to camps or executed for having ties with them, known traitors and spies (as they were described in the documents). Naum Levin, the editor at JAC, was sentenced to execution by firing squad on November 22, 1950, as "one of the active participants in the Jewish nationalistic underground in the USSR. . . . Together with enemies of Soviet power Mikhoels, Fefer, and other conspirators, under cover of JAC, he did espionage and nationalistic work [whatever that is] against the Soviet state." Arrested on January 18, 1949, the writer Samuil Persov was shot on November 23, 1950 (the day after sentencing), "for ties with Lozovsky, Mikhoels, and Fefer." With the same formulation the poet and playwright Samuil Galkin received a mere ten years from a Troika on January 25, 1950. Another writer, Samuil Gordon (in the naïve hope of hiding from the storm, he got a job as an accountant in the Izmailovo Park of Culture and Rest named for Comrade Stalin, but he was found even there), got fifteen years in the camps on July 30, 1952, for "passing espionage information [on the rides at the park?] to Fefer and Bergelson." On the same day as Levin and Persov, the journalist Mariam Aizenshtadt (Zheleznova) was condemned to death "for criminal ties with Fefer, Kvitko, and Galkin," and two days later it happened to Aron Tokar, deputy chief of the Directorate for Awarding Military Ranks in the Ministry of the Armed Forces, "for ties with M. S. Aizenshtadt (Zheleznova), and through her with enemies of the people Fefer and Kvitko."

The trial of the men called enemies of the people on these charges took place a full two years later. But no one paid attention to these legal "formalities." According to Lidia Shatunovskaya, Colonel Vladimir Komarov told her openly during her interrogation, "Now you're a smart woman, but you don't understand the policy of our organs. You keep saying that you're only accused but not convicted. You must understand that this distinction does not exist for us. Everyone's guilty."

Shatunovskaya and her husband Tumerman were sentenced to twenty years in the camps. Yevgenia and Anna Allilueva* got ten and

---

* Anna Allilueva was arrested on January 30, 1948, and condemned by the summary court on May 29 of the same year, the same day as her sister, Yevgenia Allilueva. When there was less than a month left to her term, on December 27, 1952, the summary court doubled her sentence to ten years, without any explanation, "for spreading slanderous thoughts about the Head of the Soviet Government." Those three capital letters in an official "court" document speak for themselves. As for Yevgenia's daughter, Kira Pavlovna, she was also convicted on the same day and sentenced to five years of exile, which she spent in the Ivanovo Oblast. She had been accused of "providing information about the family's private life to persons working in the American embassy." All the Alliluevs were rehabilitated in 1954 with an astonishing phrase, "On instructions of the government Instance."

five years, respectively, and the "investigation of the JAC case" continued. It grew to gigantic proportions.

The JAC case consists of forty-two volumes of preliminary investigations, nine volumes of trial transcripts, and three volumes of additional checking. Formally it began with the arrest on December 28, 1947, of a committee staff member, Zakhar Grinberg, who was named by I. Goldshtein after vicious torture. In June 1953, when there was a sharp change in policy and the sadist Komarov, who was in charge of the investigation, ended up in prison himself, he wrote this statement in his own hand, "Abakumov announced that Goldshtein was interested in the personal life of the Head of the Soviet Government and of his family not on his own initiative and that foreign intelligence was behind it. We had no materials supporting that, nevertheless Goldshtein was interrogated in that direction. At first he did not admit this charge, but after he was beaten on Abakumov's orders, Goldshtein made a statement. . . . Abakumov announced that he could not hold on to Goldshtein's statement and had to report it to the Instance. . . . As a result of Goldshtein's unchecked statements, obtained as a result of beating him, Grinberg was arrested, and his statements served as the start of the well-known case of the Jewish Antifascist Committee."

Z. G. Grinberg first succumbed not to beatings but to flattering blackmail. Colonel Likhachev, Komarov's colleague, promised him immediate release for the statements they wanted. He received the statements quickly but did not keep his promise. The investigators stopped seeing Grinberg. He appealed to Likhachev in pleading but restrained letters. "Four months ago," he wrote to Likhachev on April 19, 1949, "you officially declared to me that my case was closed and that I would soon be released, but unfortunately that has not happened. I have been in prison for 16 months, and my strength is less and less." On December 22, 1949, before the promised release or sentencing, Grinberg died of a heart attack in the Internal Prison.

Another prisoner accused of ties with the unconvicted "spies" died before his sentencing—the literary critic Professor Isaak Nusikov. Four years earlier one of the leaders of the Writers' Union of the USSR, the poet Nikolai Tikhonov, had called the professor a "passportless vagabond" in a newspaper only because in his book on Alexander Pushkin, Nusikov dared to maintain "that the Russian national genius had predecessors in the West." On October 31, 1950, prison physicians certified Nusikov's death from "paralysis of the heart." The fact that it took place in Lefortovo makes one doubt the diagnosis. And in the archives I found the results of an autopsy (marked "Top Secret"). It is surprising that one took place; they were usually forbidden since they inevitably revealed the true cause of death. It states that Nusikov died "of swelling of the hard shell of the brain." In other words, the professor had been beaten on the head with a stick.

A close reading of the archival materials leads to the conclusion that no matter how falsified the documents within them, they still shed some light on the secrets of the Kremlin. The investigation of the JAC case was completed by late March 1950. (For instance, a precise fate is given for Solomon Lozovsky, defendant number one. His investigation ended on March 24.)

We have been examining the JAC case, or the case against its leaders, members, and all those who fell into the sphere of interest of the all-seeing Lubyanka, as a separate issue, outside its relation to what was going on inside the Kremlin. For each person in the case, that makes sense. But the leader had a broader and deeper view. All those petty and insignificant cases, as far as he was concerned, were part of a grand scheme that was ripening in his feverish brain.

There are contradictory, unconfirmed reports that someone else was to be added to the large case of "Jewish conspirators"—either with them or separately. The disgraced Maxim Litvinov, in his apartment in the House on the Embankment, was quietly fading away from boredom and depression. As his biographer, the recently deceased Zinovy Sheinis, contends, Litvinov had been removed from work at the Ministry of Foreign Affairs and pensioned off after a frank talk in the summer of 1946 with the left-wing American journalist Jessica Smith, who had created the American magazine *The Soviet Union Today* back in the thirties. Litvinov gave her a far-from-official point of view on Soviet-American relations.

But, naturally, that could have been just the excuse and not the reason for his final fall. Neither Litvinov nor Maisky was needed anymore. On the contrary, they were in the way.* And now the time had come to deal with them. Maisky would be arrested on February 19, 1953, two weeks before Stalin's death. Litvinov would die earlier, on December 31, 1951. According to Stalin's translator, the diplomat and historian Valentin Berezhkov, he was told by Anastas Mikoyan that Litvinov had not died a natural death, but was killed in a car accident. In other words, he was run over by a Lubyanka car not far from his dacha in Firsanovka, outside Moscow. Beria testified to this during his trial in December 1953.

But here, as in many recollections, the chronology is confused. Beria could have planned (and in fact did) such an accident in 1939, when Stalin decided against a trial as a way of dealing with Litvinov for political reasons, but did want him exterminated physically. Later, as we have discussed, he gave up that idea too, but only temporarily. In the late forties, the idea of "accidental" death was revived, even though Beria had nothing to do with its implementation. But as a deputy of Stalin's and with his people at Lubyanka, he knew about it (or could have known). It is most likely that they gave up the accident idea not because Litvinov had stopped going out to the dacha that had been a gift from Stalin (they could always have gotten him out into the street if necessary) but because he was close to dying a natural death after two heart attacks. That end could be hastened by a simple "medical" intervention, and that is the most likely story. No one came to Litvinov's funeral—not Maisky, an old friend, not Alexander Troyanovsky, the first Soviet ambassador to Washington. The funeral oration was given by Andrei Gromyko, whom Litvinov had hated. There was no obituary in *Pravda*, not even from "a group of comrades," only insulting "biographical information."

Stalin's pathological paranoia made him see conspiracies and intrigues everywhere. Things were clearly moving in the direction of new major political trials, with the first violin played by the now-disgraced Molotov. An innocent fact that came to Stalin's attention—

---

* According to Sheinis, when Litvinov paid a final call on FDR before leaving Washington forever (1943), he handed him a personal, confidential letter with the explanation, "Stalin has unfolded an anti-Semitic campaign in the country. This will lead to grave consequences." He allegedly handed a similar letter to Vice-President Henry Wallace. Yet the anti-Semitic campaign had not been unleashed in 1943. If these letters do exist, they should be available in American archives. Their publication would be of great historical interest.

that Molotov had once traveled in a private railroad car from New York to Washington—elicited a morbid reaction and strengthened his suspicions. Perhaps the Americans had done it to show how much they valued the emissary from Moscow, where, as they knew, leaders did not ride with the common folk on trains. Perhaps it was easier for them to bug the conversations of their guest and his entourage. But certainly it was not a sign that Molotov had sold himself to American intelligence. I doubt any secret service in the world would give away its agents so stupidly. But Stalin, when he heard about the train, turned it into a major issue. He queried Vyshinsky, who was at the UN, through top-secret cipher. When he got confirmation, he drew his conclusions.

In the defendant's box, along with Molotov, would sit Mikoyan and Voroshilov. Beria, no longer in charge of the MGB, was insecure. Abakumov, who knew this well, played on the leader's weak points. Now that they had activists of the scope of Lozovsky and the leaders of JAC, they did not need to part with them so quickly. The completed investigation (which had found them all guilty) was reopened. The reason: "additional materials received on the hostile activity of Lozovsky and other prisoners."

They had received nothing new. But they could "receive" anything they wanted. Anything that the Party, in the person of its leader and teacher, wanted.

ACCORDING TO MY CALCULATIONS, a minimum of thirty-eight to forty people directly took part in the investigation of the JAC case. But I am certain there were many more. I would like to name all of them, even though there is little practical significance to that, since their full names (or even initials) were not recorded in a single document, thereby making identification extremely difficult. However, I am listing them with their names when they are known to me: Senior Lieutenant Strugov; Captains Demin, Khrebtaty, Mikhail Zhirukhin, Marchukov, Merkulov, Oshkaderov, Rodin, and Smelov; Majors Burdin, Boris Kuzmin, Lisitsky, Metelenko, Progrebnoy, and Vassily Zaitsev; Lieutenant Colonels Artemov, Alexei Gerasimov, Pavel Grishaev, Kazhdan, Konyakhin, Kuzmishin, Ivan Lebedev, Makarov,

Nosov, Putintsev, Anatoly Rassypninsky, Shishkov, Shvets, Smolyakov, and Evgeny Tsvetaev; Colonels Kholin, Vladimir Komarov, Mikhail Likhachev, Alexander Romanov, Mikhail Rumin, and Georgy Sorokin; Major Generals Leonov and Evgeny Pitovranov; and also the chief of the secretariat of the Summary Court of the MVD USSR Ivanov and officer Zhigalov, whose rank I could not learn. I repeat, there were many more, but I have listed all the names that are in the archives to which I have had access.

The investigative team was headed by Lieutenant Colonel Pavel Ivanovich Grishaev, chief of the investigation section for important cases. He was the youngest in the group at age thirty. He reached the heights of his career in a single bound.

Investigator Grishaev combined his work with correspondence study in law school. He reportedly managed to take notes on scholarly monographs and even write his papers during the long hours of interrogations, thereby giving his exhausted prisoners a rest. His work went even faster when his subordinates "employed illegal methods of conducting an investigation on the prisoners" (as the official euphemism has it), and he sat in the same room and wrote his legal tracts.

After Stalin's death, when he was exposed, Grishaev nevertheless managed the move from the Lubyanka cellars to the law institute where he had studied. He became a professor and received the title of Honored Worker of Scholarship, very rare among jurists. Of his numerous books, I find one particularly touching: *Repression in the Countries of Capital*. Never did he mention anywhere the fact that there was so much blood on his hands.

Until I exposed his secret on the pages of *Literaturnaya Gazeta*, he went on teaching law to his students and enjoyed a reputation for honorable scholarship. All my attempts to elicit information from him on the secrets of the JAC investigation or any other case were in vain. "I remember nothing," was his categorical answer to every question. Now retired, Grishaev is alive and well.

BUT WHAT HAD SLOWED down the reprisals against Lozovsky's "group"? Why was the major case planned for the middle of 1950 postponed for twenty-four months and done very quietly? It was terrible and tragic but not public.

There were many reasons. I will dwell on three.

First, the attention of the Lubyanka and, most important, of Stalin shifted completely to the "Leningrad case," which was bigger in scope and frightened the Boss much more. Between July and September 1949 almost all the Leningrad Party, administrative, and management leaders were arrested and accused of a conspiracy against Stalin. Central Committee Secretary Alexei Kuznetsov (whom Stalin allegedly saw as his heir in the Party) and Politburo member Nikolai Voznesensky (who was supposed to succeed Stalin as head of state) were declared the leaders of the conspiracy. Georgi Malenkov, another pretender to the throne, started this case and blew it out of proportion with the support behind the scenes of Lavrenti Beria. This "Kremlin conspiracy" fixed Stalin's attention more than the Zionist plot to get the Crimea. They had dealt with the Alliluevs one by one, and JAC could wait its turn. The names of the investigators working on JAC also appear in the Leningrad case. They were moved to the more important business at hand.

After October 1950, when the second of the two main trials in the Leningrad case took place, the JAC case would resurface, but a scandalous intrigue at the pinnacle of the Lubyanka broke out, which once again shifted the leaders' attention away from the committee and also called for a hasty change in the scenario.

While the JAC case slowly metastasized in all directions, waiting for the investigators to focus on their work, an "active Jewish nationalist" came into the Lubyanka's orbit of interest through the denunciations of their informers. Professor Yakov Etinger of the Second Moscow Medical Institute was not involved with JAC and there was nothing in the denunciations but "anti-Soviet conversations" with a narrow circle of friends, and so he was not arrested right away. He was taken in November 1950. Abakumov interrogated him personally, but did not see any opportunity to turn this molehill into a mountain. Etinger had studied medicine in Berlin, so the investigators tried to turn him into a German spy. Usually they could invent and prove anything they wanted at the Lubyanka, but Etinger was stubborn, and Abakumov, who had failed to see the potential there, did not give his subordinates any special instructions. Traditionally the stubborn cases were sent to Lefortovo Prison to be worked over. Etinger ended up there. He soon died in Lefortovo of heart failure, that is, he was killed by his torturers.

This is a very ordinary story for the mores and practice of the Lubyanka. But a mid-level Chekist, Mikhail Rumin, senior investigator of important cases, used it craftily. He took a crazily bold step. In a personal letter to Stalin he challenged his omnipotent minister, asserting that Abakumov was helping terrorists who were planning to kill dear Josif Vissarionovich and his closest comrades-in-arms, and that this was the explanation behind the sudden death of Professor Etinger, who knew too much about the planned killings and was therefore liquidated by Abakumov, who feared exposure.

There are various theories on whether that letter was the act of a single madman who decided to risk everything. It is unlikely, but possible. More likely is the theory that there were forces behind Rumin who directed his hand, using his immense ego. By then the struggle for power in the Kremlin among those comrades-in-arms was at its peak. Beria, who hated Abakumov, had been removed from control of the MGB in 1946. His obsession with returning to that key post pushed him into making hasty, decisive moves. But this is an independent theme worthy of extended study and will lead us away from our topic. All we need to observe here is that events in the Kremlin and at the Lubyanka affected the course of investigation of the JAC case—if only because Abakumov had started the case and was suddenly a prisoner, a state criminal.

For reasons that have never been established, Rumin's letter bypassed all the usual barriers and found its way to Stalin's desk. This is very strange. Unless it was hand-delivered by someone with access to Stalin, it would have had to go through a filter such as Stalin's personal secretary, Alexander Poskrebyshev, who was a Chekist himself. Therefore, he must have been working on the side of Beria, despite the fact that he knew Stalin wanted to keep Beria away from the Lubyanka. In the end, Poskrebyshev was fired for his years of faithful service and punished. After Abakumov, those arrested included his deputies, Nikolai Selivanovsky and Yevgeny Pitovranov, and the main creators of the JAC case—Leonov, Komarov, Likhachev, and Shvartsman. The last was charged with the same crimes as the ones he had attributed to his "clients": nationalist Zionism, hostile activity, etc.—the full range.

It is very clear that there had to be changes made in the case against JAC. Rumin was now in charge of the investigation, a huge career jump for him. He became a general and was put in charge of the investigation department, and then moved into the office of Deputy Minister of State Security. The case shows the influence of his personal, and very vivid, creative presence.

Almost unnoticed, but quite symptomatic and vicious, was the arrest by Rumin of the pathologist Professor Boris Zbarsky, who was in charge of preserving Lenin's mummy. Since the mausoleum holding Lenin was part of the state security system, the scientist if for no other reason was part of the Lubyanka staff. Even though he dealt only with corpses, he was still accused of espionage and planning terrorist acts. The main reason for Zbarsky's arrest was his work on the head and mutilated face of Mikhoels before his body could be seen. He knew better than anyone what damaging evidence there had been before the body was cremated. Of course, "terrorist Zbarsky" could expect to be shot, but on December 30, 1953, months after the tyrant's death—and thanks to it—Zbarsky was released.

That was the second reason for the holdup in the JAC case. The third and perhaps most important reason flows from the second.

It became obvious that neither the business with the Crimea, nor the transfer of allegedly secret papers to unidentified Americans, nor even the gathering of information about the leader's personal life would impress the masses—not enough to cause popular wrath that would serve as the basis for the "final solution" of the Jewish question. These indictments had become standard and unimpressive in view of the emotional inflation in the country. They would not be enough.

The soil was prepared. All that was lacking was a simple, guaranteed plot that would stun the public consciousness and be a battle cry for patriots for an action that would make Kristallnacht in 1938 in Nazi Germany seem like child's play. Rumin found the plot—killer doctors. And this case became his life's work. A public case—not one behind closed doors. The JAC affair would be a prologue to the real case, the important one. The first act of a two-act bloody tragedy. Act One took place. Act Two did not. God's will intervened.

FIFTEEN PEOPLE WERE TURNED over to the court. The list was headed by Solomon Lozovsky. He was followed by writers Itzik Fefer, Lev Kvitko, Peretz Markish, David Bergelson, and David Gofshtein; Academician Lina Shtern, Dr. Boris Shimeliovich, actor Veniamin Zuskin, historian Iosif Yuzefovich, journalist Leon Talmi, and JAC editors and translators Ilya Vatenberg, Chaika Vatenberg-Ostrovskaya, and Emilia Teumin. The fifteenth defendant, Deputy Minister of State Control of the RSFSR Solomon Bregman, was gravely ill and died a natural death, if a death in a prison cell after torture and humiliations can be termed natural.

Lina Shtern may seem a bit incongruous in this list. Born in Latvia, she graduated from Geneva University in 1903 and stayed on as an instructor and later a professor of chemical physiology. Revolutionary romanticism captivated her. In 1925, at the age of forty-seven, she moved to the Soviet Union to work for the good of the great country of socialism, and she considered the date of her arrival her greatest personal holiday. In 1938 she joined the Party and less than a year later was made an academician. A short while later she became a "double academician," with her election to the Academy of Medical Sciences.

Stalin gave Shtern her own institute with a large staff, and in 1943 awarded her his prize. Her brother lived in the United States—he used to send her streptomycin, which she needed for her experiments, even though in those days it was considered a strategic material and its distribution was within the competence of higher authorities. Two powerful anti-Semites disliked her very much—Shcherbakov and Malenkov, even though the latter pretended to have only good feelings for her. When Shtern, as head of an institute, was given orders at the start of the anti-Semitic campaign to "get rid of Jews," she called Malenkov and asked, "What am I supposed to do with myself?" Malenkov laughed and replied, "Don't be silly, Lina Solomonovna, I'll talk with Josif Vissarionovich, and we'll take care of it."

They did. Lina Shtern remained as director for a year, and then was arrested. And yet, Stalin decided to spare her—she was the only one. After his death she returned to Moscow from exile in Kazakhstan. She died in 1968 at the age of ninety.

Iosif Yuzefovich was a historian only because once he was fired from all his official posts he was given a job as a junior researcher at the Academic Institute of History. In fact, he had been a Bolshevik since 1917 and was known as a major union activist, who was head of various industrial unions over the years. But, most important, he was Lozovsky's right hand as secretary of the Profintern. Lozovsky—to Yuzefovich's misfortune—brought Yuzefovich with him to JAC. But Yuzefovich had another job as well. To save his own life at the height of the Great Terror, he allowed himself to be recruited by the Lubyanka and was its agent at JAC, keeping an eye on Fefer, just as Fefer kept an eye on him.

The case was heard by the military collegium of the Supreme Court of the USSR, chaired by Justice Lieutenant General Cheptsov. With him were two other military judges, Major Generals Dmitriev and Zaryanov. There were neither prosecutors nor defense attorneys. Stalin's law of December 1, 1934, was still in force. The sessions took place primarily at the Lubyanka—at the Dzerzhinsky Club, in the presence of investigators and other employees of the organs. The trial lasted from May 8 until July 18, 1952, even though the sentences indicate, for mysterious reasons, that the trial was only one week long, July 11–18. Why was it necessary to lie so blatantly in top-secret documents?

I will not describe the trial or what went on backstage. Instead I will cite in full (without any changes or corrections of errors) a letter from General Cheptsov to Marshal Zhukov, Minister of Defense of the USSR, written for an investigation of the Party responsibility of those found guilty of falsifications (which is why the letter is addressed to Zhukov in his Party position, rather than his government one).

TO COMRADE ZHUKOV, G.K.,

   MEMBER OF THE PRESIDIUM OF THE CENTRAL COMMITTEE OF THE COMMU-NIST PARTY OF THE SOVIET UNION

   At your request I am reporting on the circumstances of the investigation and judicial consideration of the case against Lozovsky S.A. and others.

At the outset I would like to point out that because of time limitations imposed on me, I cannot fully illuminate all the facts, but I will relate the issue truthfully and objectively.

In late March 1952 or early April I was called in by former MGB Minister S.D. Ignatiev, who in the presence of his former deputy Rumin (convicted in 1954 for falsifying criminal cases) told me that he and Rumin were going to report on the Lozovsky case at the Politburo of the Central Committee CPSU. The latter had previously decided to turn over to the courts for anti-Soviet activity Lozovsky and by the same decision to propose sentencing defendants Lozovsky, Fefer, Yuzefovich, Shimeliovich, Kvitko, Gofshtein, Markish, Bergelson, Vatenberg, Vatenberg-Ostrovskaya, Zuskin, Talmi, and Teumin to be shot, and defendant Lina Shtern to three years of exile to a distant part in the USSR.

It must be noted here that as it is now known, it was common practice, starting in 1935, for the directors of the NKVD USSR, later the MGB, to report on particularly important political crimes to Comrade Stalin or to the Politburo of the Central Committee, where the questions of guilt and punishment of the prisoners were decided preliminarily.

And the judicial employees who would be hearing these cases were not familiarized with the evidence until the directive organs had made their decisions and they were not invited to the discussion of these questions at the CC.

With this practice, the Military Collegium often carried out sentences that did not correspond with the materials obtained in the court. The judges did not bring their doubts to the attention of the CC, either out of fear or out of trust in the infallibility of Comrade Stalin's decisions, even though the judges could have seen in a number of cases that the information had not been reported objectively to the directive organs.

However, I must note here, that during my time as Chairman of the Military Collegium, from the beginning of 1949 through 1956 and in a number of cases, which were the subject of pretrial discussion in the directive organs, whenever I disagreed with the preliminary decision, I reported my point of view to the CC, which is what happened in the Lozovsky case, which I will relate below.

On instructions of the leadership of the Supreme Soviet USSR the case was heard in the court session under my chairmanship along with two other members of the court during a long period—from May 8 through July 18, 1952, i.e., over two months—and in the course of the trial we judges developed many doubts about the veracity of the charges made against Lozovsky and others.

At that time the Supreme Court of the USSR did not have its own building where trials could be held, and we were forced to hear this case in the club of the MGB USSR, where, as we later learned, former Deputy Minister of the MGB SSR Rumin not only did not help us examine the case objectively, but also interfered and frequently threatened me for my desire to examine the case thoroughly.

After a study of the materials of the investigation before the court sessions, I determined the following history of the origins of this case.

In 1946 employees of the CC CPSU apparat researched the activity of the Jewish Antifascist Committee. The note composed as a result of the examination asserted with detail and many facts cited that the committee's activities were sharply nationalistic in character and that it had gone far beyond the limits of its competence (propaganda of the struggle against fascism, propaganda of our economic and cultural achievements), and as a result it had become a center of attraction for Jewish nationalists. The note's conclusion was to disband JAC. In 1947 that note was sent by former Secretary CC CPSU Kuznetsov to former Minister MGB USSR Abakumov for examination.

In 1947 Lozovsky was dismissed from his job in Sovinformburo for manifestations of nationalism and malfeasance and then expelled from the Party by a decision of the CC CPSU.

In 1947 Abakumov arrested Goldshtein and Grinberg, who in numerous interrogations at the MGB USSR stated that under the leadership of the JAC presidium anti-Soviet, nationalistic and espionage activity was under way in the USSR. In September 1948 Gofshtein, a member of the JAC presidium, was arrested and in December 1948 JAC's executive secretary, Fefer, who both gave detailed statements in early interrogations on the anti-Soviet activities of the members of the JAC presidium, performed under the leadership of Lozovsky, who headed the committee's work since 1946.

In January 1949, Abakumov had Lozovsky and other persons convicted in this case arrested.

All the detainees, including Lozovsky, when interrogated admitted their guilt in nationalistic and espionage activity for the USA and that allegedly JAC was an underground center of nationalism and espionage. Toward the end of the preliminary investigation four of the prisoners—

*Bregman, Shimeliovich, Shtern, and Markish—recanted their state-
ments and denied their guilt. This circumstance was hidden by Rumin
from the directive organs.*

*In the investigation of this case, besides Abakumov and Rumin, who
was finishing up the investigation of the case and reporting it to the
Central Committee, there were 34 investigators (some of whom were
convicted). Several military procurators supervised the investigation and
participated in the interrogations of the prisoners.*

*Before the trial began, we, the judges, Rumin, and the procurators
were told that for a long period (six months) all the prisoners had been
in a prison supervised by the former Chairman of the Committee of Party
Control Shkiryatov and who also checked the indictment by personally
interrogating the prisoners (the case has transcripts of such interrogations
of Lozovsky and others). It must be noted that Lozovsky gave Shkiryatov
vivid details on his and the others' anti-Soviet activity.*

*All this—the results of the examination performed by the group from
the CC apparat, the facts of JAC's nationalistic activity, the confessions
of guilt during interrogation of almost all the prisoners, the statements of
many witnesses, the participation of military procurators in the investigation, former Chairman KPK Shkiryatov's checking of the case (whom
we trusted then), and finally the above-mentioned decision of the Politburo—created the impression before the trial that the case had been
examined objectively and that all the prisoners had been charged correctly.*

*And it must be added that a negative public opinion towards the
prisoners in this case had been created, as you know.*

*For objective support of the charges, Rumin had literary experts testify
that in their literary works the accused pushed nationalistic activity,
other experts confirmed that through the efforts of the defendants many
articles were sent to the USA with information that was a state secret.
The experts, members of the Party, were also major specialists in their
fields.*

*For greater conviction, Abakumov and Rumin had selected defendants
who had been besmirched before Soviet rule in the past.*

*Thus Kvitko, Gofshtein, Markish, Talmi, and Bergelson (writers)
had fled to Germany, the USA, and Palestine after the October Revolution and some of them returned only in 1930, defendants I. Vatenberg
(in the past a leader of the Poalei-Zion Party in Austria and the USA)*

and his wife, Ch. Vatenberg, came back to the USSR from the USA in 1938. The other defendants had come out of parties alien to us and had close family ties abroad.

As proof of Lozovsky's guilt we were given the information that he was twice, in 1914 and 1917, expelled on Lenin's insistence from the Party for anti-Party activity and that in 1918 and 1919 he was the organizer and leader of a party of social democratic internationalists.

These biographical data of all the defendants were confirmed at the trial and reflected reality, but nevertheless, by themselves, they could not be basic proof of guilt without other objective facts that substantiated their anti-Soviet activity in the period of their work in JAC in 1942–1946.

In the very first days of the trial the court had immediate doubts about the fullness and objectivity of the examination of the case.

When the court asked its first question—do they admit their guilt—5 of the 15 defendants denied it completely, saying that their statements during the investigation were incorrect and given under duress, under physical force from the investigators. The other defendants admitted their guilt either fully or partially.

While all the defendants admitted individual facts of the manifestation of nationalism in their literary works and in the activity of JAC, Fefer stubbornly for many days accused all the defendants of anti-Soviet activity, including Lozovsky, as the organizer and leader of this criminal organization. However under cross-examination Fefer began to give confused testimony that did not inspire trust.

After a long and thorough examination at the court of the case materials in order, I decided to have separate closed interrogations of the defendants, witnesses, and experts outside the walls of the MGB, in one of the rooms of the Military Collegium. This was necessary also because former Deputy Minister MGB USSR Rumin was interested in the outcome of the trial and interfered with an objective hearing. From the behavior of individual defendants one could conclude that the investigators were influencing them during the recesses. Rumin had bugging devices installed in the judges' chambers, and he and his assistants told us lies in response to our numerous questions about the investigation.

At a closed individual interrogation, a month after the trial had started, Fefer told the court that he had been a secret employee of the

MGB since 1944,* *that he had signed all the interrogation transcripts prepared by the investigators after his arrest and threats of beatings, and that he had been warned by an investigator before the trial that he had to corroborate his statements in court. Later in the trial he corroborated only separate facts of nationalistic manifestations in his own and the others' literary works and in their work at JAC.*

Yuzefovich gave analogous statements, having been a secret employee of the MGB since 1938.

The literary experts called into the court confirmed discrete facts of nationalistic manifestations in Jewish literature and JAC activities on the part of each of the defendants. These included propagandizing the exclusivity and isolation of the Jewish nation, the idea of a non-class unity of Jews of the world and the praise of biblical images and so on, raising the question of the creation of a Jewish Autonomous Republic in the Crimea, finding work for Jews, demanding special schools for Jews, discussing questions of the standard of living of Jews, discussing questions of aiding the state of Israel, and other questions going beyond the competence of JAC.

However, at the trial there was no proof of the existence of an underground nationalist-Jewish center, since all these nationalist manifestations were done legally and, I would say, with the connivance of the appropriate organs. But in turn this practice in the work of JAC was the result of the fact that nationalist elements did group themselves around the committee.

This supposition of the court was subsequently confirmed by the general procurator of the USSR when he examined the case in 1955.

Charges of espionage for the USA were also not sufficiently proven in the court, and in individual facts disproved. All the defendants denied these charges. The experts called into court on this point of the indictment sharply changed their previous conclusions under questioning and could not authenticate the secrecy of the information placed in various articles sent to Britain and the USA by JAC; could not explain what relation the defendants had to the authorship of those articles and their trans-

---

* On Cheptsov's initiative the Military Collegium checked and determined that this statement was true. Fefer ("Zorin") performed assignments from his masters not only until but also during the trial. He realized too late that they would deceive him and that the same fate awaited him that did the others on whom he had snitched. Fefer finally told the court the truth, but his fate was sealed.—A.V.

mission to the USA; did not offer proof that these articles actually were sent to the USA; admitted that they had overreached their competence by stating in their expertise that the defendants were involved in espionage; and, finally, two experts who signed the certification of expertise admitted that they had never seen each other before the trial.

When I asked Rumin and his assistant Grishaev to present evidence to us that the Americans Goldberg and Novik, who had been in Moscow for some time, were American spies, as the indictment contends, they declined to do so.

Yet Lozovsky and the other defendants were accused of passing espionage information to these Americans, and in particular Lozovsky was accused of giving Goldberg a paper on the colonial policies of Britain, compiled by Institute 205 of the Party, and allegedly containing secret information.

I inquired at the Party section and determined that Novik was at the time of the trial a member of the U.S. Communist Party and that Goldberg was a progressive activist in the USA, with positive feelings for the USSR. Witness Pukhlov—a Party employee—told the court that the paper was written by him, that it did not contain secret information, and that it was given to Lozovsky to give to Goldberg with the knowledge of the Party.

At the preliminary investigation Fefer maintained that when he and Mikhoels traveled in the USA in 1943, at the instigation of Lozovsky and JAC they entered into relationships with certain American capitalists, agreed with them on financial aid and support of nationalistic activity in the USSR, and handed them espionage information.

However, in court he denied this and stated that all their meetings in the USA with Americans had been controlled by employees of the USSR embassy and he named them, but none of them was questioned during the investigation.

This was all revealed toward the end of the trial. Clearly, it was impossible to pass sentence in this case with such unchecked and dubious materials.

In the course of the long trial I often went during recess to see former MGB Minister Ignatiev, whom I informed of what was happening in the trial, since I trusted him as a Party worker, as I now trust that he was and is an honest Party worker. I told him the case had been falsified by Rumin and his investigators and that Rumin was deceiving him. This made Rumin furious. It was only after Stalin's death that I learned from the explanations given by Ignatiev to the Party in the doctors' case that Rumin had the complete trust of Stalin, who at that time did not trust Ignatiev. This is only to explain that Ignatiev could not have supported me in the JAC case then or perhaps this was the result of his inexperience in the MGB.

Postponing the case in early July 1952, I appealed to former Procurator General Safonov with a request to go with me to the Party and report on the necessity of returning the case for further investigation. However, he refused, telling me, "You have instructions from the Politburo CC, so obey them!" I did not get support from former Chairman of the Supreme Court USSR Valin. Then I appealed by telephone to former Party Chairman Shkiryatov, who was in charge of the investigation of Lozovsky and others, but upon learning from me that I wanted to raise the question of sending the case back for more investigation, he informed me that he was convinced of the guilt of Lozovsky and the others, refused to see me, and recommended that I appeal to the Central Committee secretaries.

Like many people, I believed in him as the conscience of our Party and I could not imagine that he could be hypocritical.

After that I informed N. M. Shvernik, then chairman of the presidium of the Supreme Court USSR, and received counsel from him to appeal with this question to Malenkov. I called Malenkov and asked him to receive me and hear me out. Learning that I wanted to talk to him about sending the Lozovsky and other cases back for more investigation, he told me he would think about it and perhaps call me in.

Before the meeting with Malenkov I gave thorough information on the state of this case to former chief of the administrative section of the Central Committee, G. P. Gromov, who approved of my position on the case and also recommended that I approach Malenkov. At that period in time I was called in to see former Central Committee Secretary Ponomarenko for negotiations regarding my possible return to work in the Party apparat, where I had worked until I transferred to the procurator's office and then in late 1948 to the Military Collegium.

I informed Ponomarenko in detail about my doubts in the Lozovsky case, in the presence of Gromov and his deputy, Egorov, and got the same response from them—appeal to Malenkov.

A few days later I was called in to see Malenkov, who also asked Rumin and Ignatiev to see him.

I assumed that Malenkov would support me and agree with my conclusion about sending the case back for more investigation for a thorough check of all the indictment materials. However, that did not happen. He apparently believed scoundrels who pushed their way into the MGB, like Rumin, more than me. He listened to my conclusions, and then gave the floor to Rumin, who began accusing me of liberalism toward enemies of the people and said that I was intentionally dragging out the hearing for over two months and thereby orienting the defendants to deny their statements made in the investigation, accused me of slandering the organs of the MGB, and denied using physical means of influencing Lozovsky and others. I once again stated that Rumin was behaving illegally. However Malenkov, after asking me a few questions about the work of the Military Collegium, stated the following, almost literally: "What do you want to do, put us on our knees before those criminals, after all the sentence in this case has the approbation of the people, the Politburo of the CC took up this case three times, execute the decision of the Politburo." I was discouraged by this reply. After all, at the time we knew Malenkov as Comrade Stalin's closest aide, and we believed him and did not allow the possibility that he was an unworthy leader of the Party, as he appeared to us after the exposure of his factional activity. Then, having assumed that before seeing me he had spoken on this issue to Comrade Stalin, for which I have certain confirmation, I told Malenkov I would pass along his instruction to the judges, and that we, as members of the Party, had done our duty by reporting our doubts about the case to the Central Committee and will follow the instructions of the Politburo with the conviction that it has its own reasons in this case.

After the conversation with Malenkov, Rumin caught up with me and, cursing me with street language, threatened reprisals. As was determined by the investigation in the Rumin case, he began preparing materials against me in August and September of 1952.

Following Malenkov's instructions and sentencing Lozovsky and the others to the methods of punishment that we had been told to give, I denied Rumin's desire for immediate execution of the sentences and offered the prisoners the right to appeal for a pardon. I made the proviso that besides these appeals being heard in the presidium of the Supreme Soviet of the

USSR, in which all the defendants categorically denied their guilt, the question would be discussed yet one more time at the Politburo, since it was customary then for decisions of the presidium of the Supreme Soviet of the USSR on commutations of the death sentence to be confirmed by the Politburo. Besides which, I sent to Comrade Stalin Lozovsky's statement after sentencing, in which he fully denied his guilt. However, no instructions followed and the sentence was executed.

I feel that I took all possible measures in the legal resolution of this case, but at that time absolutely no one supported me and we judges, then, as Party members, were forced to submit to the categorical instructions of Malenkov.

Member of the CPSU since 1927, Party ticket No. 04521575
15.08.1957   *A. CHEPTSOV*

Little needs to be added to this document, which speaks for itself. I will note that among the so-called experts mentioned in Judge Cheptsov's note was the "honorary member of the Komsomol" young people's poet Alexander Bezymensky, popular since the 1920s, to whom Stalin had officially entrusted the announcement of the closing of the Jewish sections of the Writers' Union and of the Jewish literary almanacs. And he found "nationalism" in the works of his friends and colleagues. Another Judas was an employee of the Writers' Union apparat—the quiet and proper Semyon Evgenov, who was liked by all his comrades at work.

But who cares about the unknown Evgenov? During the trial, Stalin asked Alexander Fadeyev, head of the Writers' Union, to give written sanction for the execution of the most celebrated Jewish writers. In this case Fadeyev was not only general secretary of the Writers' Union but the creator of the image of the fearless Red commander Levinson, the Jewish hero of his novella *The Rout*, which was declared a classic of socialist realism and was studied in schools along with Pushkin's *Eugene Onegin* and Tolstoy's *War and Peace*. According to the Russian writer Arkady Lvov, now living in the USA, he personally heard from Konstantin Simonov that Fadeyev tried to split the shame with Simonov, but when the latter refused, had to sign alone. Simonov told him, "You put together the lists, Sasha, you sign them. I won't. *Basta!*"

The only one to withstand the suffering and the torture was Boris Shimeliovich. We do not have the right to blame anyone who could not endure torture, but we must give their due to those whose threshold of tolerance is very high. In his final word, Shimeliovich said, "I ask the court to appeal in the appropriate instances to ban physical punishment in prisons. . . . To teach workers of the MGB from thinking that the investigative part is the holy of holies. . . . On the basis of what I have said in the court I ask some people from the MGB, including Abakumov, to be brought to strict accountability." This request was honored, in fact, but not by the Military Collegium that tried Shimeliovich. It was just a short time before the tyrant's death and changes in the Kremlin. The victims of the most shameful anti-Semitic trial in history missed them by little over a half year.

The executions took place on August 12, 1952. The relatives, close and distant, of the defendants were arrested or exiled—they were not even informed of the trial or its results. Some were misled into delivering parcels for their arrested husbands long after they had been shot.

Fifteen years before his tragic death, Peretz Markish wrote in *Literaturnaya Gazeta* on February 1, 1937, about the trial of Pyatakov-Radek, "Not a drop of pity for the rabid wolf pack!" David Bergelson seconded him, calling the deposed Bolshevik leaders a "vile gang" that "stank unbearably." "Who knows," asked one of my readers, Genrikh Elbaum, in Montreal, "perhaps in demanding no pity for 'enemies of the people,' Markish and Bergelson were pronouncing their own death sentences?"

No, their death sentences were pronounced by others. But Elbaum is right about one thing. All of Stalin's slaves had "equal opportunities," but the executioner's bullets preferred those who sought the limelight, letting live those who had the courage to stay in the shadow, doomed to hide their talents under a bushel. Can this sacrifice be demanded of anyone, especially if by the rules of the tyrant's game, he must pay with his life for wanting to be someone?

The men executed in August 1952 were guilty of only one thing—of being born Jewish.

10

TOP SECRET

THAT WINTER OF 1952, I was a graduate student at the All-Union Institute of Juridical Sciences—the youngest of all my friends. Actually, I was a *corresponding* graduate student, which in this particular case is a fundamental difference. The institute was part of the Ministry of Justice and was in essence one of its departments. Working there (graduate school was considered being in the service of the ministry) endowed a person with the status of a Soviet bureaucrat who had gone through the filter of the personnel department, that is, the Lubyanka representative at the ministry. Corresponding graduate students did not have that status because the personnel people of the MVD were not interested in them.

But the personnel departments where they worked were supposed to be interested. A mandatory condition for acceptance in the corresponding graduate school was a certificate from your workplace and a "characterization," a long document about your reliability, signed by the administration and the Party representatives from your workplace. It is astonishing but true that the directors of my institute (abbreviated VIYuN) disregarded this rule. While it did not accept a single Jewish candidate into the graduate school, it accepted every Jewish candidate into the corresponding school, without demanding documents from them that would have protected the respectable institute from alien elements. Moreover, the "corresponding" students were not treated any differently at the institute except for one thing: they did not receive a monthly stipend. At the time that did not seem like a serious problem.

The institute was headed by a man whose name lawyers of that generation knew well. Ivan Golyakov first came to people's attention when he became a reserve judge at the first Moscow show trial (the Zinoviev-Kamenev case). He rose from an ordinary member of a military judicial collegium who had signed hundreds and perhaps thousands of death sentences by firing squad to chairman of the Supreme Court of the USSR, and then completed his upward trajectory as director of VIYuN. If I were writing a novel in which the protagonist was modeled on Golyakov, I would try to create a complex, contradictory man who combined focused ruthlessness and bloodthirstiness with gentleness, amiability, and a willingness to help. And also with erudition: Golyakov was a book lover, owner of a priceless collection, and author of historical literary works.

But all that falls beyond the confines of this book. This long digression is merely to explain how even on the crest of the murky anti-Semitic wave I ended up at the prestigious research and scholarly center where even then a good third of the professors were Jewish and how, because of my own stupidity, that wave almost engulfed me. The episode I am leading up to occurred in January 1953. It was the night of January 10.

Why do I remember the date? Before leaving on Christmas vacation (winter break, it was called then), the leader of the seminar on Marxist-Leninist dialectics, Professor Karl Troinikov, collected our papers to review them at leisure and discuss them when we returned to class.

My paper was on the Marxist-Leninist interpretation of nationality problems and, naturally, it was based on Stalin's "Marxism and the National Question," discussed at length in Chapter 1. A section of the paper dealt with anti-Semitism, and that social phenomenon was interpreted exclusively from the official Stalinist position that it was the worst form of cannibalism. In passing, the young author, showing off his erudition, mentioned in rather sketchy form the Dreyfus case, citing the little-known letter from Chekhov to his publisher and then friend, Alexei Suvorin, dated February 6, 1898: ". . . they've cooked up a mess of porridge on the soil of anti-Semitism, on soil that smells of the slaughterhouse. When something is wrong with us, we seek the causes outside us and soon find them: 'It's the Frenchman spoiling things, it's the Yids, it's Wilhelm . . .' Capital . . . Masons—they're specters, but they ease our anxiety! They are, of course, a bad sign. If the French are talking about Yids, that means . . . that a worm is digging away at them, that they need those specters in order to soothe their troubled consciences. . . . The first to raise the alarm had to be the best people, at the forefront of the nation—and that's what happened." This was Chekhov's response to Emile Zola's "J'accuse!"

A few minutes before the seminar on January 9, Troinikov ran into me in the hallway, grabbed me by the elbow, and pulled me into an empty room. "You've lost your mind!" he hissed, pulling my manuscript out of his briefcase. "Child! *Frondeur!* Are you a fool or a provocateur?"

Will today's reader believe me when I say that I did not understand—not a thing—of this almost hysterical reaction? What was wrong? How had I angered the professor? The paper was nothing more than a conscientious exposition of Stalin's dogmatic views and if it was flawed, it was by excessive compilation. But the professor, holding the paper fastidiously between thumb and finger, as if it were an eel, pushed it at me and went on hissing: "Hold on to it and show it to no one! Destroy it! Rewrite it! Pick a different subject! Madman!"

He flew out of the room and opened the seminar a few minutes later, red and sweating. He started by upbraiding me publicly: everyone had turned in their papers except for me! Violation . . . Failing grade . . . Unfortunately, one of the students came to my defense. He had personally seen me hand in my paper and personally heard me apologize for not having time to retype it. A scandal was brewing, made worse by the fact that I had confirmed the professor's criticism, trying to explain my "lateness." The vigilant student suspected something. He knew that it was not forgetfulness and absentmindedness on the professor's part, but something else. A conspiracy! "The paper was on national problems," he thundered.

"No!" I cried.

"What do you mean no?" My "helper" was choking on his anger. Troinikov clutched his chest. The seminar ended before it began.

The next morning Golyakov called me in. "Let's see this paper of yours," he said with feigned weariness. "Come on, come on . . . Troinikov filled me in." He leafed through the manuscript. "Well, where's the sedition?" He found it but he didn't read it. He told his secretary not to let anyone into his office—and lit a match. In about ten minutes the several pages of "sedition" had turned into a mound of ashes, filling the director's large ashtray. He shook it out the window and completed the scene with a brief instruction: "While Karl Iosifovich is out sick, you write a paper on a different topic. Unless you want to spoil your dissertation defense . . . or worse. And if you do, then we will not keep you."

That same evening my mother said, "You'll be better off getting sick tomorrow too." She didn't know what tomorrow would bring. "Stay out of their way: that's the best thing to do now."

I was "sick" until March 5. Stalin died on March 5.

PERHAPS I SHOULD not have interjected this tiny episode into this account of the tragic events that posed a real threat to millions of people and led to a bullet for hundreds and even thousands. But I would not like to regard the events of these years as a historian. Personal recollections of an eyewitness fill out a picture and give it added dimensions. After all, things did not happen only countrywide, they also took place on the micro-level, touching literally everyone who by virtue of his birth was doomed to be blacklisted.

This became quite obvious to me very quickly—on January 13, the fifth anniversary of Mikhoels's death. Stalin marked the occasion with the announcement of the arrest of the killer doctors, which went down in history under the headline in one of the newspapers: "Killers in White Coats." This was the official beginning of the final act of a drama created by the crazed imagination of the Kremlin playwright. The act was supposed to end with the realization of Hitler's unfinished dream—the final solution of the Jewish question. It would not be global, but limited to the territories in Stalin's power: the Soviet Union and Eastern Europe.

The act had begun a year earlier, in circumstances that were dark and still capable of supporting several versions.

Let us remember that killing unsuitable people through medicine had been part of Stalin's arsenal since at least the mid-twenties. The death on the operating table of Mikhail Frunze* (1925), sent under the knife on the decision of the solicitous Politburo, had become even then the subject of Boris Pilnyak's "Tale of an Unextinguished Moon." It elicited Stalin's fury, which would have been puzzling had the writer not hit his sore spot. After Frunze comes a long list of medical murders, done in various ways on Stalin's orders and often culminating in the murderers being charged with their crime. Since Stalin inspired, organized, and directed this well-known practice, he easily could have believed that it was to be used against him. Especially since he was in an acute phase of maniacal aggressive psychosis, aggravated by high blood pressure and arteriosclerosis of the brain.

It was this diagnosis that had started it all. At his regular—and last—checkup, Stalin's physician, Professor Vladimir Vinogradov, noted an increase in the disruption of circulation in the brain, which in view of his recent strokes, presented a grave danger to the leader's health. Vinogradov wrote in the patient's file, "Complete rest, freedom from all work." This recommendation was reported to Stalin. Amazingly, his vanity was stronger than his concern for his own health, or his life. The man was smart, but his need to see conspiracies everywhere, his thirst for power, suppressed his natural instinct for self-preservation and pushed him to take a fatal step: fatal for his victims and for himself.

"Leg irons! Put him in leg irons!" he shouted, trembling with rage when he heard the doctor's advice. Khrushchev describes the episode this way, and his story is supported by facts. Vinogradov was arrested and shackled, which had never been done by the sophisticated Lubyanka torturers in the thirties and forties. Another Kremlin physician, Professor Vasilenko, was shackled the minute he crossed the threshold in response to a summons: he was also considered a conspirator by Stalin. His emotional and metaphorical response when he was struck to the heart by his sudden awareness of treachery was taken literally. At least this way, they could not be accused of disobedience.

These arrests, in early 1952, did not reveal any overt anti-Semitism,

---

* Mikhail Frunze, in that period People's Commissar on Military and Naval Affairs, chairman of the Revolutionary Military Council of the USSR, replacing Trotsky in these posts; candidate member of the Politburo. Stalin's enemies discussed him as a possible alternative to the dictator.

since the first names were not Jewish. This leads the last surviving "killer in a white coat," Yakov Rapoport, a professor of pathology, to conclude that the doctors' case was originally devoid of national coloration, that it was "merely" about a conspiracy of doctors against the leaders of the party and the government, a conspiracy by people of different nationalities: the profession was more important than the nationality. It was only later, through the efforts of Mikhail Rumin, whom Stalin came to like and elevated to Deputy Minister of State Security (where he overwhelmed the less energetic Minister Semyon Ignatiev), that the case was given a Jewish tone, and the iron broom started sweeping up Jews.

That is so, but not really so. It is hard to determine precisely, to the day, when the Lubyanka started writing the scenario for the killer doctors. Vinogradov was not the first. Professor Yakov Etinger, as we recall, had died in the torture chamber a year earlier. He had not been arrested as a conspirator, but Rumin made him one after his death, accusing him of killing his patient Alexander Shcherbakov. Rumin also made sure of the arrest of Abakumov, who allegedly killed Etinger because they were co-conspirators and Abakumov needed to get rid of a witness who knew too much and might break under the pressure of interrogation.

And this theory of Rapoport's is careless with dates, thereby making it impossible to reconstruct the chronology properly. Vinogradov's diagnosis of Stalin (and the recommendation for complete rest) came at the beginning of the year, but this does not automatically mean that Stalin was told about it immediately. We do not know who took it upon himself and when. In any case, Vinogradov was not arrested until November 7, 1952. It is impossible to imagine that the cry "Put him in leg irons!" could go unobeyed for over half a year.

Yet the arrests of Jewish doctors had begun in the early summer of 1952, when the trial of the Jewish Antifascist Committee was in full swing. And the new concept is clearly connected to the old one. On June 4, Yevgenia Lifshits, a pediatrician at the Kremlin polyclinic, was accused of providing improper treatment to the children and grandchildren of Soviet leaders, an assignment given to her by American Zionist circles. The KGB tried to force Dr. Lifshits to admit that she got her instructions from her colleague Professor Vovsi. The courageous woman refused to denounce Vovsi and even attempted to hang herself in her cell. She was then transferred for "treatment" in the soon-to-be notorious Serbsky Forensic Psychiatry Institute. But even after psychotropic drugs were used on her, Lifshits stood firm: despite blackmail and torture, she refused to give evidence against Vovsi. Besides which, Vovsi himself was arrested only on the night of November 11. An avalanche of arrests followed Vinogradov's.

Meer Vovsi was a lieutenant general in the medical service and during the war was chief physician of the Red Army. This outstanding Soviet doctor was known throughout the land and abroad not only as a notable specialist but as the cousin of Solomon Mikhoels. He was also a member of JAC, thereby serving as a link in the Lubyanka fantasy between the medical conspirators and the Zionist conspirators. In trying to get Lifshits to condemn Vovsi, the Lubyanka was clearly preparing for a "logical" and "convincing" transition from the trial under way to a new, bigger one.

Beginning in mid-November, renowned physicians were arrested almost daily. It was Stalin's wise advice being put into practice. When he was told of the arrest of one of the conspirator doctors, Stalin said, "Look for a group, it's impossible that he acted alone." (Sukhanov, for many years Malenkov's assistant, heard about these instructions from his boss.) The Lubyanka had a wealth of experience in fabricating groups. Rumin was very quick to pick up Stalin's orders and hints, and a few days later could report on results.

Apparently, the idea of a medical conspiracy came to be blended into the Zionist conspiracy. The large number of Russian surnames in the "Jewish" list is explained by the fact that the Lubyanka cells were already full of doctors, Russian and Jewish, and the Russians were no less celebrated than their Jewish colleagues. The specific Jewish orientation of the action is explained by the fact that Stalin had come to his decision by then to realize his life's greatest task, and he could not have found a better excuse for it.

While this medical scenario was building up, the Lubyanka agents remembered a letter written four years earlier and not taken seriously at the time.

In August 1948, while vacationing in the resort of Valdai, Andrei Zhdanov had a massive heart attack. The best Kremlin doctors were flown in to treat the Party leader—including Vasilenko, Vinogradov, and Egorov, and the electrocardiographer Lidia Timashuk. There was a disagreement among the consultants: examining the cardiogram, Timashuk was of the opinion that Zhdanov had suffered an infarction, while the cardiologists diagnosed it as "acute myocardiodystrophy" and consequently prescribed injections of digitalis, which is contraindicated for infarctions.

Frightened and super-vigilant, Timashuk, who was also a secret informant for the Lubyanka, wrote a denunciation and asked Zhdanov's guard to pass it immediately to his bosses, that is, to the MGB. Disagreeing with her distinguished colleagues and in the best traditions of the Great Terror, she accused them of an intentional attempt on the patient's life. Her report could have been all the more serious since Zhdanov died a few days later. But an autopsy showed the correctness of the doctors' diagnosis. Therefore Abakumov shrugged off Timashuk's report and sent it to the secret files. His reaction is the more interesting because he was a Zhdanov man, and if he had had the slightest suspicion, he would not have missed this chance.

But the patient and the physicians were too famous for the denunciation to be forgotten. Abakumov was not the only one who knew about it. And now, the report was remembered: everything fit. Rumin began developing the case feverishly, hoping to build his career on it. He got the report out of the archives and sent it upstairs. This was also a neat piece of evidence against Abakumov: the former minister had intentionally hidden an alarming report from the vigilant Timashuk in order to protect the conspirators.

Again, it is very important to follow the exact chronology—so as not to fall into the trap of trying to fit a priori versions of the events. What prompts this mention here is the very substantial work of Christopher Andrew and Oleg Gordievsky, who maintain in their book, *The KGB*, that Lidia Timashuk wrote a letter to Stalin in late 1952 accusing the Kremlin doctors, primarily Jewish ones, of wanting to take the precious lives of the leaders. In fact Timashuk never wrote such a letter—they are referring to her report written four years earlier, which had been resuscitated by Mikhail Rumin for new political purposes. All the names of the killer doctors listed by the vigilant informant back in 1948 are Russian. But the time had come for the denunciation to play its historic role.

Timashuk's resuscitation dates to the fall of 1952, just two or three months before she drew attention around the world: right around the time of the Nineteenth Party Congress, at which Stalin sat in total silence, almost without stirring, and gave an extremely brief and almost incomprehensible speech toward the end. Many people recognized that he was gravely ill, both physically and mentally. Right after the congress there was a plenum of the newly "elected" Central Committee, where Stalin attacked Molotov and Mikoyan, who were not part of the small bureau of the CC presidium. Stalin's strategic plans at that time included both the "final solution" and the liquidation of some of his "closest comrades-in-arms," and apparently the two conspiracies, Zionist and Kremlin, were tied in. We can be sure that Molotov would have been reminded of his wife, Zhemchuzhina, and both he and Mikoyan of their support for the Jewish Republic in the Crimea.

There is one more bit of convincing evidence that allows us to place the reanimation of the Timashuk denunciation to the fall of 1952 rather than January 1953. In December General Nikolai Vlasik, former chief of Stalin's personal bodyguards, was arrested. Seven months before that he had been demoted and sent to Asbest, a distant city in the Urals, as deputy chief of the local concentration camp. At that time Stalin had got rid of Vlasik with the excuse that he had violated Party ethics by attending the illegal gargantuan feasts the Chekists threw for themselves. Now things were much worse: Vlasik was charged with treason, since he, like Abakumov, had "hidden" Timashuk's denunciation in 1948 and therefore was also part of the medical conspiracy against Stalin and involved in the killing of Zhdanov and Shcherbakov. Stalin made the same charges against another of his most loyal satraps—the chief of his personal secretariat, Lubyanka General Alexander Poskrebyshev, who was also suspected of concealing the important patriotic warning. He was fired and awaited his arrest at any moment.

The expert commission created by Rumin on Stalin's orders would sign anything, but yet even it came to the conclusion that medicine could not have saved Shcherbakov. And as a result? The killer doctors were still accused of getting rid of Scherbakov, Timashuk's denunciation about Zhdanov's "murder" was declared a highly patriotic act, and Stalin fired Rumin, finding him to be a scoundrel. From the heights of his job as Deputy Minister of State Security, he plunged to the lowly position of senior inspector at the Ministry of State Control—also in November 1952. This is the month that should be considered the time of the informant Timashuk's brief revival.

THE PRESS CARRIED INFORMATION on the arrest of nine doctors, two of whom (Etinger and M. Kogan) were already dead: the first in prison, the other of cancer. But actually, many more were arrested. It would not have been possible to publish the entire list, because it would have contained all the celebrities of Soviet medicine of the day—internists and surgeons, laryngologists and ophthalmologists, neurologists and psychiatrists, pediatricians and urologists. And pathologists. And allegedly they were all killers— poisoning people with drugs, killing them on the operating table. Among the prisoners were Academician Vladimir Zelenin, whose name is on the popular drops taken in Russia for heart trouble, and Professor Mark Sereisky, whose clinic treated thousands of people for nervous stress. The complete list could not be published for another reason as well: there were many Russians on it, many more than necessary just to balance things. This would spoil the Zionist conspiracy theory, because it would be hard to explain to the average reader why these elderly, distinguished, and famous doctors, pampered by the Soviet regime, wreathed with all possible awards and titles, would suddenly sell out wholesale to international Jewish organizations.

But a short version of the list was printed and the desired effect achieved. The official campaign of anti-Semitism was launched, and the next blows would certainly follow the first. The greatest threat was that this was the first instance since 1938 of public listing of selected victims to be classified as spies and terrorists: in the intervening fifteen years thousands of people had been executed, not only without any notice appearing in the press, but without their families being informed. Moreover, the relatives (and the public) were constantly deceived with the illusion that the prisoners were in fact alive and incarcerated "without the right to correspondence." Even the trial of Lozovsky and the other JAC members was held in secret, and not a word appeared in the newspapers about it. When the rare "emissaries of Soviet literature" were sent abroad and then asked about Markish or Kvitko, they replied according to their instructions, that the Jewish writers were doing well. One of them (the writer Boris Polevoy) replied to a question in the United States about an arrested Jewish poet, "I just saw him a few days ago, he feels fine and is writing a new poem."

But now it would be impossible to deceive people about the health of the medical professors. Nor was it necessary: that is why the press announced the coming trial, because it was planned to be open and with far-reaching consequences. The anti-Semitic seeds fell into prepared, plowed soil. Much has been written about the fear in society, how people refused medical attention, afraid of becoming victims of the killers in white coats. Thousands volunteered additional information to the Lubyanka on Jewish doctors killing their patients. The future editor-in-chief of *Literaturnaya Gazeta*, then a young writer who had been a war correspondent, Alexander Chakovsky, reported to the organs that Professor Vovsi, his neighbor in the country, was the cousin of Mikhoels. That was as revealing and secret as reporting that he knew from highly placed and reliable sources that General Eisenhower had been elected President of the United States and that its capital was Washington, D.C. The significance was not in the contents of the information but in the fact of its transmission: he had checked in, he had underlined his loyalty and vigilance.

Marshal Ivan Konev sent a passionate letter from the hospital to Stalin. A newspaper account had mentioned him as one of the military leaders the "criminal doctors . . . were trying to disable"—along with Marshal Vasilevsky, Marshal Govorov, General Shtemenko, Admiral Levchenko, and others. The "and others" category was all-embracing and quite useful. And Konev, whose health was not good, did not feel great improvement after his treatments and so he rushed to tell Stalin that his Jewish doctors were trying to poison him, thereby depriving Comrade Stalin of his most faithful soldier. This letter will remain a part of the marshal's biography as much as his exploits in battle.

The public reaction to this not-unexpected psychological attack from the Soviet propaganda mills was mixed. On January 15 or 16 I came to the Central House of Workers in the Arts, a hospitable place where I had been known since my childhood, for an evening with the puppet theater directed by Sergei Obraztsov. The regular coatroom attendant looked at me sharply with his murky eyes and said, calmly but firmly, "Here's what . . . You don't come here anymore." He refused to take my coat, and there was no one nearby to help me. And would anyone have helped? I had to leave my coat in the director's office, where his staff recognized me and paid no attention to me.

The audience was overflowing: even in those terrible days, Moscow's cultural life went on. The curtain parted and the whole troupe was standing onstage. Polite applause. Sergei Obraztsov came forward and spoke words that were totally inappropriate to the beginning of the show. "I ask you to welcome," he said, pronouncing each syllable clearly, "the best artists of our theater, Semyon Solomonovich Samodur and Zinovy Efimovich Gerdt." He took the artists by the hand, led them out to the footlights, and then took a few steps back. Thunderous applause shook the theater. It continued for several minutes. My friend Zinovy Gerdt still recalls that spontaneous manifestation of solidarity. The ovation would not stop. Everyone realized that it was not directed only at those brilliant puppet artists. Obraztsov, pale, stood far back on the stage. Tears rolled down his cheeks and he did not try to hide them.

Forty years have passed, but I remember it all to the tiniest detail: the figures standing in the spotlights, their bewildered faces, the clamor of the audience—the only possible form of collective protest, and not without its danger. Those minutes formed one of the strongest impressions of my life.

For the first time, Mikhoels was mentioned in the newspaper accounts of the arrests of the killer doctors as "the famous Jewish bourgeois nationalist," and Dr. Boris Shimeliovich, according to these stories, gave his colleagues "directives to annihilate the leadership cadres of the USSR." This way the public trial would also remove the secrecy from the JAC case: they were going to be connected and the executions would be announced. The fact that the JAC case had been heard behind closed doors could have been explained away by a concern for preserving state secrets, since the vile traitors had sold great military and economic secrets to their American masters.

The anti-Semitic campaign in the press bypassed Mikhoels and concentrated on the medical issues. That is easy to explain: the actions of the white-coated monsters (the term used in an official communiqué) impinged on literally everyone—no one could feel safe from them. This had a powerful effect on the masses and brought them to a state of fury that played into Stalin's hands for the realization of his plan.

For the same reason—the need to inflame anti-Semitic hysteria quickly—the published materials did not touch on global issues or theoretical bases, but dealt on the most primitive level. *Pravda*, which did less in this campaign than other newspapers, printed a small article by Party journalist Olga Chechetkina, "Lidia Timashuk's Mail." On January 20, Stalin bestowed the Order of Lenin on the "patriot" for her exploit of almost five years earlier, creating a personification of the hero of our times. The official statement read, "For aid to the Soviet Government in exposing the killer doctors." Lidia Timashuk was proclaimed the Russian Joan of Arc. The press did its job. "Lidia Timashuk's name," enthused Chechetkina, "has become the symbol of Soviet patriotism, high vigilance, resoluteness, and courage in the struggle with the enemies of our Homeland. . . . Lidia Feodoseyvna Timashuk became a close and dear person for millions of Soviet people."

The other newspapers formed a chorus railing against the "despicable gang of killer doctors"—*Izvestia, Komsomolskaya Pravda,* and *Trud.* Another hysterical journalist, Elena Kononenko, demanded that her readers be like that marvelous Soviet woman, the great daughter of the Russian people, Lidia Timashuk. The satirical magazine *Krokodil*, very popular with an unsophisticated audience, fumed and exhorted. The writer Vassily Ardamatsky (a Lubyanka officer) composed a foul anti-Semitic lampoon, "Pinya from Zhmerinka,"* which could seem funny only to Neanderthals. "Do you know Sarah Shmerkovna Pestunovich?" asked another hooligan lampoonist, Semyon Narinyani, a turncoat Georgian Jew. "We do, we do!" replied his protagonists. "She's the one who pisses in the neighbors' soup in their communal kitchen." This was the ground-preparing work on the minds of the public for the coming bloodbath.

---

* Zhmerinka was a small Ukrainian town in the center of the Pale of Settlement in pre-revolutionary Russia and was the negative term for small-town Jews.

It should not be surprising that the Soviet propagandists and journalists who wrathfully exposed the killers in white coats were joined by the West's professional friends of the fraternal USSR, the homeland of the world's proletariat. The strong support on the part of left-wing Frenchmen was touching. As usual, they were in the front rows singing Hallelujah! Georges Cogniot, Pierre Hervé, Maxim Rodinson, Francis Cremier, and Annie Bess (who later became Annie Krigel, the name by which she is known to this day) all expressed their anger against the despicable slaves of Zionism.

Similar claques were found in other countries. Their fidelity to the Kremlin, which was right because it was always right, is amazing. Even a year later, after this mad anti-Semitic operation was publicly revealed, Howard Fast, the American writer and recipient of the International Stalin Prize, said in the *New York Times*, "This is the greatest honor a person can receive in our times." As a member of the American Committee of Jewish Writers he might have had something else to say about the bacchanalia begun by the man whose prize so delighted him. But it was another three years before he finally regained his sight, which was cleared by the materials of the Twentieth Party Congress. And as soon as he did, the name of this faithful friend of the Soviet Union vanished forever from all Soviet reference books, encyclopedias, and dictionaries, and his novels from the shelves of bookstores.

BUT EVEN ONCE HE took his historic decision, Stalin did not lose his presence of mind and did not shed his characteristic hypocrisy. He managed to come up with an alibi for himself. Even as the Lubyanka's "black Marias" were carting away the remaining killer doctors and the scandalous revelations about the Jewish plot were only three weeks away, Stalin reached for his magic wand—Ilya Ehrenburg. Not the man for now, just his name. On December 20, 1952, the resolution on the award of the International Stalin Peace Prizes was published (the prize was later renamed the Lenin Prize and eventually it just vanished into oblivion). Among the laureates was the tireless fighter for peace Ilya Ehrenburg. This greatest honor was shared by the American singer Paul Robeson, the French leftist Yves Farge, and East

German writer and Communist Johannes Becher. Who could suspect Stalin of being an anti-Semite now that the great foe of anti-Semitism was awarded the prize bearing Stalin's own name?

Now the problem was to keep Ehrenburg's name from being lost in the flood of Jewish names appearing in the newspapers for a completely different reason, to keep his voice from being drowned out by the drums beaten by Party minions setting barking dogs against an entire nation. On January 23, *Pravda* gave half a page to Ilya Ehrenburg's article "Decisive Years," which included not a word about the killer doctors or about the programmed propaganda engulfing the country. But it contained an abundance of cliché invectives against "American imperialists." "Never before have the rulers of America been so cynical, so brazen." This pathetic example of standard agitprop came from the pen of the brilliant essayist. But this time Stalin did not care about his pen, he needed his name.

In another four days the award ceremony took place at the Kremlin. Ehrenburg's picture was printed in *Pravda* and other newspapers. The German writer Anna Seghers and the Colombian writer and diplomat Jorge Zalamea attended the event and kissed Ehrenburg before the cameras. But the most toadying speech, unparalleled in its sycophancy, at the height of the anti-Semitic campaign, was Louis Aragon's. This speech must not be forgotten, especially since the orator dared to say that he spoke "on behalf of the French people."

"This prize," exclaimed Aragon, "bears the name of a man the peoples of the whole world connect with the hope for the triumph of peace; a man whose every word is heard round the world; a man to whom mothers appeal in the name of the lives of their children, in the name of their future; a man who brought the Soviet people to socialism. This prize bears the name of the greatest philosopher of all time. Of the one who rears man and transforms nature; the one who proclaimed man the greatest treasure on earth; the one whose name is the most beautiful, the dearest, and the most extraordinary in all countries for all people who are struggling for their human dignity—the name of Comrade Stalin."

Aragon's delirious babble was spoken while the Soviet press was choking on anti-Semitic curses. The French writer Elsa Triolet, born Elizaveta Kagan, listened to her husband's speech. Her father, the

Moscow lawyer Uria Kagan, must have been spinning in his grave.

But Ehrenburg was right behind Aragon. I think this was his most impassioned and bilious speech against Americans. "The rulers of America," intoned the laureate, "are prepared to destroy everything and everyone in order to stop the course of history. The rulers of America do not want to listen to the voice of reason. We can still hear their vicious curses, their hostile activity is still visible. There is no base action to which they will not stoop. There is no crime that they would not commit. They are losing their heads because they have lost their hope." Ehrenburg did not always find such strong words for the Nazis and Hitler himself.

He did not overlook the national issue—after all, that was his hidden agenda (as he understood so sensitively). "Whatever the national origins of any Soviet person," Ehrenburg boldly declared, "he is first of all a patriot of his homeland and he is a true internationalist, a foe of racial or national discrimination, a supporter of brotherhood, a fearless defender of peace."

But he saved the best for last: "I have been given a high honor—the right to wear on my chest a depiction of the man whose image lives eternally in the hearts of all Soviet people, all peace-loving people of our times. When I talk about this great, prescient, and just man, I think of our people: they are inseparable."

A bit later Stalin had another opportunity to prove to the world that there wasn't even a hint of anti-Semitism in his country. He was lucky: Lev Mekhlis, one of the last Jews in his entourage, who took every opportunity to demonstrate that he did not belong to that "vile tribe," died on February 13. His co-workers at *Pravda* recall that Mekhlis liked to say, "I am not a Jew, I am a Communist." Nevertheless, for foreign observers he was a Jew, which was most important in this case. Neither Stalin, whom Mekhlis had served with slavish fidelity, nor Molotov came to say good-bye to their "close comrade," but Stalin did have a lavish funeral for him in Red Square, which he could have avoided, since Mekhlis no longer held any important government posts. But he did it, knowing that it was too good an opportunity to miss.

There is a theory (that period is filled with theories and versions, which more than one generation of historians will have to try to straighten out) that Mekhlis was arrested, charged with ties to the Zionist conspirators, and died in a prison cell after confessing. This version has no corroboration. Why bother with the pomp of the funeral if he had confessed? He could have been declared a scoundrel posthumously, as was done with Mikhoels. No one can guarantee that he had not been helped along in his death, but he did die at a good time for Stalin and Stalin needed him as a respected Jewish corpse shown the esteem that was his due, and not as a conspirator.

The anti-Semitic hysteria grew faster than anything done by Soviet propaganda before, for all its mobility and organization. The sphere of activity was all-encompassing. A GULAG inmate and founder of a theater behind barbed wire, the playwright Matvey Grin, recalls how the camp authorities reacted to the campaign. One evening it sent all the Jewish inmates, and only Jews, out into the taiga to a faraway felling site, that is, to almost certain death away from the minimal shelter and rations of the camp. Only a few survived. He is certain that there had been no direct instructions to the camp authorities on the matter—it's just that they sensed the atmosphere of the times. And it was that way all around the country. Stalin counted on that sensitive and swift reaction.

The campaign expanded and spread across the borders of the Soviet Union. In the colonial countries of Eastern Europe—the People's Democracies—it was just as open. And it was divided into two stages, just as in the Soviet Union: state anti-Semitism covered with the fig leaf of proletarian internationalism, and state anti-Semitism covered by nothing. "Even in the first days of incarceration," Artur London, the former Deputy Minister of Foreign Affairs of Czechoslovakia, later recalled, "I came across naked anti-Semitism, purely Hitlerite, but at the time I was prepared to write it off as the personal foibles of individual investigators. . . . As soon as a new name would come up, the investigator would demand to know whether the person was Jewish. . . . If that person was in fact a Jew, he would be included in the transcript under any excuse and written down with the ritual 'Zionist,' which replaces 'Jew,' in front of the name. The final transcript will also have the formulation 'Jew by descent' (this will be said about eleven of the fourteen defendants; the others were two Czechs and one Slovak). Once I asked the investigator how they could call a group of former interbrigadiers [members of the international brigades that fought on the republican side during the Civil War in Spain] Zionists, especially since there were no Jews except for me and another comrade. He replied with total seriousness, 'You've forgotten about their wives. They are all Jewish. Where Judaism could not penetrate directly, it went by an oblique path, forcing Jewish wives on you.' "

The reader is ahead of me by now. I am discussing the group put on trial in the case of Rudolf Slansky (Zaltsman), the General Secretary of the Central Committee of the Communist Party of Czechoslovakia; Berdzhikh Geminder; Rudolf Margolies; and others. Jews held positions of authority in the other "people's democracies," as well: Hungary (Matyas Rakoszy), Poland (Eduard Okhag, Yakub Berman, Gilyari Minz), and Romania (Anna Pauker), countries with long traditions of deep-rooted anti-Semitism. It was not difficult to fan the flames of anti-Semitism there. Stalin knew that a new wave of anti-Semitism in the satellites would also be a wave of anti-Sovietism. That did not worry him. Once he had settled the Jewish question, he would have quashed any manifestations of anti-Sovietism, explaining through his propaganda that the Jews had perverted the idea of Stalin's socialist paradise instead of promoting it.

The hand of Moscow sowed the seeds of anti-Semitism even where there was no soil for them. Before the war around forty-eight thousand Jews lived in Bulgaria, and they were never subject to discrimination. When an attempt was made in 1940 to pass anti-Jewish laws under pressure from Berlin, the Bulgarian intelligentsia protested indignantly. The great majority of Bulgarian Jews were saved by Bulgarians from deportation to death camps. There were many Jews among the major Resistance fighters, and they were all revered by the new regime. It took incredible efforts to force this tolerant country to dance to Stalin's anti-Semitic pipe.

On my first trip to Bulgaria in 1960, the memory was still alive about events that had taken place years earlier, and my new acquaintances begged me never to mention my Jewish ancestry to anyone and to respond to the inevitable questions about my surname by saying it was German. I was swayed by their friendly advice, and to my great amazement, people took that nonsense at face value. Albert Coen, an old Bulgarian Communist and a partisan, told me that on orders from

Moscow, a purge of Jews in the apparat began in 1952 and reached its apogee in early 1953. He was dismissed from his job as head of national radio. Almost all the Bulgarian apparatchiks had been trained in Moscow (at Party schools, methodological courses, etc.) and brought back direct instructions and the atmosphere of suspicion toward Jews. A systematic removal of Jews from key posts and a purge of them from all vital social spheres was under way.

These seeds yielded noxious shoots for a long time. In the late sixties Bulgarian television produced one of my historic-revolutionary plays, a typical piece of hack work done solely for the money. Just before air time, my friend Pavel Pisarev, head of television, asked me to come outside for a confidential talk. The "artistic council" (the censors, in other words) had banned the show, since the play's hero, Yakov Sverdlov, was a Jew. Pisarev asked me to help him help me.

After much thought I came up with an absurd move. "Tell them that you called Moscow and found out that Sverdlov's Jewish ancestry was not confirmed. Otherwise they would have removed his name from Moscow's main square and the Urals' biggest city long a time ago." Despite the idiocy of this suggestion, it worked: the Bulgarian keepers of racial purity could not imagine a Jew's name on such important sites in the Soviet Union. They found the argument quite convincing.

IN NEW YORK FOR a session of the UN General Assembly, Andrei Vyshinsky was constantly challenged by his Western colleagues, who used the only means at their disposal to protest the pogrom actions in Russia. The Soviet mission to the UN received innumerable letters and telegrams daily protesting the spree in Moscow. Albert Einstein sent a letter filled with bitterness, incredulity, and indignation, both in the name of the American Committee of Jewish Writers, Artists, and Scientists and in his own name. Even he got no reply. A small bomb went off at the Soviet embassy in Tel Aviv, allegedly causing "light wounds" in several diplomats. The cheap provocation was so obvious—it gave Stalin a chance to increase the anti-Semitic hysteria. And of course, he used it as an excuse to break off diplomatic relations with Israel. International reaction no longer interested Stalin. The euphoria that followed the theft of American atomic secrets and the successful progress in the creation of a domestic weapon of destruction blinded him. His idée fixe, the Stalin solution to the Jewish question, pushed every other consideration into the background.

No later than mid-February Stalin began the realization—detailed and in stages—of his plan. The massive propaganda campaign was supposed to culminate in a public trial: naturally, all would receive the death sentence. The execution would take place on Red Square, where dozens of scaffolds would be set up. The furious crowd would tear the victims away from their guards and lynch them, despite the soldiers' heroic attempts to control the mob. Immediately thereafter, pogroms would begin throughout the country.

There is corroborating evidence supporting this version. One of Stalin's bodyguards, who does not hide his continuing admiration for the Father of the Peoples, MGB Major Alexei Rybin, was present at two secret meetings where the details of this operation were developed. He recalls being sent to the passport office of the Moscow militia, to determine personally that the list of non-Aryan doctors and their addresses was accurate and complete. These addresses were to be given to the pogrom leaders.

Lev Sheinin talked about this in my presence. When he was released from prison after Stalin's death, he reactivated his old ties with people in the MGB and the procurator's office involved in this operation. They also confirmed the existence of lists in every police precinct—not only of doctors but of all Jews. Sheinin talked about this at a modest dinner at the home of our mutual friend, a colonel in the justice department, Professor Arkady Poltorak, with whom he worked in the Soviet part of the prosecution at the Nuremberg trials. Poltorak knew a lot too, and there were some other informed people at the table. This was in the mid-sixties, and the events of 1953 were still fresh in their minds. I remember that the guests and Poltorak not only confirmed the lists and the construction of barracks and the freight trains being made ready, but also added this detail to Sheinin's account: they planned to give people only two hours to pack, only one bag per person, and all those who would have trouble surviving the rigors of the journey—without food or heat—would be tossed over the side when the trains were in deserted fields or forests in the thirty-below Siberian winter.

The political scientist and American specialist Academician Georgy Arbatov writes in his memoirs that Boris Afanasyev, the celebrated intelligence officer, said that "in early 1953 orders were sent to increase the capacity of prisons and camps in view of the coming influx of prisoners and to prepare additional rolling stock for the transportation of prisoners." Afanasyev, whose real, non-Russified name was Atanasov, told me this too. The old Bulgarian revolutionary, who worked at the Lubyanka, was brought to me by the writer Konstantin Kulumov, who combined his literary work with a major post in Bulgarian state security. Afanasyev, who had almost forgotten Bulgarian completely and was a survivor of Stalin's harsh school of purges, spoke reluctantly at first but then, when his inner brakes were released, told me that Stalin planned to have all the Moscow Jews deported in just three days and to find "some other way" for those who did not get loaded up on the trains in that time. It is not hard to imagine the other way.

The operation was not meant to be secret. The course of events would unfold in this manner: Right after the start of the pogroms, *Pravda* would write and the radio would broadcast a request to Stalin from distinguished Jews to save their compatriots from the just wrath of the people by deporting them to the deserted regions of the Far East, where they would expiate their guilt as murderers and traitors. Stalin would paternally agree to this request. The nation that did not exist would then truly cease to exist.

Credit for the idea of deportation belongs to Dmitri Chesnokov, Ph.D., editor-in-chief of the journal *Questions of Philosophy*, who quite unexpectedly in 1952, at the Nineteenth Party Congress, was made a member of the presidium of the Central Committee (that is, the Politburo) and was moved to the editorship of the journal *Kommunist*, which was a much higher post in the Party hierarchy. This leap up the career ladder was the result of his philosophical ideas. In early 1953, Chesnokov had prepared a theoretical work with scientific justification from the Marxist-Leninist perspective for the historical inevitability and justice of the measures taken by the Party and Comrade Stalin personally.*

The trial was planned for March, but by February thousands of barracks unsuitable even for cattle had been hammered together in Birobidzhan (there is an unverified version that they had been prepared even earlier), reserve tracks around Moscow were filled with freight cars, militia headquarters in large cities were writing lists of citizens subject to deportation—those of 100 percent and 50 percent Jewish blood, and two other famous scholars—historian Isaak Mintz and philosopher Mark Mitin, both academicians—together with journalist Yakov Khavinson, who at one time had been director of TASS and had written under the name Marinin, were composing the text of the letter to which Comrade Stalin was to respond so generously.

There have been suppositions that the letter was initiated by eminent Jews, seeking salvation for themselves and most of the miserable Jewish population. But that is unlikely, in fact impossible. The scale of the operation and of the propaganda campaign could leave no doubt who was behind it. And no one would dare to act so boldly without orders or at least approval from Stalin. The headquarters for the operation was at *Pravda*, the largest department of the Central Committee, where the smallest, most insignificant initiative from below was categorically forbidden. Who would dare, without permission to do so, call Jewish luminaries into the *Pravda* offices and demand that they sign such a risky document? General David Dragunsky, twice Hero of the Soviet Union, was recalled urgently from Tbilisi (where he commanded a tank division relocated in the Transcaucasus) to add his autograph. The general went to Moscow by military plane. Who would take on that kind of responsibility in Stalin's day? No one. This was all part of a well-designed plan and done on the instructions of the person who created the plan. †

---

* The philosopher's sojourn on the Party Olympus did not last long. By March 6, 1953, the day after Stalin's death, he was expelled. But his career continued. He held such important positions as first secretary of the Gorky Regional Party Committee and chairman of the State Committee on Radio and Television. Until his death in 1973 he never mentioned his most brilliant philosophical conception.

† Research has failed to turn up this letter in the archives. I think it is because the letter did not go through the bureaucratic procedure of registration at each level—with a number and other mandatory attributes. It would not have settled into a file without it. But this invalu-

Jews living in the USSR, the letter said, have all the rights guaranteed by the constitution of our land. Many of them work successfully in institutions, scientific institutes, factories, and plants. And nevertheless, as a whole, they are infected with the spirit of militant bourgeois nationalism, and this phenomenon cannot be treated indifferently. Damning the killer doctors and demanding the severest punishment for them, the signatories appealed to the Politburo to spare the Jewish people, to protect them from the nation's wrath, and to send them for reeducation to remote reaches of the country. In other words, the "authors" not only rejected the existence of anti-Semitism in the USSR but justified the coming mass arrests, torture, and exile to camps of innocents; they supported this villainy in advance, in essence becoming part of its realization, since it had to be performed with the complete approval of those whose names appeared at the bottom of the letter.

The center of activity was the *Pravda* offices of its leading staff members, Yakov Khavinson and David Zaslavsky. It is hard to decide which of them was more odious, but I would give Zaslavsky the edge. He could win the gold medal among all the Jewish scoundrels bustling near the throne. Few elicited the revulsion that Zaslavsky did. A militant Menshevik who had energetically attacked Lenin (personally, not Bolshevism in general) in the press of his party, Zaslavsky then switched to the winning side and like any convert became more Catholic than the Pope. He continually proved his loyalty.

Stalin seemed to forgive him his past sins precisely because he had attacked Lenin, which pleased Stalin. Besides which, he knew that Zaslavsky was a faithful slave. In 1928 he gave him a job at the Party's central publication, *Pravda*, six years before Zaslavsky was accepted into the Party (1934)—a unique event. Zaslavsky was the ringleader in the persecution of Osip Mandelstam (1929), which elicited a collective protest from writers of every political hue. And this man sat with Khavinson at the dispatcher's switchboard, calling in the people who were given the great honor of signing a letter of such enormous social import.

able historical document must be in some file or other and eventually will surface. We can judge its contents from an outline made by the writer Veniamin Kaverin, who was among the people invited to sign it.

Many agreed to sign, but I do not believe that any should be reproached for doing so. They were all unfortunate victims of the unthinkable situation that the leader of the most free and most happy country had created. We do not know everyone who signed, and where there is any doubt about accuracy, it is better not to mention the names. But even those whose signing is verified, I repeat, do not deserve a belated rebuke: God spare us all from the trap into which Stalin cornered his chosen people. Academician Alexander Frumin signed. So did General Boris Vannikov, former People's Commissar of the Defense Industry and Supplies (he had gone through hell in the Lubyanka prison in 1941). And the aviation engineer Semyon Lavochkin. Two-time Hero of the Soviet Union David Dragunsky signed. And the marvelous poet Samuil Marshak signed (and then tormented himself for the rest of his life over it). The writer Vassily Grossman signed. (Just three days before the summons to the *Pravda* offices, he was humiliated on its pages by the vicious anti-Semite Mikhail Bubennov, followed by the other newspapers, and Grossman, according to his friends, decided that "at the cost of a few lives we can save the wretched nation.") One of the most sophisticated and respected poets, Pavel Antokolsky, signed. And so did the composer of the popular song "Katyusha," Matvei Blanter. Then he opened the paper in horror every morning, looking for his name under that letter. Many others signed whose names will mean little to the contemporary reader. Margarita Aliger, who died recently, told me she had signed too. "It was very terrifying, and not everyone is capable of being a suicidal hero." Fragile and sickly, Margarita was then suffering a series of personal tragedies.

According to Rapoport, a major figure of the old music school, the composer Reinhold Gliere agreed to sign the letter, but warned them frankly that he was not Jewish but German (on his father's side) and Ukrainian (on his mother's). They denied him the honor of signing.

But there were others who refused consciously and voluntarily. In that situation it was an act of great personal courage, no matter the reasons and rationales of the brave. General Yakov Kreizer refused. So did Stalin's favorite singer, Mark Reizen. So did writer Veniamin Kaverin. Academician and economist Yevgeny Varga, an old Hungarian Communist who had settled in Moscow, refused to sign; he had permitted himself to argue with Stalin back in the thirties and forties too. The extremely popular poet Yevgeny Dolmatovsky, a former German POW and son of an executed "enemy of the people," a famous Moscow lawyer, refused to sign. A man with that background would have been better off not sticking his neck out. But Dolmatovsky (who is still alive) did stick his neck out. Without demagogy but not without reason, he noted that everyone knew him as a Russian poet, and only as a Russian poet. His verses set to music had become Russian songs. He was a proponent of assimilation and considered himself a member of a new nation: the Soviet people. (Much later the great theoretician and thinker Leonid Brezhnev would develop this idea as his own discovery.)

Several other non-signers have been mentioned in the memoirs of various people and in circulating rumors. Mentioned were Academician Iosif Trakhtenberg, an economist; composer Isaak Dunaevsky; and a few others. There is no confirmation yet. I interviewed Mikhail Botvinnik, then world chess champion, to learn what his position had been. Botvinnik denied the existence of such a letter and insisted that he, at least, knew nothing about it. Yet there is the testimony of a few people who saw Botvinnik in a group at the long table in Zaslavsky's office.

But the true historic event was the position taken by Ilya Ehrenburg. No one expected anything but sycophantic agreement from that faithful Stalinist who had just played his role as laureate to perfection.

Did he know, did he guess, not only that he could end up (that could happen to anyone) among the American spies and agents of the Joint Distribution Committee, but that there was a seat for him in the defendant's dock? I am convinced that Stalin would have left that place empty. Ehrenburg was much more useful as a flourishing Jew than as an executed one. But the energy with which the Lubyanka gathered materials against Ehrenburg in the thirties, forties, and early fifties, the confidence with which they named him as ringleader of a spy gang when they interrogated other prisoners (there are many witnesses to that), speaks of the sword that was raised over Ehrenburg's head.

Avraam Kleiner, an engineer convicted of "Jewish nationalism," who survived the GULAG, recalls that Investigator Dubok stubbornly

called Ehrenburg the head of the "All-Union Anti-Soviet Jewish Nationalist Organization" during interrogations. "If Ehrenburg is head
of the organization, why is he out free?" Kleiner asked.

Without hesitation, Dubok replied, "He was arrested a long time
ago and is here."

Investigators often used such lies to confuse their victims and get
the information they wanted. But perhaps Dubok was not lying then.
A former colonel in the MGB, Mark Spektor, who eventually became
deputy chairman of the Moscow Collegium of Advocates (the bar,
where he showed himself at his best), told me in a frank moment that
many of his colleagues (and he himself) were certain that Ehrenburg
would be arrested any day, that it was all prepared. Some thought he
was already under arrest and writing his articles from prison, to create
the impression that all was well.

Ehrenburg had to be aware of his precarious situation: the shells
were hitting very close. He maneuvered as best he could on the edge
of the knife. But even that tactic (if waiting for the blow can be called
a tactic) has its limits. Which makes the step he took all the more
significant.

The information that came to us second- and thirdhand does not let
us determine if Ehrenburg had been summoned to *Pravda* or if mes-
sengers had been sent to his house (or dacha). But in any case he
refused to sign the letter slapped together by Zaslavsky-Mintz-
Khavinson-Mitin. And he wrote his own—a completely different one.
Some sources indicate that he did it in one sitting, in the office of
Dmitri Shepilov, editor-in-chief of *Pravda*, who offered to bring it to
its addressee: Comrade Stalin. Ehrenburg's letter was thought to be
lost and was always given in a brief recounting (some people even
thought that it was apocryphal). But it has been found.

Dear Josif Vissarionovich!
In view of the extreme importance of the problem that I am facing and
which I cannot resolve on my own, I am daring to disturb you.

Comrade Mintz and Comrade Marinin today showed me the text of
the letter to Pravda *and suggested that I sign it. I feel I must share my*
doubts with you and ask for your advice.

I feel that the only radical solution to the Jewish problem in our socialist state is assimilation and the blending of people of Jewish ancestry with those peoples among whom they live. I am afraid that the collective initiative coming from a certain number of representatives of Russian-Soviet culture, who are not united by anything except their origins, is in danger of making nationalistic tendencies more acute.

I am very concerned by the blow the letter to the editor could cause to our efforts to deepen and broaden the world movement for peace. Whenever I was asked in various commissions and at press conferences about the disappearance of Yiddish schools and newspapers in the Soviet Union, I always replied that the Pale of Settlement was destroyed completely after the war and that new generations of Soviet citizens of Jewish origin do not wish to be isolated from the people among whom they live. The publication of this letter, signed by scholars and composers of Jewish origin, could reanimate a vile anti-Soviet campaign.

For progressive Frenchmen, Italians, or Englishmen, the term "Jew" does not refer to nationality but exclusively to religious affiliation, and slanderers could use this letter to the editor for their base ends.

You understand, dear Josif Vissarionovich, that I myself cannot take any categorical decisions and that is the only reason why I dare write to you. We are talking about an important political step and that is why I allow myself to ask you to have someone inform me about your attitude toward my refusal to sign this document. If responsible comrades inform me that the publication of this letter and my signature could benefit the Homeland and the Peace Movement, than I will sign the letter to the editor.

There is evidence that the "responsible comrades" whom Stalin entrusted to have a talk with Ehrenburg were Malenkov and Kaganovich. According to other evidence, it was only Malenkov, which is what Ehrenburg had hoped for. But that is not so important. Much more important is that the operation was slowed down. It might even have been rescinded. Perhaps—since we do not know what would have happened if the trial had taken place. It did not because Stalin died (whether of natural causes or with the help of Beria is outside the scope of this book). Alexander Yakovlev, in an interview with French Sovietologist Lilly Marcou, said that Ehrenburg's letter played an important role in the decision Stalin made.* Does that mean that the trial would not have taken place? That would have been impossible. It would also have been impossible to conduct the trial behind closed doors. But a public hearing inevitably presupposed some *conclusions*. What would they have been?

THE STORY OF THE never-published letter to the editor of *Pravda* from eminent Jews is overgrown with rumors. One has two versions: (1) the list of signatories was headed by Lazar Kaganovich; (2) Stalin asked Kaganovich to sign, but he refused indignantly, insulted Stalin, and left, slamming the door.

The first is out-and-out ridiculous: there is nothing for a Politburo member to do among "public figures," and the letter was addressed to the Politburo. The absence of Kaganovich's signature is obliquely confirmed by Ehrenburg. In his letter to Stalin he mentions "scholars and composers," and he would not have used that formulation if there had been a Politburo member among them.

The second version is apparently a distorted reflection of another account, ascribed to Ilya Ehrenburg himself, who was supposed to have told it to Jean-Paul Sartre (Abdurakhman Avtorkhanov refers to it in his book *The Mystery of Stalin's Death*, published in West Germany in 1976) and to Panteleimon Ponomarenko (1902–1984), former secretary of the Central Committee, who shared his reminiscences with Polish journalists when he was ambassador in Warsaw. In this version Stalin gathered the bureau of the Presidium of the

---

* We cannot leave in silence a shameful episode that occurred almost ten years later. At a meeting between Nikita Khrushchev and the creative intelligentsia on December 17, 1962, the writer Galina Serebryakova, back from seventeen years in the camps, and despite that and the execution of her two husbands a flaming Communist, attacked Ehrenburg. She accused him of being an accomplice of Stalin's in the rout of JAC, in the destruction of Jewish writers, and in the planned reprisals against the doctors. She referred to some apocryphal testimony of Alexander Poskrebyshev, Stalin's secretary, which had never been published anywhere and was unknown to everyone but Serebryakova. Khrushchev's faithful lackey Leonid Ilyichev, then ideology secretary of the Central Committee and later Deputy Minister of Foreign Affairs, readily supported the speaker, while Dmitri Shostakovich supported Ehrenburg. There is no doubt that this was a planned provocation. Its goal was not only to weaken the effect of Ehrenburg's just-published memoirs, *People. Years. Life*, but to smear his role in derailing Stalin's bloody plan to solve the Jewish question.

Central Committee (remember, neither Molotov nor Mikoyan was a member) in late February or early March to get a formal endorsement of his plan for a trial of the killer doctors and the deportation of Jews to remote areas of Siberia and the Far East. But instead of endorsement he met with resistance. And it is allegedly then that Kaganovich, with others, was rude to him and even tore up his membership card in the Presidium of the Central Committee. Even Beria, who "was quiet at first," supported the rebels, and a shocked Stalin fell unconscious, after which he gave up his sinful soul to God.

Molotov avoided a direct answer when pressed by Felix Chuev, merely saying that "Beria was involved in that business" and that he himself saw Stalin for the last time four or five weeks before his death. "He was perfectly healthy." The perfectly healthy part is more than an exaggeration. Vinogradov's diagnosis from early 1952 is known to us, and Stalin, who then remained without medical aid, got worse, not better. But in effect Molotov did not deny the Ehrenburg-Ponomarenko version, he simply declined to answer, even though he certainly had more information than most people.

There are many rumors about Stalin's final days, and little is known reliably. But it is still possible to reconstruct events schematically. On the evening of February 27 Stalin watched *Swan Lake* at the Bolshoi Theater, completely alone, hidden from the eyes of the audience behind heavy drapes in the government box. On the 28th, according to his last living bodyguard, MGB Major Rybin, Stalin came to the Kremlin just to watch a film and spent two hours in the screening room with Beria, Malenkov, Khrushchev, and Bulganin. Afterward, the entire group headed for Stalin's dacha in Kuntsevo, where they stayed up all night. The guests went off to rest after four in the morning, and only late in the evening on March 1 did the guards, worried by his silence, dare to enter Stalin's room to find the Leader of the Peoples unconscious on the floor.

Rybin's statement, which has been checked and found accurate on the facts known to him (I am disregarding his interpretation of them, which is purely Stalinist), is also confirmed by other published materials. In particular, the fact that the foursome spent the night with Stalin before he fell into a coma. Therefore, we can determine that there was no meeting before Stalin's stroke (or certainly none that precipitated it). And that means that the version in which Lazar Kaganovich acted heroically or at least with inspired desperation has no basis in fact.

Nevertheless, Stuart Kahan, Kaganovich's American relative, relates a similar story in his book. This version is based on Kaganovich's account; in his final years, he tried to clean up his name a bit. Added to the incident of the demonstratively torn-up membership card (did the "closest comrades-in-arms" get identification? Did Stalin have an ID card too?) is the chilling tale of Kaganovich's sister, Rosa (unceremoniously called "Stalin's last wife"), a doctor who on the orders of the killers gave Stalin rat poison or some other drug and thereby saved her people from annihilation.

I do not know the reaction in America to Kahan's book, *The Wolf of the Kremlin*. In Russia, the translation published by Progress Press and the excerpts in weekly magazines merely added to the voluminous mounds of "penny dreadfuls" that flooded the perestroika book market. Since the book (and therefore the version of Stalin's death that it contains) does exist, and Lazar Kaganovich's role in Stalin's last days requires clarification, I will cite a few passages from a letter sent to *Literaturnaya Gazeta* but, for reasons I am unable to fathom, not printed.

The author of the letter is a nephew of Lazar Kaganovich, authenticated by my colleagues who have known him for decades and by my own checking. Mikhail Kaganovich was a Kiev journalist (for *Vecherny Kiev* and *Kievsky Vestnik*) who wrote under the pseudonym K. Mikhailenko. He is the son of one of Lazar's four brothers, Aron Moiseyevich Kaganovich. He is now living in Israel. Here is what he wrote:

> "*I don't know Jack Kahan or his son, Stuart, I never met them or talked to them,*" my Uncle Lazar said not long before his death about Stuart Kahan. "*In all my years of retirement no one except my real and close relatives have crossed the doorway to this apartment, I have never given an interview to a journalist, including this Stuart Kahan who allegedly talked with me in September 1981.*"
>
> Lazar had four brothers, and not two as S. Kahan writes, and his sister Rakhil, whom the author calls Rosa, died in Kharkov back in 1925, and therefore, naturally, could not have become Stalin's next wife

*after Nadezhda Allilueva died in 1932. For that same reason she could
not have given him poison.*

These lines from the letter of Mikhail Aronovich Kaganovich,
which are corroborated by the information on the death of Rakhil
Moiseyevna Kaganovich, rejects the story about the place of "Lazar's
sister" by the throne and her role in Stalin's murder. There is yet
another interesting passage in Mikhail Kaganovich's letter that I
would like to quote. The nephew asked his uncle if Ehrenburg's
story was accurate, whether in late February 1953 Lazar tore up his
Politburo card and gave Stalin an ultimatum because he was so incensed over the doctors' case.

*"You might say yes and no," replied Uncle Lazar. "A delegation came
to see me with a request to sign the letter to the newspaper, wrathfully
condemning the Jewish poisoner doctors. There already were signatures of
Jews—famous scientists, writers, and actors. I was told in confidence,
'Comrade Stalin wants the first signature to be yours, Lazar Moiseyevich.'*

*"That outraged me to the bottom of my heart . . . I categorically
refused to sign the letter, which brought horror to the faces of my visitor
(after all, Stalin 'himself' had ordered it!), and I decided to tell him
my attitude toward the case and the letter. In fact, to tell the truth, I
had been thinking that Stalin was losing his mind in those days. He was
weakening physically very noticeably, he was having memory lapses, he
forgot the names of people he had been seeing for decades. Perhaps he was
simply intoxicated and was not in control of his actions. . . .*

*"Stalin received me austerely. Apparently he sensed that the conver-
sation would not be a pleasant one, he knew that the events had to elicit
a rebuttal from me. I took the bull by the horns, as they say:*

*" 'Have you forgotten who Kaganovich is, Comrade Stalin?' I asked
harshly, raising my voice, looking him right in his yellowish eyes, as he
always demanded. 'I can remind you that Lazar Moiseyevich Kaganovich is a member of the bureau of the Presidium of the Central Committee
of the Party, recently elected, by the way, at your suggestion at the CC
plenum after the Nineteenth Congress. Besides that I am deputy chairman
of the Council of Ministers of the USSR, that is, your deputy, and that
means you entrusted me to be a Party and state figure. Is that not so,
Comrade Stalin?'*

" 'It is, it is,' he said softly, realizing of course what state I was in and my readiness to speak bluntly. I have to tell you that I had never talked to him like that before. I think only Marshal Zhukov during the war dared raise his voice at the Leader.

" 'Then why,' I continued, 'have you suddenly decided to make me a public figure? What am I—an actor or a writer? Do you really want me to sign a letter with cultural figures to a newspaper with a condemnation of the so-called poisoner doctors?'

"Stalin, who was pacing in his office, as usual, stopped and interrupted me sharply.

" 'Don't be upset, don't be, Comrade Kaganovich. I agree with you. Consider the question closed: Comrade Stalin' (he often talked about himself in the third person) 'does not insist on your signature on the letter to Pravda.'

" 'But that's not all,' I interrupted him. 'I think that there is no need for such a letter. It's absurd, everyone will realize that it was fabricated in the CC and that people were forced to sign it, because no one believes the charges against those innocent doctors.'

" 'They all confessed,' Stalin replied.

"As I was preparing to leave, I blurted angrily, 'You certainly know how those confessions are beaten out of people! You'd confess yourself if you were being tortured by Beria and Ignatiev (he was Minister of State Security then) that you had worked in the tsarist secret police, were a Hitlerite spy, or worked with the Zionist organization Joint. Good-bye, Comrade Stalin!'

"Those were my last words to Stalin, that was our last conversation over decades of work and personal friendship. I saw him turn black and he seemed to be ready to faint.

"I left his office and sent in the secretary sitting in the reception area. I went to my dacha because I felt that I couldn't work after a conversation like that. . . . I walked along the fir path from the house to the gate and back again about fifty times.

"Stalin grew ill a short time later and, practically without regaining consciousness, died in his dacha in Kuntsevo."

I thought it necessary to use such a long quotation from an unpublished letter to the editor because it is interesting in many ways. Kaganovich's reported dialogue with Stalin is like an excerpt from a cheap novel intended for a simpleton reader with a primitive worldview. At the time that Kaganovich shared his memories with his nephew, none of the other "closest comrades-in-arms" was alive to dispute this story, and it is not surprising that he paints himself acting so heroically one-on-one with Stalin. But if he had not prepared for collective safety ahead of time, this would have been impossible: the rebel could have walked out of the Kremlin and joined the despicable Zionist gang as their leader at the trial.

Obviously Kaganovich needed to clear his name of the bloody filth attached to it not only toward the end of his life, but right after Stalin's death, which is when he started spreading these rumors about himself. Since it he did it so clumsily, without the help of the experienced people at the Lubyanka, the rumors were so contradictory and unlikely that no one believed them. Kaganovich's results were just the opposite of what he wanted.

But there is still some use to be made of these apocryphal statements. Apparently there was no scandalous meeting of the Presidium of the Central Committee, where Stalin was rebuffed: otherwise, Kaganovich would not have missed a chance to talk about it and ascribe the role of first fiddle to himself. And the shameful episode with the letter to *Pravda*, which came to nothing, did happen and was given great weight. No matter why it misfired, the failure had a significant effect on Stalin, who had planned to use the letter and was unable to make it happen (for almost the first time in his life).

ON MARCH 5 HISTORY'S bloodiest tyrant died. Hundreds of books will try to solve the mystery of whether anyone helped him along. If someone did, no matter how many other crimes and sins were on his conscience, this act was a mitigating factor. An innocent people was saved, not just from persecution but from annihilation.

I remember that on the night of March 5 my mother was having heart trouble and I called an ambulance. The doctor was a long time in coming, and we used up all the medication at home. At last a plump and noisy lady with a medical bag arrived. She took Mother's pulse and gave her a shot. Mother said something in a weak voice about taking so long. The doctor did not get angry or embarrassed—

she smiled. "Do you know how many calls I've had tonight? You're the sixteenth and look"—she waved a piece of paper—"nine or ten to go. And they're all people of your nationality. And they've all got heart problems. Did you get agitated out of fear or joy?"

Unwilling to reply, Mother pretended to be sleeping. After the doctor left I asked her the question Professor Troinikov had put to me, "Is she a fool or a provocateur?"

"A valuable informant," Mother answered cheerfully, and I realized that the crisis had truly passed.

In some sense it could be said that the Jews were "guilty" of Stalin's death. He got the anti-Semitic bonfire blazing monstrously and then burned in its flames. On May 7, 1945, Hermann Goering gave himself up to an American lieutenant named Shapiro and said with a sigh, "A Jew here, too." If Stalin had any moments of clarity before his death, he may have had a similar thought. Having sent the best doctors of the time into the cells of the Lubyanka, he was left at a critical moment alone with death. Even if his comrades had called for medical aid, who would have been available to render it?

The few doctors, far from first-rate, who were at the leader's bedside gave the last diagnosis he would ever have: Cheyne-Stokes breathing, that is, sounds that show the patient is losing strength. His comrades wanted to know what it meant, and from real authorities. But all the real authorities were in prison. So the investigators suddenly began asking questions that had nothing to do with the Zionist conspiracy: "My uncle is very sick and they said he has this Cheyne-Stokes breathing. What do you think that means?" One beaten professor who still had his sense of humor replied, "If you're expecting to inherit from your uncle, consider that it's in your pocket."

The inheritance left by this uncle was royally generous: the lives of hundreds of thousands, perhaps millions.

On March 5, before Stalin's body was cold and clinically it was not yet a corpse, Beria's euphoric hundred days began: with Malenkov and Molotov, he formed the fragile and doomed triumvirate. The ministries of State Security and Internal Affairs became a single, mighty organism once more, headed naturally by Beria, and all his gang members took key positions. Beria's deputy was Bogdan Kobylov; the head of the Main Directorate of State Security, General Goglidze; the Minister of Internal Affairs of Ukraine, Meshik; of Georgia, Dekanozov.

The temporary leader's first, unpublicized act was the release of Polina Zhemchuzhina. Stalin was buried on March 9, which by a strange coincidence was Molotov's birthday. Coming down from the mausoleum in a cheerful mood, Beria congratulated Molotov and asked what he would like for his birthday. He knew what the answer would be and he was prepared for it. "Return Polina," Molotov said curtly. The question had been decided. Despite what Stuart Kahan has to say, Zhemchuzhina was not under house arrest—on Stalin's decision, without any sentence, she was sent to the Kustanai region of Kazakhstan for five years, where she was given the code name "Object No. 12." Stalin received regular reports on that object. In January 1953 Zhemchuzhina had been transferred to Moscow to be included in the doctors' case. They had already obtained statements against her from Vovsi, Vinogradov, and B. Kogan. On March 10, Beria personally handed Polina over to her husband and beat him to the first kiss. "A heroine!" he proclaimed in his falsetto with a heavy Georgian accent. Upon hearing that Stalin was dead, Zhemchuzhina fainted right in the office.

But even more important and urgent was the release of the doctors. Naturally, Beria wanted to wring as much political capital as he could out of this necessary act. The transcript of the meeting of the Presidium of April 3, 1953, is extant; Beria proposed dropping the case against the doctors, releasing the innocent prisoners, and bringing the falsifiers to justice. The same date is on the letter quoted in Chapter Eight, "The Murder of Solomon Mikhoels," relating who committed the murder, where, and how, the punishment of Tsanava, and taking back the decorations the killers were awarded for their work. The decision to drop the doctors' case now needed to go through the Party bureaucratic machine. The formalities were observed and that same night all the prisoners who had gone from wretches to fortune's children, still reeling from the zigzags of the last few months, were driven to their homes in luxurious Lubyanka limousines. In the morning the newspapers and radio informed the world of an unprecedented event in Soviet history: "It was been determined," the official statement read, "that the evidence given by the prisoners allegedly confirming the charges against them was obtained by investigators of the former Ministry of State Security by methods that are intolerable and strictly forbidden by Soviet law." No explanation of the intolerable methods was needed.

The information on the rehabilitation of the doctors gives fifteen names, instead of just nine. The additions were Russian (Professors Vasilenko, Zelenin, Preobrazhensky, Popova, Zakusov, and Shershevsky), which emphasized the tendentiousness and anti-Semitic nature of the report given on January 13. But the later report still did not mention the other rehabilitated Jewish doctors (even such eminent ones as Sereisky and Rapoport), who were buried in the handy "and others": they were unwilling even then to reveal the scope of the anti-Semitic operation.

I know no fewer than seven people who declared April 4 as their birthday and mark the holiday annually. There were, of course, many, many more. And the holiday was not simply personal but far-reaching. As were the ramifications of divesting Lidia Timashuk of the Order of Lenin "in connection with the true circumstances now apparent." But the heroine who had once been a close and dear friend of millions of Soviet citizens and had fallen on bad times was soon awarded a consolation prize (second in importance in the hierarchy of state awards), the Order of the Red Banner of Labor, for her many years of fruitful work. She continued to work fruitfully at the Kremlin hospital for many more years (around twenty), demonstrating her astonishing medical illiteracy and an equally astonishing indifference to what had happened to her.

IN THE VERY BRIEF period between Stalin's death and the rehabilitation of the doctors, there was yet another mysterious accidental death that is directly involved with the case.

In the last week of March, the French activist Yves Farge, a friend of Ilya Ehrenburg, came to Moscow to receive the Stalin Prize. Today this name is almost forgotten, brought up only in connection with the doctors' plot, but back then Farge was well known and popularly read in France. He was a resistance leader, a commissar of the republic in Lyon, and had the reputation of being an honest, objective, left-wing political figure. After the war he was Minister of Foodstuffs for a while. In 1948 with Emmanuel d'Astier, Charles Tillon (then a member of the Politburo of the French Communist Party) and Abbé Jean Boulier, he founded the movement called Combatants de la paix et de la liberté.

Circuitously, via Prague, Ehrenburg brought Farge from Paris to Moscow. He was one of Ehrenburg's closest friends. On March 26 Ehrenburg handed Farge the Stalin Prize in the Kremlin, and on the 28th the guest flew to Georgia. Ehrenburg, who devotes an entire chapter to his friend in his memoirs, does not talk at all about why Farge insisted on going to Georgia, why he categorically demanded (while still in Paris) to visit Tbilisi, or what story went around as soon as Farge died in a car crash on the road from Gori, Stalin's birthplace, where they made him go, to Tbilisi—even though in the mid-sixties when Ehrenburg wrote and published (with great difficulty) his memoirs, it was possible at least to hint broadly about these things.

A widespread version held that Yves Farge demanded a meeting with the arrested doctors, that he was given permission for this and noticed that one man (the name was even given) had no more fingernails (in another he was shocked by the prisoners' nails, blackened by torture). And that was why Beria decided to get rid of a dangerous witness.

The absurdity of this story is glaringly evident: Farge came to Moscow when the question of releasing the doctors had been decided and Beria, the evil man with the pince-nez, had no intention of hiding the barbarism of his vanquished rivals, whom he intended to blame for every illegality possible. Besides, none of the memoirs or testimony that reached us ever mentions black or ripped-out fingernails. There is no direct or oblique evidence to verify a visit to the Lubyanka by Farge. No "white coat" ever mentioned meeting Farge in prison. And yet that temptingly nasty story continues to agitate people. Even Yevgeny Yevtushenko develops it uncritically in his film Stalin's Funeral, without trying to cast doubt on its obvious internal contradictions. Some Russian journalists, relying on their memory, persist in spreading this story too.

On the other hand, there is no doubt that Farge was murdered. There is recorded eyewitness testimony—about the ride to Tbilisi down a mountain road in the middle of the night, after an unscheduled dinner party. Ever polite, Farge could not refuse. Contrary to safety rules, he was put in the front passenger seat. On one of the most dangerous turns, in a mountain pass, the road was blocked by a truck that blinded the driver with its headlights. Driving around the obstruction at full speed, the driver did not notice the other car, parked by the edge in the darkness, with its lights off. The blow came just where Farge was sitting. No one else was injured. The escort car pretended to chase the perpetrators of the accident, but quickly faded. No other attempts to find them were made. Ehrenburg later insisted that he had been assigned to write the obituary while Farge was still alive. Ehrenburg got into a lot of trouble under Khrushchev when he revealed that secret.

What was the point, then? How does this planned murder fit in with the fact that Farge had nothing to do with the doctors? The answer is in the files on the Beria case. But since it is still basically inaccessible, and until just recently could not be read even in excerpts, the secret has been hidden from historians. But it is not difficult to figure out from the fragments of the questioning of Beria and witnesses in his case. However, the mystery has nothing to do with the doctors' plot. Nevertheless, since Farge's tragic death has been connected with the story of the Jewish catastrophe, I will deal with it briefly, to put an end to the legend at last.

During the war, in 1942, the Germans captured Tiemuraz Shavdia, the nephew of Nina Teimurazovna, Beria's wife, and the family favorite. Distinguished not by high moral qualities or steadfastness, but by zealotry and cruelty, Teimuraz quickly agreed (or more likely volunteered) to collaborate with the Nazis and joined the "Georgian legion," which was part of the Nazi security forces. He was at his best in France, where he punished members of the resistance and prisoners of war from the Red Army and other Allied troops. In 1944, during the liberation of France, he became an American POW.

Through his Lubyanka agents and diplomatic channels (one of Beria's closest colleagues, Vladimir Dekanozov, was Deputy Commissar of Foreign Affairs), Beria learned that his nephew was in France. He sent to Paris his most trusted hand, Petr Sharia, who was involved in the murder of Nestor Lakoba, Party chief of Abkhazia, whom Beria hated. Sharia made secret contact with the leaders of the Georgian émigrés in Paris, Noi Zhordania and other Mensheviks who headed the government of independent Georgia in 1918–1921. Beria knew many of them well—they must have shared more than nostalgic reminiscences. This is confirmed by the fact that three years later, the Politburo approved Beria's proposal to give permission to fifty-nine émigrés and their families to return to Georgia.

With the help of Zhordania and his comrades, Sharia managed to make contact with Teimuraz, who was with German POWs, get him out, and fly him back to Moscow by special plane. Teimuraz Shavdia lived happily under his uncle's protection until 1952, when someone's pressure (Beria's file says vaguely, "the demand of public opinion") led to his arrest and the camps. At that time Beria was "away" from the Lubyanka and could not bring real influence to bear. But as soon as he was back at the helm—almost instantaneously—Shavdia was transferred to Tbilisi for a review of the case. And in Tbilisi, it was Beria's friend Dekanozov who was now Minister of Internal Affairs.

It was at that moment that Yves Farge arrived in the USSR. He had been a commissar in the very region where Teimuraz and other Georgian legionnaires had had a free hand during the Nazi occupation. According to reports received at the Lubyanka, Farge was bringing incontrovertible evidence of the atrocities committed by Beria's nephew. The visitor did not hide his intention to get a public trial of the killer of resistance members and have him handed over to France, since Shavdia had been brought out illegally and before an investigation. This was a real threat to Beria.

The word that the car accident had been planned spread instantly, and Beria could not stop it. But it was much more crafty and treacherous to shape the rumor to his purposes. The doctors' case was still a very hot topic. And so the story of the ripped (or black) nails was accepted instantly, readily, without any critical evaluation. This version was no threat to Beria. On the contrary. He had liberated the doctors. And it led away from his criminal nephew. And who could have suspected anything this complicated from the face value of the events?

And so this was the final scene, absurd but bloody, of the monstrous mystery play of the twentieth century, which will be known in history as the case of the Jewish killers in white coats.

. . .

THE MAN WHO IS credited with starting this whole case (even though he was no more than a zealous executor of Stalin's will), Mikhail Rumin, was arrested on March 16, just ten days after the death of his patron, who had thrown him down in the first place.

In November 1952, disappointed in Rumin, Stalin transferred him to the Ministry of State Control as senior state comptroller. The minister was Beria's man—Vsevolod Merkulov. Beria may have chosen this post for him: to keep the comptroller under control.

Rumin was arrested on March 16 by Colonel Khvat, the torturer of the geneticist Nikolai Vavilov, on the orders of Beria's closest aides, Bogdan Kobulov and Pavel Meshik, who were executed along with Beria at the end of that year. Another of Beria's men, Lev Vlodzimirsky (who would also be executed with him), took the post recently vacated by Rumin (head of the investigation group for specially important cases) and ran the investigation of Rumin's case. He wrote a report to Beria (May 15, 1953) that speaks for itself eloquently: "Rumin behaves challengingly at interrogations, loudly denying his guilt. . . . He brazenly rejects the rightness of the facts presented to him, and this is his mode of behavior during interrogation. . . . We [it was signed jointly with Colonel Sokolov] consider it necessary to punish Rumin, in the solitary confinement cell of Lefortovo Prison." Beria marked it "agree," thereby confirming that no changes were expected in his ministry.

I do not know whether it was the solitary confinement, the torture, or his conscience, but Rumin admitted in July 1953 that the investigation of JAC

> had been done unobjectively . . . the statements of prisoners were falsified in many cases. . . .
>
> I personally interrogated prisoners Shimeliovich and Markish. . . . The evidence on the most important questions, in particular, espionage and also the creation of the Jewish Republic in the Crimea, was strengthened in the editing. When signing the transcript Shimeliovich complained about the unobjective recording, however I managed to persuade him and only in one case, where it dealt with the creation of the Jewish

Republic in the Crimea, I allowed him to make corrections in his own hand in the text.

A while after signing the transcript Shimeliovich wrote a statement renouncing all his evidence. . . . The refusal was not registered officially. And at this same period, when Shimeliovich's case was in the hands of another investigator, cruel measures of physical coercion were used on the prisoner.

I must admit that in 1952, when I was already Deputy Minister of State Security, many prisoners in the JAC case tried during interrogation to deny their statements as being invented, but I forbade any reinterrogations or writing down their denials, and said that the investigators should not give the prisoners their statements for revision, as they had in the past. . . .

When the court tried to send the case back for additional investigation, I insisted that the sentence be handed out on the materials before the court. . . . I felt and understood that sooner or later the investigation team, including myself, would have to bear responsibility for these crimes.

Rumin's file, comparatively small and reflective of an apparently hasty investigation, is notable for its mix of astonishingly frank statements with ordinary reports from investigators, like this one from Investigator Kuzyaikin: ". . . starting in September 1953, Rumin behaves insincerely, blackmailing investigators with his alleged closeness to leaders of the Soviet state, and utters threats."

Did he realize that those who had him arrested—Beria, Kobulov, Meshik, Vlodzimirsky, and others—were themselves under arrest and that things had shifted around with dizzying speed once again?

But there was no hope for Rumin. The new temporary leaders did not need him. In July 1954 Rumin was turned over to the courts. He was judged by Lieutenant General of Justice Zeidin and Major Generals Stepanov and Suldin: these names rarely appear in cases seen by the Military Collegium of the Supreme Court of the USSR during the period of the "cult of personality." (Zeidin was a member of the special court office that tried Beria and company.)

A long trail of evil deeds follows Rumin—just listing them would lead us far afield, for each doomed fate on his conscience deserves a separate tale. I will cite only one document from the archives of the main military procurator's office, because it deals with one of the protagonists of this book. Pavel Grishaev confirms on April 15, 1953, that "with Rumin I did the paperwork on October 19, 1951, for the arrest of Raikhman,* Eitingon, and Sheinin, even though there were no materials on them at all. Rumin told me then that the arrest was 'allegedly taking place on the orders of the head of the Soviet government, who having looked through the statement of Schwartzman, made the decision.' " Alas, I will have to defend both Rumin and Grishaev: it did happen this way, not "allegedly," but actually—the orders came from Stalin.

The court found that Rumin had personally tortured Professors Busalov and Vasilenko, the members of JAC arrested in the doctors' case, with metal rods and a hot iron.

Rumin could not appeal the death sentence given on July 7, 1954 (the law does not allow appeals of sentences given by the Supreme Court of the USSR), but he entered a plea for clemency, which was rejected by the general procurator of the USSR, Roman Rudenko. On July 22, 1954, Rumin was shot. His victims—those who were alive—gradually reappeared. The Alliluevs returned, Academician Lina Shtern returned from exile in Dzhambul, the relatives of people executed in the JAC case ended their exile. Even though they were permitted to return, they were still subjected to humiliations and persecution. They could not get information on what had happened to their husbands, fathers, and brothers, and then they were refused permission to live in Moscow and forced to move quickly. Minister of Internal Affairs Stakhanov wrote with poorly hidden surprise to General Procurator Rudenko on November 10, 1954, that Ivan Serov of the KGB demanded that all relatives of people sentenced under the JAC case be forbidden "to live in all the regimented cities of the

* Leonid Fedorovich Raikhman, a lieutenant general in the KGB. He sometimes used the pseudonym Zaitsev in his operative work. He was directly involved in the Katyn tragedy, in dirty business around the Nuremberg trial, and other Lubyanka affairs. In the fifties he was arrested twice and released twice. They tried to make him part of the Zionist conspiracy inside the MGB. Shvartsman testified against him, perhaps inspired by the investigators who were following Rumin's orders. Robert Conquest writes in his book, *Stalin's Secret Police* (1985), that Raikhman was executed. Actually, until his death on March 16, 1990, he lived in his Moscow apartment, working at an almost professional level in cosmology. In the forties and fifties he was married to the ballerina Olga Lepeshinskaya, a People's Artist of the USSR, who had started as his secret informant and then became his legal wife. His arrest ended their union.

USSR" (that is, Moscow, Leningrad, republic capitals, major cities, resort areas, and so on) "even though there was no legal basis for this." The procurator general—the chief supervisor of legality—did not deign to answer this letter (even though there is a note from his assistant on it: "Given to Comrade Rudenko").

"How long can innocent people be persecuted?" demanded Lev Bergelson, son of David Bergelson and future corresponding member of the Academy of Sciences, an outstanding biochemist, in his letter to Rudenko. Someone's anonymous resolution is written on the letter: "No answer needed, the militia is acting correctly." This mockery came to an end only after there was a formal rehabilitation.

The procurator's office did a new lengthy and thorough check, even though the absurdity of the charges made against honest people was obvious to any unprejudiced person. They waited for orders from above. I'd like to name at least some of the people who appealed over and over to Khrushchev, Molotov, Voroshilov, and other leaders— some with demands, some with requests, some with pleas—for the speedy rehabilitation of the condemned and an end to the mockery of their families: the composer Dmitri Shostakovich, Academician Ivan Nazarov, and the writers Alexander Fadeyev, Yustas Paletskis (deputy chairman of the Presidium of the Supreme Soviet of the USSR), Kornei Chukovsky, Samuil Marshak, and Lev Kassil. It was only on November 22, 1955, that the military collegium met, actually chaired (and this was almost unique) by the chairman of the Supreme Court of the USSR himself, A. A. Volin. The sentence of 1952 was repealed for lack of real evidence.

This act of elementary and belated human justice was marked "Top Secret." It remains classified to this day.

STALIN IS DEAD, BUT
HIS WORK LIVES ON

IT IS HARD TO DECIDE which day should be celebrated as Liberation Day: March 5 or April 4. Probably March 5: without it, April would not have happened, and I am not speaking only about chronology. "I'm the one who saved you all," Beria whispered to Molotov as he came down from the mausoleum on May 1 after the parade. Whether this was boasting in the hope of saving himself or whether the words contained a hidden truth is still a mystery. But it is not that important. Fate saved the Jews from Stalin's plan for them either at Beria's hands or someone else's.

That Beria had no direct connection with the fabrication of the doctors' plot seems obvious now, but even back then people who were informed or simply observant knew it. Moreover, if Stalin's scheme had been taken to its logical conclusion, deporting Jews and destroying all his "closest comrades-in-arms," they would have pinned contacts with Zionists on Beria, Molotov, Voroshilov, and Andreyev (through their wives): Beria's entourage and protégés were all charged with being part of the Zionist conspiracy in the MGB.

By starting the final, euphoric lap of his bloody career with the release of the doctors, Beria was not acting out of altruism or a sense of justice. It was simply an urgent and necessary action that would allow him to present himself as a savior and humanist, hurl the dead Stalin from his pedestal, separate himself from Stalin's crimes, and begin reprisals against those who had kept him from taking back the command positions in the Lubyanka. His personal aims were clearly at work. But nevertheless, it was he who released the doctors and gave the criminal plot notoriety. His "inseparable friends," who got rid of him very quickly, were not frightened by the fact that Beria had deprived them of the chance to claim credit for exposing Stalin's provocation. They were frightened by the generalizations that any reading, thinking, and analyzing person would make of the newspaper accounts of the end of the doctors' case. The release of "mistakenly" arrested people—that was a fine, correct measure. But the torture in prison cells, the planned deportation of the Jewish populace, the blatant state anti-Semitism—none of that had happened. Lavrenti Beria had made it all up to further his own treacherous plans. Stalin was gone, but Stalinism had not gone away.

The transcripts, published forty years later, of the Central Committee plenum (July 1953) that took place right after Beria's arrest, show the fear that the "collective leadership" felt facing the possible exposure of even the partial truth about the failed plot. Central Committee Secretary Shatalin expressed it best: "It is perfectly clear that they [the doctors] must be released, rehabilitated, and allowed back to work. No, this perfidious adventurer managed to get published the special communiqué of the Ministry of Internal Affairs, the question was studied up and down in our press. It must be said that it all had a depressing effect on our public. A mistake is being corrected by methods that have wrought a lot of damage to the interests of our state. The reactions abroad were also not in our favor."

It is pointless to wonder what reactions in their favor the Kremlin could have expected from abroad. The best reaction is none at all. Release the doctors quietly, without any publicity, and if the damned bourgeois propaganda finds out that there's something wrong with them, then expose the bourgeois press and declare it slanderous, and even get a statement from one of the victims that he had never been arrested. That he had spent a few months secluded at a resort.

The next few years were marked by a weak healing of the wounds made by Stalinism on the country and the people—and part of it was the return to normal life for the victims of the planned genocide. Many, probably most of them, were not bitter. In the summer of 1957 or 1958, at the Koktebel writers' resort in Eastern Crimea, I saw some Jewish writers in a friendly conversation with Vassily Ardamatsky, a Lubyanka colonel and vicious anti-Semite: it was only four years since the publication of his filthy racist lampoon *Pinya from Zhmerinka*. But no one wanted to stir up the past: it seemed gone forever.

Anti-Semitism was not condoned, it was not fanned from above, but it was not condemned either. The whole topic was simply forgotten. In his depiction of the changes in the Soviet Union, in the novella *The Thaw*, Ilya Ehrenburg touched on the events of late 1952–early 1953 in a very euphemistic way, referring to "people of a certain nationality." Which nationality was perfectly clear to the reader, but the very fact that he needed to resort to circumlocutions reflected a shameful moral atmosphere in which a return to chauvinism seemed quite possible.

For a while it was considered good form in high Kremlin circles to boast of one's Jewish friends, especially childhood pals whose friendship had never faded. Khrushchev said something like that in his meeting with the intelligentsia, and the comrades from the Central Committee and even ministers toed the same line. At the Twenty-second Party Congress—the culmination of the official exposé of Stalinism—Khrushchev gave the floor to only one victim of political repressions (although there were quite a few alive at the time), the Old Bolshevik Dora Lazurskina, referring to her by her name and patronymic, Dora Abramovna, which made it very clear that she was Jewish.

But a new wave of anti-Semitism was already rising, about to crash down on Soviet Jews who were still recovering from the last one, and Khrushchev was its father and inspiration. That should come as no surprise. Anti-Semitism was more than the outcome of a single individual's evil intent; it was an organic part of the system that played on the sensitive strings of the dulled and embittered masses. Whenever politics reaches a dead end, when good intentions come to naught, when promises are not kept and cannot be kept—the leaders reach for the soiled anti-Semitic card from the same old deck, which always wins the hand.

This time the stumbling block was economic failure, and Khrushchev took the Stalin path with a light heart. Lacking Stalin's brains, craftiness, and treachery, he did not bother with ornamental screens of ideological demagoguery to cover his blatant plans. Stalin's planned tragedy, which failed when he died, was repeated under Khrushchev as a farce, bloody but pathetic and tacky. The script was the same, but the director was inept.

By 1961 it was becoming clear that Khrushchev's dilettante forays into economics were failing. The "mastery of virgin lands," that is, the cultivation of lands covered with natural vegetation for centuries in Kazakhstan, Siberia, the Urals, and the Volga regions, was a flop. Khrushchev thought he had found the panacea to end the country's permanent grain shortage: he had 48 million hectares of unfertile land plowed by the forced labor of hundreds of thousands of young people. The operation was extremely costly and unprofitable.

The corn fiasco was another example. Khrushchev wanted to apply the "American experience," without taking into consideration such factors as climate, techniques, and technology, and plant corn everywhere, promising general prosperity in a year. The government's eternal "Jew de jour," Alexander Bezymensky, who had announced the closing of the Jewish sections of the Writers' Union and had been an expert witness at the JAC trial, hastily transformed himself from a Stalinist to a Khrushchevite and wrote toadying verse along the lines of "And I am proud, that loving life, my lyric muse has the honor of singing your praises, O corn!" But even with his praises, the corn refused to grow where it could not grow.

Khrushchev's scandalous plan "to catch up with and pass America in meat and milk production" also failed. Moscow's wags had their own response to the idiotic slogan. When the highway patrol started a new safety campaign that required all trucks to have a sign in the back: "If you're not sure, don't pass," hundreds of trucks hit the roads with the warning, "If you're not sure, don't pass America." Dozens of jokesters ended up in jail for that.

The crowning moment of silliness was Khrushchev's announcement that the country would be living in Communism, the goal of the socialist USSR, in another fifteen years. People practically laughed in his face: unlike Stalin, who inspired fear, he inspired disgust. He was quick to take revenge for his failures. The victims—as usual—were the same.

The brief thaw misled not only intellectuals but craftsmen, tradesmen, and businessmen of varying sorts. The shadow economy had existed as part of Stalinist socialism, filling the gaps in the market and easing the permanent deficit of the most needed commodities. But the Khrushchev era was a relatively charitable one toward business, and many people, especially in the provinces, thought that it was time to expand. The "left" (that is, illegal) factories began working at top capacity, supplying the market and swelling the pockets of good producers and clever tradesmen.

This subject requires book-length investigation, but I will give a brief outline here. I am not writing a history of Russian anti-Semitism or a history of Soviet illegality. I am interested only in how just a few years after Stalin's death, the seeds he had sown which seemed to have been rejected, condemned, and ruthlessly weeded, were suddenly sprouting new shoots. And the old model remained in place; it worked well in the new conditions. This time, instead of ideological crimes, the victims were charged with economic ones.

The great majority of "left" businessmen were Jewish. They did the same things that businesspeople in Russia are doing now; in the Gorbachev and Yeltsin era, businessmen are given honorary degrees and awards, invited to sit on the dais at ceremonial functions, advertised on television, and promoted to government posts. But in Khrushchev's time, business was a crime. Khrushchev decided to blame all his failures on Jewish "crooks" and "shylocks," turning society's wrath down familiar channels. The wrath would be particularly violent because the fall guys were branded currency speculators. For perfectly sound reasons, the underground businessmen wanted to convert their earnings into a sound currency, and the authorities managed to make people think that there was no greater evil than that.

Moscow lawyer Yevgenia Evelson counted 290 economic cases of an openly anti-Semitic character in the campaign unleashed by Khrushchev and continued under Brezhnev (1961–1967). Under Stalin the victims were well-known Jews, mostly writers, who used Russian pseudonyms that required decoding. The targets now were Jews who were known only within their business circles. They had no pseudonyms, which made it much easier for the paid journalists to write their trash: they merely had to copy accurately the names on the defendants' passports. Many did not use their Hebrew names, but they were there in the passport: Borukh, not Boris; Srul, not Sergei. The authors of the vicious articles (often employees of local state security, internal affairs, or procurator's offices) enjoyed using the Hebrew names, like red flags for Russian bulls.

Here are a few examples of Soviet journalism from that period: "Ber Paisakhovich Frid is good at defrauding, he charges higher prices for his goods. His assistants are M. Gir, D. Shteiman, A. Mardukhlin, A. Linder, A. Rudzitser"; or "Leib-Khaim Yudovich is an enterprising dealer who built himself a five-bedroom house with palatial furnishings on unknown income"; or "Currency speculators Yuda Goldenfarb, Mikhail Shnaider, Khaim Kats, Shlema Kuris, Yankel Poizner, Sarra Grinberg, Fanya Koiferman, Aaron Gerter, Elik Kushnir, Pitel Veitset, Ida Nudelman, and Naum Feldman have been indicted.".

The peak of Khrushchev's anti-Semitism (his feelings toward Jews had been known since the early thirties) came with an unprecedented application of severe laws with retroactive force. Stalin could (and did) kill millions of people secretly and without any regard for the law, but he never allowed a formal clash with the law. Appearances had to be kept up. Khrushchev did not bother about this. When he was told that two "currency speculators"—Rokotov and Faibishenko—had been sentenced to fifteen years in the camps, he demanded indignantly, "Why weren't they shot?" He was told that the defendants had been given the maximum sentence allowed by law. "We write the laws, we'll change them. No need to coddle those Yids." A law was passed immediately, setting the death penalty for economic crimes, and the court was ordered to review Rokotov's and Faibishenko's sentences, giving them the death penalty: Brezhnev, chairman of the Presidium of the Supreme Soviet of the USSR, signed a paper "allowing" the court to apply the law retroactively to the defendants. The newspapers gleefully reported their execution.

Out of auld lang syne, Khrushchev paid special attention to the Jewish trials in the Ukraine. The newspapers in the city of Lvov were particularly anti-Semitic. *Lvovskaya Pravda* accused "hardened swindlers" like Khaim Kitaigorodksy, Khaim Breitman, Moisey Ioffe, Lev Vaiman, and Sonya Shkolnik of "vulpine passion for profit." The reader had no rest from Jewish names in the paper. Several people say that Khrushchev demanded that "the Yids in Lvov in economic trials be exterminated."

Naturally, this campaign did not go unnoticed in the West. On February 3, 1956, *Pravda* published a letter from British philosopher and mathematician Bertrand Russell, highly esteemed in the USSR. The eighty-three-year-old Nobel laureate wrote to Khrushchev: "I am deeply concerned by the capital punishment meted out to Jews in the Soviet Union and the official condoning of anti-Semitism that seems to be taking place." A month later *Pravda* printed Khrushchev's reply, written in the best Stalinist tradition: "The attempt by reactionary propaganda to ascribe to our state the policy of anti-Semitism or of condoning it is not a new phenomenon. Class enemies resorted to this slander on our reality in the past, as well. There is no policy of anti-Semitism and never has been in the Soviet Union, since the character of our multinational state excludes the possibility of such a policy. . . . Our constitution states: 'Any propaganda of racial or national exclusivity or hatred or neglect is punishable by law.' Our society's motto is man is man's friend, comrade, and brother."

As we recall, Stalin in his replies to foreigners was also quick to blame Western slanderers who invented anti-Semitism in the Soviet Union and was quick to condemn anti-Semitism, so inimical to the most humane society in the world, the land of true internationalism. Khrushchev used Stalin's tricks and followed the old outline. His correspondence with Russell did not hamper the aggressive Judeophobia that was spreading to every republic in the Union. Yevgenia Evelson's data show that there were 163 death sentences for Jews for "economic crimes." And there were 5 "persons of non-Jewish nationality" shot for the same crimes. These figures apply only to those cases that made it into the newspapers. Naturally, there were many more.

This revival of state anti-Semitism in the USSR also fostered the publication of openly anti-Jewish books, like Trofim Kichko's *Judaism Without Embellishment*, a booklet now forgotten that made a big stir in its time, and the organized persecution of Yevgeny Yevtushenko, whose poem "Babi Yar" had thundered throughout the world. The authorities were not as incensed by the reminder that "there are no monuments over Babi Yar" as by the fact that the poet called himself "a true Russian" precisely because he was the enemy of all anti-Semites. Valery Kosolapov, the editor-in-chief of *Literaturnaya Gazeta*, which had published the poem, was fired. This traditional Soviet method of punishment was a better measure of the Party's fright caused by the blasphemous freethinking poem than the nasty articles written by toadies ordered to express their disgust with their colleague's anti-patriotic poetry. But there was yet another fine stroke of fidelity to the old Stalinist tricks: Kosolapov's replacement as editor-in-chief was Jewish—Alexander Chakovsky was now to play the role enacted by Ehrenburg under Stalin. The actors had changed, but the play was the same.

The paradox of this situation under Brezhnev was in the combination of the uncombinable: they wanted to get rid of the Jews, but they made every effort to keep them from emigrating to Israel. Every leader brought his own creativity to the problem. The absurdity of Brezhnev's contribution smacks of senility, but its shameless cynicism is merely a development of Stalin's immortal idea. The absurdity was that Jews had nowhere to go in Soviet society, they were doomed never to be able to grow as individuals. At the same time the desire to leave the country, free it of their presence, and move to Israel or, even worse, the United States, was considered treason and a base treatment of their homeland.

The word "refusenik" came into being, and the struggle of Soviet Jewry to gain the right to leave expanded. This story is well-known and all I can do is to point out that even here the Soviet authorities returned to Stalin's methods, which outlived their inventor.

Forty-two years after the Jewish Antifascist Committee was founded in 1941, the idea was reanimated under different circumstances. Stalin's plans of the late forties and early fifties resurfaced without the decorative veneer. And like everything else that followed him, it was in a caricatured manner. The resolution of the secretariat of the Central Committee CPSU dated March 29, 1983 (No. T-101/82, marked "Top Secret") states: "Agree with the proposal of the Propaganda Section of the CC CPSU and the KGB USSR [sic] to create an Anti-Zionist Committee of the Soviet Public. Ratify staff, salary, and nomenklatura of positions of the CC CPSU on the Anti-Zionist Committee. Ratify Comrade Dragunsky, D. A. (without salary) as chairman and Comrade Zivs, S. L. as first deputy.* Appoint the propaganda section of the CC CPSU jointly with the KGB USSR to examine the plans of the committee's work and give it the necessary support."

In an interview shortly before his death, General Dragunsky admitted that after the war he had been a victim of anti-Semitism himself and that because he was Jewish he had trouble advancing in his career and could not get a promotion to general for a long time. "It was only after Stalin's death, under Khrushchev, when the anti-Semitic plank was lowered somewhat," Dragunsky said, "that I managed to move ahead. But the anti-Semitism remained." Realization of this fact led the general to fight, not anti-Semitism, but the people whose lot it was to become its victims: such are the mind-boggling paradoxes of Soviet thought.

At least JAC had a timely excuse for its existence, for seeking contacts and even unity with fellow Jews abroad. The Anti-Zionist Committee of the Soviet Public (AKSO) had just the opposite goal. Instead of uniting, it was to splinter, slander, and condemn. JAC gathered the best forces of Jewish Soviet culture, AKSO mobilized scoundrels in the Lubyanka sphere of influence, happy to persecute anyone who tried to escape discrimination.

Anti-Semitic Jews, ready to outdo the most rabid chauvinists, are not a new phenomenon, but in the Brezhnev-Andropov era they were an exceptionally mediocre and pathetic lot. Instead of the heinous Zaslavsky, the sleek cynic Khavinson, the professors and academicians, there were now mostly people like the untalented playwright Tsezar Solodar or the wretched journalist Viktor Magidson, whose texts sprinkled all the newspapers with screechy hysteria in exposing Zionists, a cheap harping on "Soviet patriotism," a total lack of anything positive to say about his fellow Jews.

From the early seventies until Gorbachev took power in the mid-eighties, the Jewish theme was uppermost in Soviet propaganda. The Jews were no longer accused of engaging in a Zionist conspiracy, but they were all considered potential traitors capable of abandoning the homeland, in whose debt they were, in search of a richer life. They

* David Dragunsky (1910–1992), general of Tank Division, twice Hero of the Soviet Union. Samuil Zivs (1923–), lawyer, professor, former deputy director of the Institute of State and Law of the Academy of Sciences of the USSR.

were not being hired, and the explanation was no longer a secret: it was question five of the application form again, but not anti-Semitism, they were told. It was merely a question of not hiring someone who could announce the very next day that he was leaving his homeland.

Much has been written on this stage of our history. I will add only that the motives for discrimination change, the terminology is cleaned up, the sanctions are eased (not mass repressions, not arrest, but second-class citizenship)—but the system's aggression remains, directed against only one ethnic group, and focused on inciting hatred.

Only a month after the failed coup of August 1991 and three months before leaving the political scene, Mikhail Gorbachev decided to speak out openly about anti-Semitism. He used the fiftieth anniversary of Babi Yar as the occasion. "Among the tens of millions who perished," the President of the USSR informed his audience, "were almost six million Jews, representatives of a great nation scattered by fate across the planet." He forgot to mention that those "almost six million" victims were killed only because they were Jewish.

But this was the first time that the country's leader officially admitted that there had been state anti-Semitism in the USSR, if only in Stalin's era. "Stalin's bureaucracy," wrote Gorbachev, "publicly disassociated itself from anti-Semitism, but in practice armed itself with it in order to isolate the country from the outside world, hoping to use chauvinism to strengthen its sovereignty." The care with which the words were chosen by Gorbachev's apparat is apparent ("balanced," as it is called in Soviet political jargon). The great tragedy of a nation is described in a flat and false tone. But still, this was a belated act of awkward repentance, with its "hope that we, our society that is renewing itself, will be able to learn from the tragedies and errors of the past."

What lessons have "we" learned? As soon as the officially sanctioned state anti-Semitism started to weaken, it reared its head in different forms. Now anti-Semitic campaigns are no longer formulated by Politburo decisions and stamped "Top Secret." They "spontaneously arise from below," a "natural reaction to Jewish entrenchment in all spheres of government, administration, and cultural life." That this statement by a leader of the "patriotic movement" was nonsense did not worry anyone: anti-Semitism was always marked by the absurdity of its arguments. Every attempt to give the arguments a sense of reality or a "decent" form is doomed, because, to use Chekhov's immortal formula, it cannot be, because this can never be.

Contrary to a widespread notion, the rejection of a state anti-Semitic policy did not come immediately with Gorbachev's rise to power, but around 1988. Before that, there were powerful moments of repression. In October 1987, *Mezhdunarodnaya Zhizn* [*International Life*], the journal of the Ministry of Foreign Affairs, published an article by Vladimir Semyonov, recently ambassador to the Federal Republic of Germany and Deputy Minister of Foreign Affairs, whose anti-Semitism was no secret. The author described with delight how in 1939–1940 Molotov and Beria "renewed the personnel" of Soviet diplomacy, "cluttered with people who had been selected by the principle of personal loyalty or *ethnic closeness* [italics mine]." No experienced diplomat or senior apparatchik would allow himself such bluntness if he did not know that the Kremlin supported such personnel and national policies. Nor would such an official journal, which to this day is read and approved by the ministry before a line is published.

It is no accident that the "patriotic movement" which calls itself Pamyat, once it got on its feet (not without the help of influential forces), made itself a defender and protector of Stalin's unfading shadow. The artist Igor Suchev, a Pamyat leader, declared publicly in 1990, "The destruction of the holy sites of the Russian people [Russian Orthodox churches blown up or vandalized by the Bolsheviks] is not the work of Josif Vissarionovich Stalin, it is the work of rootless cosmopolites: Kaganovich, Ginzburg [Semyon Ginzburg was Commissar of Construction under Stalin], and others. . . . The start of the struggle against rootless cosmopolites put an end to the destruction of the holy sites of the Russian people. . . . The key positions in the government were in the hands of Jewish Marxists, or as they are called here, Red Zionists. The penetration of the Khazar khanate was so deep that Josif Vissarionovich Stalin in fact created a revolution to overthrow the Khazar khanate, realizing that no revolution can avoid having its victims."

The appeal to Stalin's authority for a theoretical basis for anti-Semitism is very eloquent and indicative, because it allows us to dispel all illusions about the alleged contradictions in the positions of post-

Soviet neo-anti-Semites. The contradiction is supposed to be that on the one hand modern patriots declare the October Revolution to be the work of Jews and Masons, quoting exaggerated figures to show the Jewish participation in the overthrow of the old regime; on the other hand, they dream of the reanimation of the Soviet Union and a return to Stalinist times. This should be a paradox.

But there is no paradox here at all. The "neo-patriots" have a simple scheme: Lenin (Blank) and the other Jews destroyed the great Orthodox state, the great Russian empire, while Stalin re-created it, both geographically and spiritually. They dream of a return to the Stalin model, not that of Lenin, for Russia and its ideological basis—as they understand both. So Pamyat and the numerous other openly anti-Semitic organizations (like the paramilitary Russian National Unity, the Russian National Legion) can be called, without their denial, the heirs and successors of Stalin—in any case, of his policies, ideas, and strategic plans.

They also inherited Stalin's shameless cynicism: even as they call openly to fight against Yid-Masons and to clear Russia of them, they blandly maintain that accusations of anti-Semitism are slanderous and offensive to them. Pamyat is even suing *Evreiskaya Gazeta* [*The Jewish Gazette*], which quoted some of their slogans and demanded that they be brought to justice. With a multimillion-ruble suit for libel, Pamyat wanted expert opinion on the meaning of anti-Semitism and announced that it has never tried to incite national hostility. Stalin, as we recall, was also an implacable foe of anti-Semitism, the "lowest form of cannibalism."

In the surge of anti-Semitic literature that flooded the "free" market during and after perestroika, Pamyat's publications do look modest and harmless. Pamyat is widely known in the West only because it was the first to declare its chauvinist ideas and because of the operetta uniforms its members affect (black shirts, bandoliers, and boots). The many new organizations of that ilk go much further, hailing the pogroms of tsarist times and seeing themselves as successors to the perpetrators.

And as the heirs of Stalin's strategy in the Jewish question and the successors of Russia's pogrom groups, today's anti-Semitic gangs are a unique hybrid of Bolshevism, terrorism, and patriotism, under the flag of superpowerhood based on racial purity. When it suits them, they pretend to be kindly disposed to the minorities living in Russia— except the Jews. But once they get rid of the Jews, they'll start in on the rest.

During the August 1991 coup, when there were tanks on Moscow's main squares and streets, young men handed out free copies of a white, black, and red brochure that cost one ruble (a lot for a booklet back then) to the crowd that surrounded the tanks and the soldiers inside them. It was written by the patriotic journalist Viktor Ostretsov and called *The Black Hundreds and the Red Hundreds. The Truth About the Union of the Russian People.* That pre-revolutionary organization, which organized mass killings of defenseless Jews and whose name became synonymous with the vilest racist filth, is elevated in this Soviet brochure published in 1991 to the ranks of the most radiant, pure, and selfless association of Russians persecuted by Jews. It invites the reader "to join *his* Russia—a martyr, truly of the people, Orthodox, and with one ruler," and tells everyone who "rolls his R's and pushes ideas that are hostile to the Russian people" to leave "the country that is alien to him." Astonishingly, this booklet with a print run of one million copies was published not by some private, semi-legal organization, but by the powerful and official Military Publishing House, under the direct authority of Marshal Yazov, Minister of Defense, and one of the coup conspirators.*

Stalin could not have dreamed about such a change from hypocritical tactics to openly racist ones. But he had more of a chance to solve the Jewish question than his heirs do. In reanimating and inflaming the country's dormant anti-Semitism, Stalin knew that he lived and acted in a society that still believed in revolutionary ideals, in a socialism under construction, in itself. The great majority took each word Stalin spoke not simply as indisputable truth but as yet another wise step for the weal of the Soviet people and of all humanity. Stalin knew his people's sore spots, the level of their comprehension, the

---

* Anti-Semites are finding support in some army circles. In 1989, at the apogee of perestroika, anti-Gorbachev Communist leaders enlisted the help of the local KGB in Yaroslavl to "establish" that Alexander Yakovlev (who was born in the region), chairman of the Commission on Stalinism, was actually Jewish and that his real name was Epstein or Yakobson. They also tried to determine the Jewish roots of Boris Yeltsin ("Yelstyn"), Anatoly Sobchak, and other democratic leaders.

readiness of the soil into which he dropped seeds. So his multi-stage plan to cleanse the Russian empire of Jews had real possibilities of success.

The calculated attempts to press on the same sore spots under the new conditions are not reaching their target. There is no new Stalin, either as an individual or as a group, and so the militant calls from the small-caliber "patriots" lack the magic power. And there is no revolutionary fervor in the masses to turn a spark into a flame. Most people do not perceive Jews as the cause of their many problems, being intuitively (if not consciously) aware of how removed Jews were from power for the last fifty years. Today's demons come from other minorities: the Chechens and Dagestanis, Azeris and Georgians, Uzbeks and Tadjiks. They are the ones Russians see selling products in markets at fabulously expensive prices. Not Jews. In 1917 the cliché Jew was a pawnbroker or tavern keeper, but today the image of Jews is as doctor, teacher, engineer. Anti-Semitism exists, but it has lost its support in the mass consciousness and requires energetic resuscitation. Stalin did not finish his work, and his heirs are having a very hard time of it.

But they do have one advantage: Stalin had to appeal to the dark, faceless masses to do his work, while his heirs are counting on the typically Soviet stratum that Solzhenitsyn calls educated but not enlightened. The university professors, writers, and Ph.D.s found among the anti-Semites should neither surprise nor frighten: these are the pseudointellectuals who got degrees in the Soviet system, the same dark masses of the land of the triumphant proletariat, the ideologists, theoreticians, and propagandists.

The occasional anti-Semitic letter will invariably turn up in my mail, from a writer who sees no need for anonymity or pseudonym, threatening and hating over his real signature, with his social status and educational baggage included. For instance, a letter from a man in Moscow, who signed this way: "member of the CPSU since 1955, member of the Union of Journalists, candidate of history." He informed me that "in our Russia virulent Vaksbergs mock our Russian people," that "all Russian Jews work for the Zionists and imperialists." He wants me to answer his question, "How many Russians were repressed for every Jew?" I quote his letter only to show the theoretical level of the learned anti-Semites of the late twentieth century. This is typical of today's anti-Semitic movement, and this fills me, an inveterate optimist, with hope: this sort of ignorant babble of the neo-Stalinist anti-Semitic wave will not find great responsiveness among the Russian masses, who have learned to think for themselves.

For many years the Soviet Union had to hear the propaganda slogan, "Lenin's work lives and conquers." To paraphrase it, I might say that Stalin's work still lives, but fortunately it is not conquering. That time is gone, and it will not return.

INDEX